Teach Yourself VISUALLY™

Photoshop® Elements 9

Visual

Mike Wooldridge

WILEY

Wiley Publishing, Inc.

Teach Yourself Visually™ Photoshop® Elements 9

Published by
Wiley Publishing, Inc.
10475 Crosspoint Boulevard
Indianapolis, IN 46256

www.wiley.com

Published simultaneously in Canada

Library of Congress Control Number: 2010937816

ISBN: 978-0-470-91961-3

Manufactured in the United States of America

10 9 8 7 6 5 4 3 2

Trademark Acknowledgments

Contact Us

For general information on our other products and services please contact our Customer Care Department within the U.S. at 877-762-2974, outside the U.S. at 317-572-3993 or fax 317-572-4002.

For technical support please visit www.wiley.com/techsupport.

Permissions
David Huss (www.davidhuss.com)
Brianna Stuart (stuartphotography.net)

WILEY   Sales | Contact Wiley at (877) 762-2974 or fax (317) 572-4002.

Credits

Executive Editor
Jody Lefevere

Project Editor
Jade L. Williams

Technical Editor
David Huss

Copy Editor
Scott Tullis

Editorial Director
Robyn Siesky

Editorial Manager
Rosemarie Graham

Business Manager
Amy Knies

Senior Marketing Manager
Sandy Smith

Vice President and Executive Group Publisher
Richard Swadley

Vice President and Executive Publisher
Barry Pruett

Project Coordinator
Sheree Montgomery

Graphics and Production Specialists
Andrea Hornberger
Jennifer Mayberry

Quality Control Technician
Laura Albert

Proofreading
Susan Hobbs

Indexing
BIM Indexing & Proofreading Services

Screen Artists
Ana Carrillo
Mark Pinto
Jill A. Proll
Ron Terry

Illustrators
Ronda David-Burroughs
Cheryl Grubbs

About the Author

Mike Wooldridge teaches computers and develops Web sites from his home in the San Francisco Bay Area.

Author's Acknowledgments

Mike thanks Brianna Stuart and Dave Huss for the use of their beautiful photographs in the examples for the book. He also thanks Brianna for her help in preparing the hundreds of screenshots. He thanks Jade Williams for her project management, Scott Tullis for his copy editing, and Dave Huss for his technical editing. Mike dedicates the book to his ten-year-old son.

How to Use This Book

Who This Book Is For

This book is for the reader who has never used this particular technology or software application. It is also for readers who want to expand their knowledge.

The Conventions in This Book

① Steps

This book uses a step-by-step format to guide you easily through each task. Numbered steps are actions you must do; bulleted steps clarify a point, step, or optional feature; and indented steps give you the result.

② Notes

Notes give additional information — special conditions that may occur during an operation, a situation that you want to avoid, or a cross reference to a related area of the book.

③ Icons and Buttons

Icons and buttons show you exactly what you need to click to perform a step.

④ Tips

Tips offer additional information, including warnings and shortcuts.

⑤ Bold

Bold type shows command names, options, and text or numbers you must type.

⑥ Italics

Italic type introduces and defines a new term.

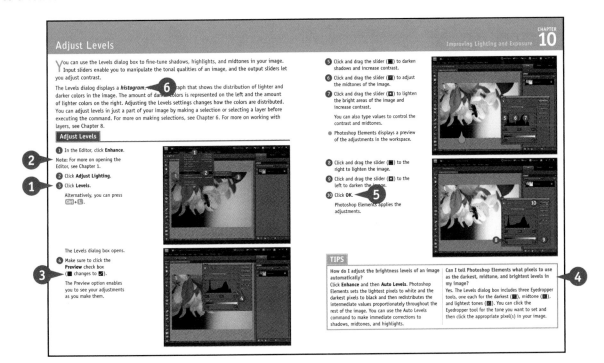

Table of Contents

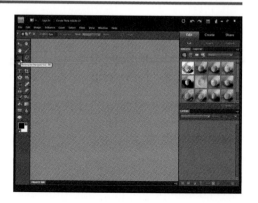

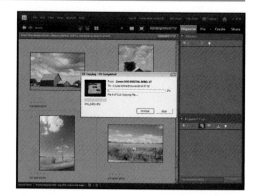

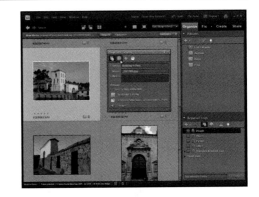

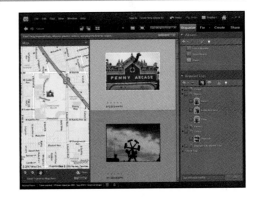

Table of Contents

Chapter 7 — Manipulating Selections

Chapter 8 — Working with Layers

Table of Contents

Chapter 9 — Enhancing and Retouching Photos

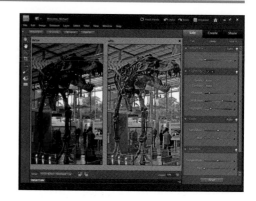

Chapter 10 — Improving Lighting and Exposure

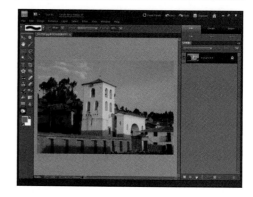

Chapter 11   Enhancing Colors

Chapter 12   Painting and Drawing on Photos

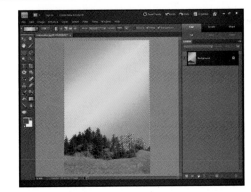

Table of Contents

Chapter 16   Presenting Photos Creatively

Chapter 17   Saving and Sharing Your Work

CHAPTER 1

Getting Started

Are you interested in working with digital images on your computer? This chapter introduces you to Adobe Photoshop Elements 9, a popular software application for editing and creating digital images. Photoshop Elements also enables you to organize your collection of digital images so you can easily find what you are looking for.

Introducing Photoshop Elements 9

Photoshop Elements is a popular photo-editing program you can use to modify, optimize, and organize digital images. You can use the program's Editor to make imperfect snapshots clearer and more colorful as well as retouch and restore older photos. With layers, you can isolate objects in your images and apply special effects just to those objects or combine multiple images into a collage. You can also use the program's Organizer to group your photos into albums, assign descriptive keyword tags, and create slide shows, online galleries, and more. When you are done with your images, you can use Photoshop Elements to save them for posting on the Web or print them out.

Manipulate Photos

As its name suggests, Photoshop Elements excels at enabling you to edit elements in your digital photographs. The program includes numerous image-editing tools and commands you can apply to manipulate the look of your photos. Whether you import photos from a digital camera or a scanner, you can apply a wide variety of editing

techniques to your images, from subtle adjustments in color to elaborate filters that make your snapshots look like paintings. See Chapter 7 for more on manipulating selected parts of your photos. See Chapter 12 for more on painting and drawing, and see Chapter 13 for more on using filters.

Retouch and Repair

You can use Photoshop Elements to edit new photos to make them look their best as well as retouch and repair older photos that suffer from aging problems. For example, you can restore a faded photo by using saturation controls to make it more vibrant, or you can use the Clone Stamp tool to repair a tear or stain. You can also use the program's exposure commands to fix lighting

problems as well as edit out unwanted objects with the Healing Brush. See Chapter 9 for more on retouching your photos.

Add Decoration

The painting tools in Photoshop Elements make the program a formidable illustration tool as well as a photo editor. You can apply colors or patterns to your images with a variety of brush styles. See Chapter 12 to discover how to paint and draw on your photos. In addition, you can use the application's typographic tools to integrate stylized letters and words into your images; see Chapter 14 for more on adding text elements.

Create a Digital Collage

You can combine parts of different images in Photoshop Elements to create a collage. Your compositions can include photos, scanned art, text, and anything else you can save on your computer as a digital image. By placing elements on separate layers, you can move, transform, and customize them independently of one another. See Chapter 8 for more on layers. You can also merge several side-by-side scenes into a seamless panorama, which is covered in Chapter 16.

Organize and Catalog

As you bring photos into Photoshop Elements, the program keeps track of them in the Organizer. In the Organizer, you can place groups of photos into theme-specific albums, tag your photos with keywords that describe where they were taken or who is in them, and search for specific photos based on a variety of criteria. See Chapters 3 and 4 for more on the Organizer.

Put Your Photos to Work

After you edit your photographs, you can use them in a variety of ways. Photoshop Elements enables you to print your images, save them for the Web, or bring them together in a slide show. You can e-mail your photos with the Photo Mail feature. You can also create greeting cards, calendars, and other projects. For more on creating and printing your photo projects, see Chapters 16 and 17.

Understanding Digital Images

To work with photos in Photoshop Elements, you must first turn them into a digital format. When a computer saves a photographic file, it turns the image content into lots of tiny squares called *pixels*. Editing a digital image is mostly about recoloring and rearranging pixels, at least on a small scale. Using Photoshop Elements can be a little easier when you remember this. This section introduces you to some important basics about how computers store images in digital form.

Acquire Photos

You can acquire photographic images to use in Photoshop Elements from a number of sources. You can download photos to Photoshop Elements from a digital camera, memory card, or photo CD. You can scan photographs, slides, or artwork and then import the images directly into the program. You can also bring in photos that you have downloaded from the Web. For more on importing photos, see Chapter 2.

Understanding Pixels

Digital images that you download from a camera consist of millions of tiny squares called *pixels*, each composed of a single color. Photoshop Elements works its magic by rearranging and recoloring these squares. You can edit specific pixels or groups of pixels by selecting the area of the photo you want to edit. If you zoom in close, you can see the pixels that make up your image. Chapter 5 covers the Zoom tool.

Bitmap Images

Images composed of pixels are known as *bitmap images* or *raster images*. The pixels are arranged in a rectangular grid, and each pixel includes information about its color and position. Most of the time when you are working in Photoshop Elements, you are working with bitmap content.

Vector Graphics

The other common way of displaying pictures on your computer is with vector graphics. Vector graphics encode image information by using mathematical equations rather than pixels. Unlike raster images, vector graphics can change size without a loss of quality. When you add shapes or text to your photos in Elements, you are working with vector graphics.

Supported File Formats

Photoshop Elements supports a variety of file types you can both import and export. Popular file formats include BMP, PICT, TIFF, EPS, JPEG, GIF, PNG, and PSD, which stands for Photoshop Document. Files that you save in the PSD and TIFF formats can include layers and other information that cannot be saved with the other formats.

For images published on the Internet, JPEG, GIF, and PNG are the most common formats.

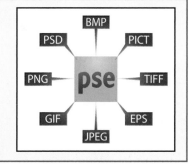

File Size

An important way file formats differ from one another is the amount of storage they take up on your computer. File formats such as PSD and TIFF tend to take up more space because they faithfully save all the information that your camera or other device originally captured. Those formats can also include multiple layers. JPEG, GIF, and PNG files, on the other hand, are built to be sent over the Internet and usually sacrifice some quality for the sake of compactness.

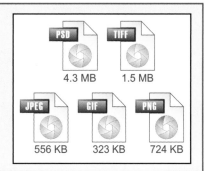

7

Start Photoshop Elements

After you install Photoshop Elements, you can start it to begin creating and editing digital images. Common ways of obtaining and installing the program include from DVD disc or by downloading it from Adobe over the Internet. On a PC, you can access Photoshop Elements as you do other programs — through the Start menu. On a Mac, you can access it through the Finder in the Applications folder.

Start Photoshop Elements

1 Click **Start**.

2 Type **Elements** in the search box.

Windows displays a list of search results.

3 Click **Adobe Photoshop Elements 9**.

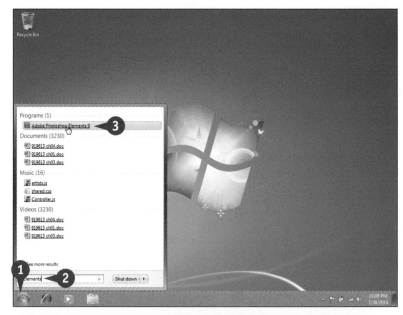

The Photoshop Elements welcome screen opens.

The welcome screen displays clickable icons that take you to different workspaces in Photoshop Elements.

4 Click **Edit**.

The Photoshop Elements Editor opens.

● You can click **Organize** to open the Organizer.

● You can also log in to or sign up for Adobe's photo-sharing and backup services. See Chapter 17 for more.

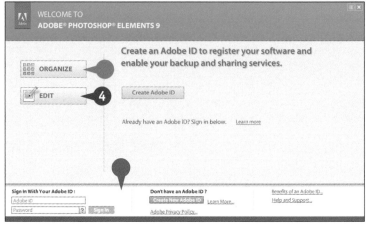

Explore the Editor Workspace

In the Photoshop Elements Editor, you can use a combination of tools, menu commands, and panel-based features to open and edit your digital photos. The main Editor pane displays the photos that you are currently modifying. To open the Editor, click Edit on the welcome screen.

● **Image Window**

Displays each photo you open in Photoshop Elements

● **Layout Button**

Opens a menu that lets you select how open images are arranged in the workspace

● **Image Tabs**

Clickable tabs for switching between open images in the Editor

● **Photoshop.com Links**

Clickable links for signing in to Photoshop.com for managing your photos online

● **Organizer Button**

Clickable button for switching to the Organizer interface, where you can catalog your photos

● **Task Tabs**

Clickable tabs for switching between workflows in the Editor

● **Panel Bin**

A storage area for panels, which are the resizable windows that hold related commands, settings, and other information

● **Project Bin**

Enables you to open and work with multiple photos

● **Toolbox**

Displays a variety of icons, each representing an image-editing tool

● **Options Bar**

Displays controls that let you customize the selected tool in the Toolbox

Tour the Organizer Workspace

In the Photoshop Elements Organizer, you can catalog, view, and sort your growing library of digital photos. The main Organizer pane, called the Media Browser, shows miniature versions of the photos in your catalog. To open the Organizer, click Organize on the welcome screen.

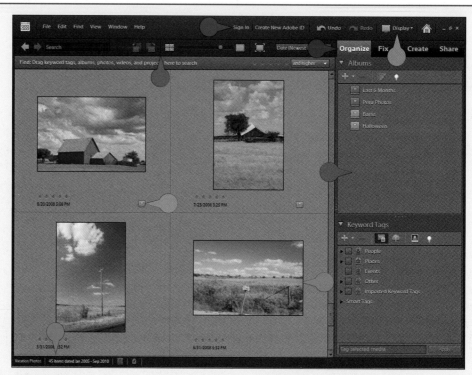

Photo Browser

Displays miniature versions, or *thumbnails*, of the photos in your catalog

Toolbar

Displays buttons and other options for modifying and sorting photos in the Photo Browser

Photoshop.com Links

Clickable links for signing in to Photoshop.com for managing your photos online

Display Menu

Contains commands for switching to different views in the Organizer

Task Tabs

Clickable tabs for switching between workflows in the Organizer

Panel Bin

A storage area for panels, which are the resizable windows that hold related commands, settings, and other information

Tag Icon

Shows which tags have been applied to a photo

Status Bar

Displays the name of the currently open catalog, how many photos the catalog contains, and other summary information

Switch Between the Editor and the Organizer

Photoshop Elements has two main workspaces: the Organizer and the Editor. The Organizer lets you browse, sort, share, and categorize photos in your collection, and the Editor enables you to modify, combine, and optimize your photos. You can easily switch between the two views.

You can use the Organizer to scan through your photo collection to find just the right images for your projects. After you select your photos in the Organizer, you can open the Editor to make changes to the colors, lighting, and other characteristics of the photos. You can switch back to the Organizer to continue browsing your collection or to choose more photos to edit.

Switch Between the Editor and the Organizer

① Start Photoshop Elements in the Organizer view.

Note: See the section "Start Photoshop Elements" for more on starting the program.

You can browse and sort your photos in the Organizer.

Note: For more about using the Organizer, see Chapters 3 and 4.

② Click a photo to select it.

③ Click **Fix**.

④ Click **Full Photo Edit**.

The photo opens in the Editor. It may take a few moments for the Editor to launch if it is not already running.

● You can click the **Organizer** icon (▦) to return to the Editor.

Anatomy of the Photoshop Elements Toolbox

Photoshop Elements offers a variety of specialized tools that enable you to edit your image. Take some time to familiarize yourself with the Toolbox tools. You can select tools by clicking buttons in the Toolbox or by typing a keyboard shortcut key. Keyboard shortcut keys are shown in parentheses.

● **Move (V)**

Moves selected areas of an image

● **Zoom (Z)**

Zooms your view of an image in or out

● **Hand (H)**

Moves the image to reveal portions of the image that are off screen

● **Eyedropper (I)**

Samples color from an area of an image

● **Marquee (M)**

Defines an area of an image by drawing a box or ellipse around the area you want to edit

● **Lasso (L)**

Selects pixels by drawing a free-form shape around the area you want to edit

● **Magic Wand (W)**

Selects pixels based on their color similarity

● **Quick Selection Brush (A)**

Selects pixels like a Magic Wand on a brush by using brush shapes

● **Type (T)**

Adds text to an image

● **Crop (C)**

Trims or expands an image to improve composition

● **Cookie Cutter (Q)**

Masks an image so only the image under the selected shape is available

● **Straighten (P)**

Straightens out crooked image or changes the orientation of an image for artistic purposes

- **Red-Eye Removal (Y)**

  Corrects red-eye problems

- **Spot-Healing Brush (J)**

  Repairs imperfections by copying nearby pixels

- **Clone Stamp (S)**

  Paints pixels from one part of an image to another part

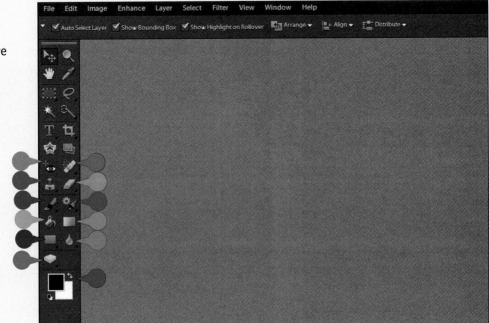

- **Eraser (E)**

  Erases pixels by replacing them with background color or making them transparent layers

- **Brush (B)**

  Paints strokes of color

- **Smart Brush (F)**

  Simultaneously selects and applies a wide variety of different effects

- **Paint Bucket (K)**

  Fills a selected area with a single color

- **Gradient (G)**

  Fills areas with blended color effects

- **Custom Shape (U)**

  Draws predefined shapes

- **Blur (R)**

  Blurs selected portions of your image

- **Sponge (O)**

  Increases or decreases color saturation or intensity

- **Foreground and Background Color**

  Sets foreground and background colors to use with tools

Work with Toolbox Tools

You can use the tools in the Photoshop Elements Toolbox to make changes to an image. After you click to select a tool, the Options bar displays controls for customizing how the tool works. For example, after you select the Rectangular Marquee tool, you can adjust the Options bar settings to determine the height and width of the tool.

Some tools include a tiny triangle in the bottom-right corner indicating hidden tools you can select. For example, the Marquee tool includes two variations: Rectangular and Elliptical.

Work with Toolbox Tools

Select a Tool

1 Position the mouse pointer over a tool.

● A screen tip displays the tool name and shortcut key. You can click the tool name to access help information about the tool.

2 Click a tool to select it.

● The Options bar displays customizing options for the selected tool.

3 Specify any options you want for the tool.

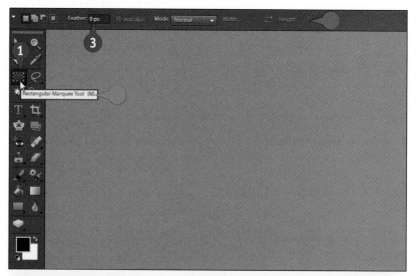

Select a Hidden Tool

1 Click a tool that has a triangle in its corner.

2 Press and hold the mouse button.

● A menu of hidden tools appears.

You can also right-click a tool to show hidden tools.

3 Click the tool you want to use.

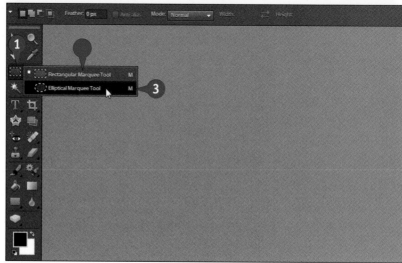

Float the Toolbox

1 At the top of the Toolbox, click and drag into the center workspace.

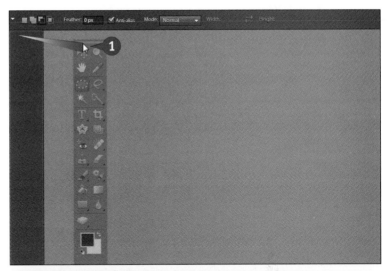

The Toolbox detaches from the side of the workspace.

● When the Toolbox is floating, you can click 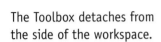 to toggle between one- and two-column configurations.

You can click and drag the Toolbox back to the side to unfloat it.

TIP

How can I hide the Toolbox?

You can hide the Toolbox by following these steps:

1 With the Toolbox open, click **Window**.

2 Click **Tools**.

Photoshop Elements hides the Toolbox.

To show the hidden Toolbox, click **Window** and then click **Tools** again.

Work with Panels

In the Photoshop Elements Editor, you can open resizable windows called *panels* to access different Photoshop Elements commands and features. By default, most panels open in the Panel Bin located on the right side of the Photoshop Elements workspace. You can float panels over the program workspace to give yourself easy access to commands.

The Layers panel gives you access to the one or more layers present in your image. Each layer can contain image content that can be moved and adjusted independent of the content in other layers. The Effects panel includes dozens of special effects that you can apply to your image to transform its appearance.

Work with Panels

Open and Close a Panel

1 Open the Photoshop Elements Editor.

Note: For more on opening the Editor, see the section "Start Photoshop Elements."

2 Click **Window**.

3 Click a panel name.

A check mark (☑) next to the panel name indicates that the panel is already open.

The panel opens.

● You can hide or show a panel by double-clicking the panel's title tab.

4 Click the panel menu.

A menu with panel commands opens.

5 Click **Close**.

The panel closes.

Float a Panel

1 Click and drag the title tab of a panel to the work area.

2 Release the mouse.

The panel opens as a free-floating window.

● You can resize a floating panel by clicking and dragging its corner (■).

● To close a floating panel, click the **Close** button (■).

● To reset the Photoshop Elements panels to their default arrangement, click **Reset Panels**.

TIP

How do I rearrange panels in the Panel Bin?

1 Position the mouse pointer over the title tab of a panel.

2 Click and drag the panel to a different part of the Panel Bin.

● Photoshop Elements highlights the area to which the panel will be moved.

3 Release the mouse button.

Photoshop Elements moves the panel.

Set Program Preferences

The Photoshop Elements Preferences dialog box enables you to change default settings and modify how the program looks. You can set preferences in both the Editor and Organizer workspaces to customize the program to match how you like to work.

When you make changes to the program in the preferences, the changes remain after you exit the program and then open it again. In the Organizer, you can restore all preferences to their original state by clicking the Restore Default Settings button in the General preferences.

Set Program Preferences

In the Editor

① In the Editor, click **Edit**.

Note: For more on opening the Editor, see the section "Explore the Editor Workspace."

② Click **Preferences**.

③ Click **General**.

As an alternative, you can press Ctrl+K.

The Preferences dialog box opens and displays General options.

④ Select any settings you want to change.

● For example, you can specify the shortcut keys for stepping backward and forward through your commands.

● You can click the down arrow (⏷) to open images in floating windows instead of tabbed windows.

⑤ Click a different preference category.

● You can also click **Prev** and **Next** to move back and forth between categories.

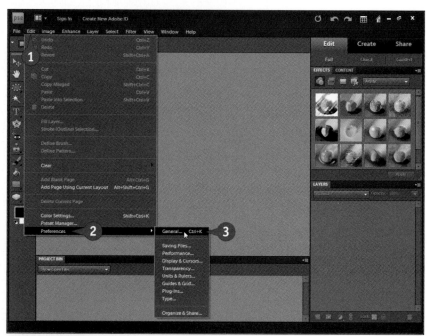

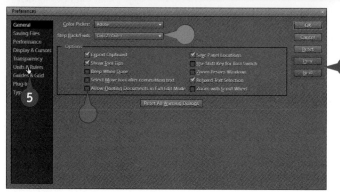

In this example, the Preferences dialog box displays Units & Rulers options.

6 Select any settings you want to change.

● For example, you can specify the default units for various aspects of the program.

7 Click **OK**.

Photoshop Elements sets the preferences.

In the Organizer

1 In the Organizer, click **Edit**, **Preferences**, and then **General**.

Note: For more on opening the Organizer, see the section "Tour the Organizer Workspace."

The Preferences dialog box opens.

2 Select any settings you want to change.

● For example, you can specify date ordering and formatting preferences.

3 Click **OK** to close the dialog box.

Photoshop Elements sets the preferences.

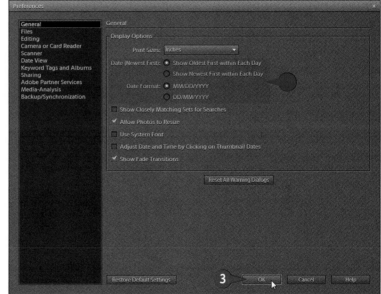

TIPS

What type of measurement units should I use in Photoshop Elements?

Typically, you should use the units most applicable to the type of output you intend to produce. Pixel units are useful for Web imaging because monitor dimensions are measured in pixels. Inches, picas, centimeters, or millimeters are useful for print because those are standards for working on paper.

How do I allocate extra memory to Photoshop Elements for opening more image files?

The Performance preferences show how much memory, or RAM, you have available and how much of it Photoshop Elements is using. The Scratch Disks preferences enable you to allocate extra memory on your hard drive, called *scratch disk space*, to use if your computer runs out of RAM.

View Rulers and Guides

You can turn on rulers and guides in Photoshop Elements to help place objects accurately in your image. Rulers appear at the top and left sides of the image window and enable you to measure distances within your image. To change the units of measurement associated with the rulers, see "Set Program Preferences."

Guides are the lines that help you position different elements in your image horizontally or vertically. These lines do not appear on your image when you save the image for the Web or print it.

View Rulers and Guides

Show Rulers

1 Click **View**.

2 Click **Rulers**.

You can also press Shift + Ctrl + R.

Create a Guide

● Photoshop Elements adds rulers to the top and left edges of the image window.

3 Click one of the rulers and drag the cursor into the window (changes to ↔).

Drag the top ruler down to create a horizontal guide.

Drag the left ruler to the right to create a vertical guide.

● A thin, colored line called a guide appears.

● You can also click **View** and then **New Guide** to add a guide.

You can use guides to align objects in the different layers of an image.

Note: See Chapter 8 for more about layers.

Move a Guide

1 Click the **Move** tool ( ).

2 Position the mouse cursor over a guide (changes to) and then click and drag.

You can also press Ctrl + # to display a grid on your image. The lines of the grid can help you align objects in your image.

TIP

How do I make objects in my images "snap to" my guides when I move those objects?

The "snap to" feature is useful for aligning elements in a row or a column.

1 Click **View**.

2 Click **Snap To**.

3 Click **Guides**.

When you move an object near a guide, Photoshop Elements automatically aligns it with the guide.

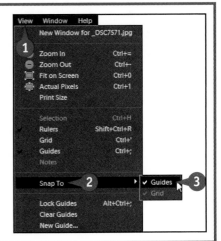

CHAPTER 2

Importing and Opening Digital Images

Before you can start working with photos in Photoshop Elements, you must first import them from a camera, scanner, or another digital device or from folders on your computer. This chapter shows you how to import photos into the Photoshop Elements Organizer and then open them in the Photoshop Elements Editor.

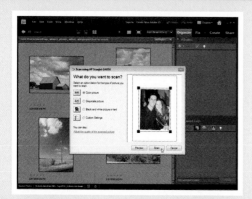

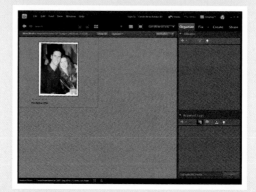

Get Photos for Your Projects

To work with images in Photoshop Elements, you must first acquire the images. You can get images and clip art to use in your creative projects from a variety of sources. Digital cameras have become ubiquitous and you can get images using expensive digital SLRs, cheap point-and-shoot cameras, as well as camera phones. Scanned art is another option as is content captured with a film-based camera. Finally, you can obtain photos that other people have posted to photo-sharing Web sites. Photoshop Elements makes it easy to bring in content from these different sources.

Digital Cameras

A digital camera is probably the most common way to take photographs and then import them into your computer. Most digital cameras save their images as JPEG or Raw files, both of which you can open and edit in Photoshop Elements. You can transfer images directly from a camera by using a USB cable, or you can transfer images by using a card reader, a device that reads your camera's memory card.

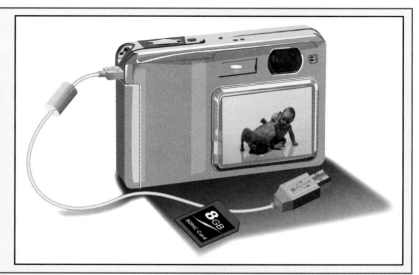

Scanned Photos and Art

A scanner gives you an inexpensive way to convert existing paper-based content into a digital form. You can scan photos and art into your computer, retouch and stylize them in Photoshop Elements, and then output them to a color printer. You can also use a slide attachment to digitize slides by using a scanner. For tips on automatically straightening scanned photos, see Chapter 5.

Web Images

If you have photos or art stored on the Web, you can easily save those image files to your computer and then open them in Photoshop Elements. In Internet Explorer on the PC, you can save a Web image by right-clicking it and then choosing Save Picture As. Inexpensive stock photo Web sites, such as iStockphoto, offer professional-grade images for download. On photo-sharing sites such as Flickr, users often allow noncommercial use of their photos.

Start from Scratch

You can also create your Photoshop Elements image from scratch by opening a blank canvas in the image window. You can then apply colors and patterns with the painting tools in Photoshop Elements, or you can cut and paste parts of other images to create a composite. See the section "Create a Blank Image" for more on opening a blank canvas.

Film Photos

If you have a film camera, you can have your photos burned to a CD or DVD during film processing. Then, you can import the photos from the disc just as you would import photos from a folder on your computer. See the section "Import Photos from a Folder" for more. Hundreds or thousands of images can be saved on a single disc, depending on the type of disc and sizes of the images. Most photo-printing services can also burn photos from digital cameras to a disc for safekeeping.

Working with Imported Photos

Images imported into Photoshop Elements are stored in the program's Organizer. There, you can browse miniature versions of your photos, called *thumbnails*, sort them, group them into albums, and assign keyword tags to them. You can edit your photos by opening them in the Photoshop Elements Editor. You can open them in the Editor from the Organizer or open them directly from folders on your computer. See Chapter 1 for more on the Editor and the Organizer workspaces.

Import Photos from a Digital Camera or Card Reader

You can import photos into Photoshop Elements from a digital camera or directly from the camera's memory card. After the import, the photos appear in the Organizer Media Browser. Most cameras and card readers manufactured today connect to a computer through a USB port. A typical PC comes with multiple USB ports. Make sure the device is properly connected before you begin. Also, some computers have special media slots that accept memory cards for transferring photos and other files.

Every camera and card reader works differently. Consult the documentation that came with your device for more information.

Import Photos from a Digital Camera or Card Reader

① In the Organizer, click **File**.

② Click **Get Photos and Videos**.

③ Click **From Camera or Card Reader**.

The Photo Downloader dialog box opens.

Photo Downloader may automatically open when you connect your device to your computer, depending on the settings in Photoshop Elements.

④ Click the down arrow (▾) to choose your camera or memory card from the Get Photos From menu.

By default, Photoshop Elements downloads your photos into dated subfolders inside your Pictures folder. The dated subfolders are based on the time stamp associated with each photo.

● You can click **Browse** to select a different download location.

● You can click ▾ to choose a different naming scheme for the subfolders.

⑤ Click ▾ to choose a naming scheme for your files.

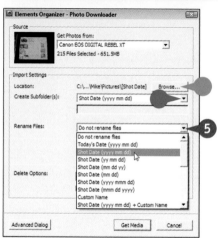

⑥ Click ▾ to choose whether to keep your photos on the device or delete them after downloading.

● You can click this check box to enable Photoshop Elements to download your photos automatically using the current settings whenever a photo device is connected to your computer (☐ changes to ☑).

⑦ Click **Get Media**.

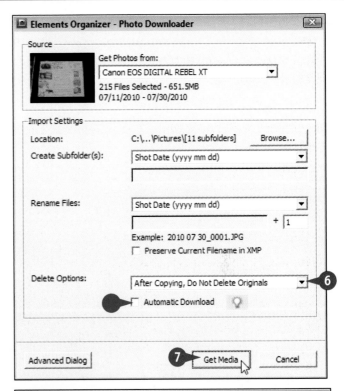

Photoshop Elements downloads the photos from the device.

After downloading the photos, Photoshop Elements adds them to the current Organizer catalog. There, you can add the photos to albums and perform other functions.

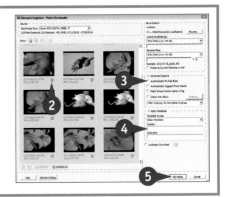

TIP

How do I use the Advanced dialog box in the Photo Downloader?

① Click **Advanced Dialog** in the bottom left corner of the Photo Downloader.

② Click each photo you want to import.

③ Click to turn on red-eye correction.

④ Type creator and copyright details to be applied to all the imported photos.

⑤ Click **Get Media**.

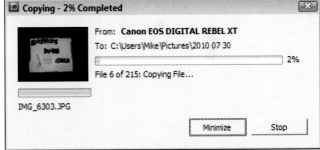

Import Photos from a Scanner

You can import a photo into Photoshop Elements through a scanner attached to your computer. After the import, the photo appears in the Organizer Media Browser. You can scan black-and-white and color photos to import into Photoshop Elements. To scan an image, make sure the scanner is properly connected before you begin. Some scanners include slide or film attachments that enable you to also digitize slides or film.

Every scanner works differently. Consult the documentation that came with your scanner for more. After scanning, you may want to rotate or crop the photo to fix any alignment issues. See Chapter 5 for details.

Import Photos from a Scanner

① In the Organizer, click **File**.

Note: For more on using the Organizer, see Chapter 3.

② Click **Get Photos and Videos**.

③ Click **From Scanner**.

The Get Photos from Scanner dialog box opens.

④ Click ▾ to choose your scanner.

By default, Photoshop Elements saves scanned photos in the Adobe folder inside your Pictures folder.

● You can click **Browse** to choose another location.

⑤ Click ▾ to choose a file format.

● If you are importing as a JPEG, it is typically best to import at a high-quality setting.

⑥ Click **OK**.

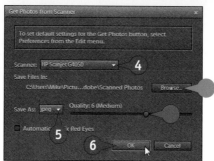

The software associated with your scanner opens. The window can look significantly different depending on the scanner make and model.

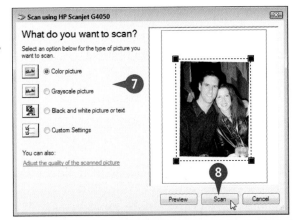

7 Change your scanning settings as needed. You may need to specify whether the photo is black and white or color. You may also get to preview the scan.

8 Click a button to scan your photo by using the scanner software.

The image is scanned and added to the current catalog in the Organizer.

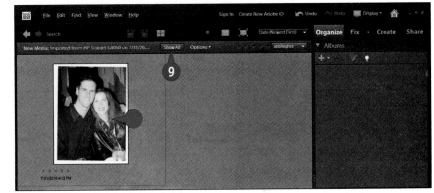

● Photoshop Elements displays the imported photo by itself.

9 Click **Show All** to view your entire catalog of photos.

Note: To crop or straighten a scanned image, see Chapter 5.

TIP

How can I adjust the default settings for importing photos?

1 Click **Edit**, click **Preferences**, and then click **Scanner**.

2 In the Scanner Preferences dialog box, adjust the default settings.

It is typically best to import scanned photos at a high-quality setting.

3 Click **OK**.

Photoshop Elements displays the updated settings the next time you scan a photo.

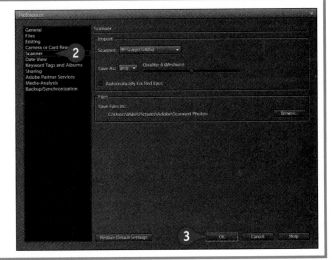

Import Photos from a Folder

You can use the Organizer workspace in Photoshop Elements to import images from a folder on your computer or a disc. You may find this useful if you already have an archive of digital photos on your PC or on photo CDs. After the import, the images appear in the Organizer Media Browser.

Although this book covers working with images, Photoshop Elements also enables you to import and organize video, audio, and PDF files in the Organizer. You can add these files to albums and also categorize them with keyword tags.

Import Photos from a Folder

1 In the Organizer, click **File**.

Note: For more on using the Organizer, see Chapter 3.

2 Click **Get Photos and Videos**.

3 Click **From Files and Folders**.

The Get Photos and Videos from Files and Folders dialog box opens.

4 Click ▼ to choose the folder containing your photos.

5 Ctrl +click to select the photos you want to import.

You can press Ctrl + A to select all the photos in the folder.

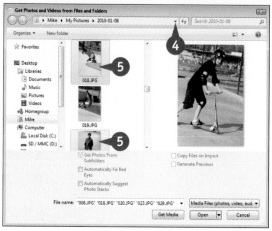

● Click this check box to have Photoshop Elements automatically fix red eye (☐ changes to ☑).

● You can import different types of files, such as PDF documents or Photoshop Elements projects, by clicking ▾.

Note: For more on creating projects in Photoshop Elements, see Chapter 16.

6 Click **Get Media**.

Photoshop Elements downloads the selected photos from the folder.

● Photoshop Elements displays the imported photos by themselves in the Organizer.

7 Click **Show All** to view your entire catalog of photos.

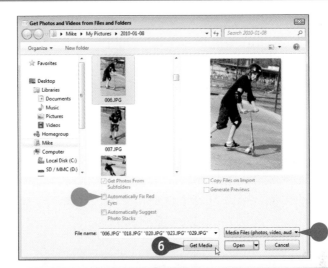

TIP

How can I quickly search my entire computer for photos to import?

1 Click **File**, click **Get Photos and Videos**, and then click **By Searching**.

2 In the Search Option section, click ▾ to choose all hard drives, a single hard drive, or a folder.

3 Click **Search**.

● Your search results appear.

4 Select one or more folders and then click **Import Folders** to get the photos. **Ctrl**+click to select multiple folders.

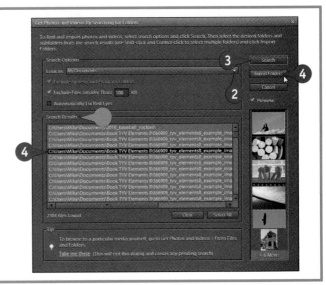

Watch a Folder for New Images

Photoshop Elements can watch certain folders on your computer for the addition of new photos. You can have Photoshop Elements notify you when it recognizes new photos, or you can have it import those photos automatically. The imported photos are added to your Organizer catalog.

Importing content automatically can save you time and effort if you know you want all the photos that you load onto your computer added to the Organizer. You can have Photoshop Elements auto-analyze the imported photos to add tags that help you sort and filter the content. See the Tip for details.

Watch a Folder for New Images

1 In the Organizer, click **File**.

Note: For more on using the Organizer, see Chapter 3.

2 Click **Watch Folders**.

The Watch Folders dialog box opens.

3 Click **Add**.

The Browse For Folder dialog box opens.

4 Choose a folder to watch.

5 Click **OK**.

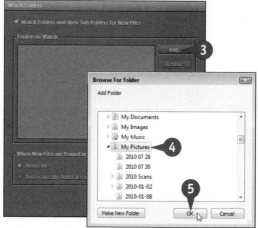

The folder appears in the watch list.

● You can click to watch subfolders inside your watched folders (■ changes to ☑).

● You can choose whether to receive alerts about new images or to have Photoshop Elements add photos to the Organizer automatically (● changes to ○).

6 Click **OK**.

● To remove a watched folder, click the folder in the Folders to Watch list and click **Remove**.

Receive a Watch Notification

1 Exit Photoshop Elements and then add new photos to a watched folder on your computer.

2 Start Photoshop Elements and then open the Organizer.

● Photoshop Elements alerts you about new photos in your watched folders.

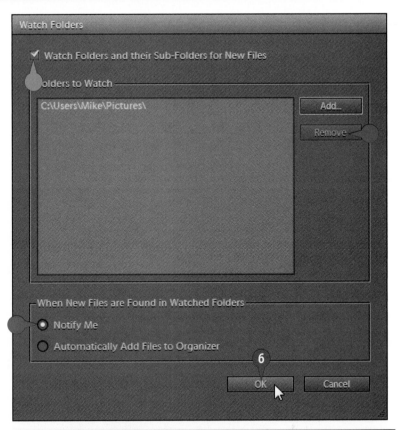

How do I run the Auto-Analyzer feature in the Organizer?

1 In the Organizer, `Ctrl`+click to select the images you want to analyze.

2 Click **Edit**.

3 Click **Run Auto-Analyzer**.

Photoshop Elements assigns relevant Smart Tags to the photos.

Open a Photo

You can open a photo in the Editor to modify it or to use it in a project. After you open the photo, you can adjust its color and lighting, add special effects, and move objects in the photo to separate layers. You can also open photos from the Organizer for editing in the Editor.

You can open more than one photo at a time in the Editor. You can switch between photos using the window tabs. Open images also appear in the Project Bin. For information about managing photos after you open them, see Chapter 5.

Open a Photo

Open a Photo from a Folder

1 In the Editor, click **File**.

Note: For more on opening the Editor, see Chapter 1.

2 Click **Open**.

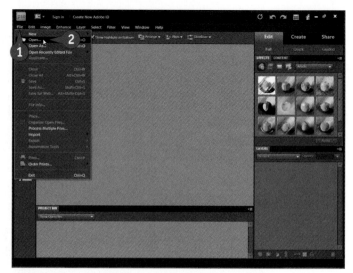

The Open dialog box opens.

3 Click ▾ to navigate to the folder containing the file you want to open.

4 Click the photo you want to open.

● A preview of the image appears.

5 Click **Open**.

Photoshop Elements opens the image.

● The filename and zoom value appear in the tab for the image.

Note: The image may also open in a floating window depending on how your program preferences are set.

● If the Project Bin is open in the Editor, the image also appears in the Bin.

● If you open multiple photos at once, you can click **Window** to view a list of the open photos.

Open an Organizer Photo for Editing

① In the Organizer, right-click the photo you want to edit.

② In the menu that appears, click **Edit with Photoshop Elements**.

Photoshop Elements opens the photo in the Editor.

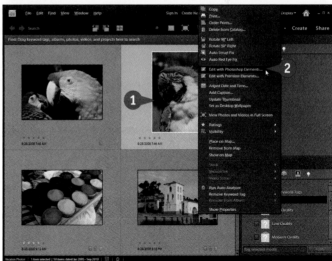

What types of files can Photoshop Elements open?

Photoshop Elements can open most of the image file formats in common use today. Some of the more popular ones are:

File Type	Description
BMP (Bitmap)	The standard Windows image format
TIFF (Tagged Image File Format)	A format for print
JPEG (Joint Photographic Experts Group)	A format for Web images
PNG (Portable Network Graphics)	A Web format that is an alternative to GIF
PSD (Photoshop Document)	Photoshop's native file format

Create a Blank Image

You can start a Photoshop Elements project by creating a blank image and then adding photographic, textual, and other content to the blank image. When you create a blank image, you specify the dimensions and the resolution. Photoshop Elements offers a number of useful preset sizes, including common paper sizes and Web browser dimensions. For more about choosing a resolution, see Chapter 5.

You can add content from other images to your blank image as separate layers. For more on layers, see Chapter 8. You can also use the Brush tool to add streaks of color. See Chapter 12 for information about using and customizing the Brush.

Create a Blank Image

1 In the Editor, click **File**.

Note: For more on opening the Editor, see Chapter 1.

2 Click **New**.

3 Click **Blank File**.

You can also press Ctrl+N.

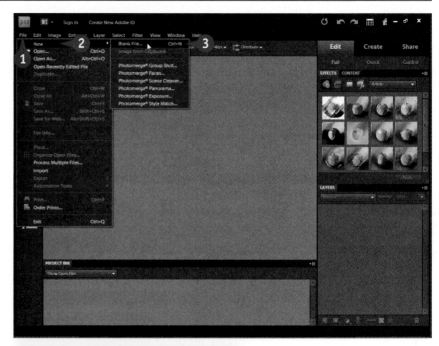

The New dialog box opens.

4 Type a name for the new image.

5 Type the desired dimensions and resolution or choose a preset dimension and resolution from the pop-up menu.

If you have just previously performed a copy command in another image window, Photoshop Elements uses the dimensions of the copied content by default.

● You can click ▾ to change the background of the blank canvas.

6 Click **OK**.

Photoshop Elements creates a new image window at the specified dimensions.

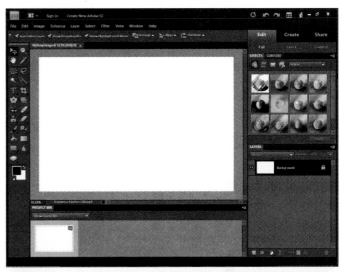

⑦ Use the Photoshop Elements tools and commands to edit the new image.

● In this example, parts of other photos are cut and pasted onto the blank image.

Note: See Chapter 7 for more on how to copy and paste into a blank image.

● The parts appear in different layers in the Layers panel.

Note: To save your image, see the section "Save a Photo."

TIPS

What should I choose as a resolution for a new image?
The appropriate resolution depends on how you plan to use the image. For Web or multimedia images, select 72 pixels/inch — the standard resolution for on-screen images. If you are printing black-and-white images on regular paper by using a laser printer, 150 pixels/inch will probably suffice. For full-color magazine or brochure images, you should use a higher resolution — at least 250 pixels/inch.

How do I open a frame from a video clip?
You can open a video frame in Photoshop Elements by clicking **File**, **Import**, and then **Frame from Video**. A dialog box opens, enabling you to browse for and open a video clip, scan through the clip, and then import a frame into the Editor. Photoshop Elements supports importing from WMV, MPEG, and AVI video files.

Save a Photo

You can save a photo in Photoshop Elements to store any changes that you made to it. PSD is the default file format for Photoshop Elements. Photoshop Elements supports a variety of other image file formats, including the popular JPEG, GIF, and PNG formats commonly found on the Web. If you have an image that includes multiple layers, you can save the image in the PSD, TIFF, or PDF format to preserve the layers.

You can have multiple versions of the same image saved as a version set in the Organizer. Version sets enable you to save copies of an image project at different stages or with different effects applied.

Save a Photo

Save a New Photo

1 In the Editor, click **File**.

Note: For more on opening the Editor, see Chapter 1.

2 Click **Save As**.

Note: For photos that you have previously saved, you can click **File** and then **Save**.

The Save As dialog box opens.

3 Type a name for the file.

● You can click ▾ to choose another folder or drive in which to store the file.

● You can click ▾ to choose another file format.

Close a Photo

You can close a photo after you finish editing it. Although you can have more than one photo open at a time, closing photos you no longer need can free up system resources and speed up your computer's performance. Closing photos also reduces clutter in your workspace because every open folder adds a tab along the top of the default workspace.

If you try to close an image that has unsaved changes, Photoshop Elements warns you before closing the image. When you exit Photoshop Elements, it closes all open images and also warns you about unsaved changes.

Close a Photo

① In the Editor, click **File**.

Note: For more on opening the Editor, see Chapter 1.

② Click **Close**.

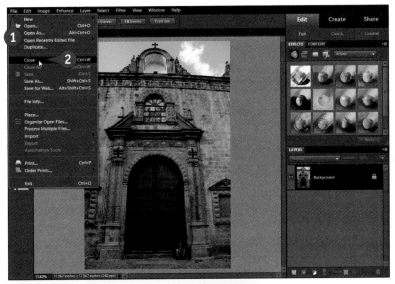

● You can also click ▣ to close a photo.

● If you have made any changes to the file and have not saved them, Photoshop Elements prompts you to do so before closing the file. Click **Yes** to save your work.

Note: See the section "Save a Photo" for more on how to save files.

After saving, if needed, Photoshop Elements closes the photo. The program remains open.

CHAPTER 3

Organizing Your Photos

Are you ready to organize your digital photos? You can catalog, view, and sort photo files by using the Organizer. A complement to the Editor in Photoshop Elements, the Organizer helps you manage your growing library of digital pictures by categorizing them in a variety of ways. This chapter shows you how to take advantage of the many photo-management features in the Organizer.

Introducing the Organizer

You can use the Organizer program to manage your growing library of digital photos. Photos you import or save in Photoshop Elements are automatically added to the Organizer catalog. In the Organizer, you can sort and filter your photo collection in different ways. You can also group photos into albums, tag them with descriptive keywords, and even place them on a geographic map.

Once you have found one or more photos that you want to edit, you can switch to the Editor interface to cut and paste objects in your photo, adjust color and lighting, or apply special effects. You can switch back to the Organizer when you are done or when you need to find more photo content.

Virtual Browser

The Organizer acts as a virtual browser, enabling you to view *thumbnails,* or miniature versions, of your pictures. The thumbnails you see in the Organizer are merely pointers to the original file locations. The images remain intact in their original location unless you decide to delete them. The Organizer enables you to view your photos from one convenient window. See the sections "View Photos in the Media Browser" and "View Photos by Date" to learn more.

Catalog

When you bring photo files into the Organizer, the program adds them to your catalog of images. Images are cataloged by date. You can keep all your photos in one catalog, or you can store them in separate catalogs. If you want to group your photos further, you can place them into albums or stacks. See the sections "Create a Catalog" and "Work with Albums" for more on these topics. For more on stacking photos, see Chapter 4.

Keyword Tags

You can use keyword tags to help you sort and track your photos. A *keyword tag* is a text identifier you assign to a photo. After you assign tags, you can search for photos that match certain tags and also sort your photos in tag order. You can assign any of the preset tags that come with the Organizer, or you can create your own. The Organizer's presets include tags for people, places, events, and more. You can also assign multiple tags to the same photo. For more on keyword tags, see Chapter 4.

Map Photos

Have you ever wanted to pull up photos that were taken in a particular location, such as a favorite vacation spot or where you used to live? The Organizer helps you associate your photos with certain places by enabling you to put them on a geographic map. Once you map your photos, the photos appear as red pins on the map. You can navigate your collection by scrolling and zooming to different countries, cities, and streets. For more on mapping photos, see Chapter 4.

Find Photos

As your photo collection grows, being able to quickly find photos becomes critically important. Although filtering photos by album or keyword tag offers one way to find photos, the Organizer also includes full-featured searching tools. You can search your catalog by date, filename, caption, camera model, map location, and more. You can even mix multiple search criteria to create more powerful searches. See the section "Find Photos" for more information.

Creations

Because it enables you to easily organize and find photos in your collection, using the Organizer is an important first step in completing various Photoshop Elements projects. For example, you can display your favorite photos in the Organizer and then create a custom slide show to distribute to friends and family. You can also create online photo galleries, photo books, postage stamps, and more. See Chapter 16 for photo projects you can build in Photoshop Elements.

Open the Organizer

You can organize and manage your digital photos in the Organizer in Photoshop Elements. The Organizer works alongside the Editor to help you keep track of the digital photos and other media you store on your computer. You can open the Organizer from the welcome screen that appears when you first start up Photoshop Elements or switch to it from the Editor.

The main feature of the organizer is the Media Browser, which features a grid of miniature versions of your photos, also known as *thumbnails*. You can select a thumbnail and then perform basic commands on it in the Organizer or open the image in the Editor to perform more complex operations.

Open the Organizer

From the Welcome Screen

1 Start Photoshop Elements.

Note: See Chapter 1 for more on starting Photoshop Elements.

The welcome screen appears.

2 Click **Organize** to open the Organizer.

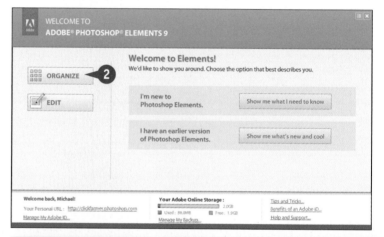

The Organizer opens.

To import photos into the Organizer workspace, see Chapter 2.

To create a new catalog with which to organize your photos, see the section "Create a Catalog."

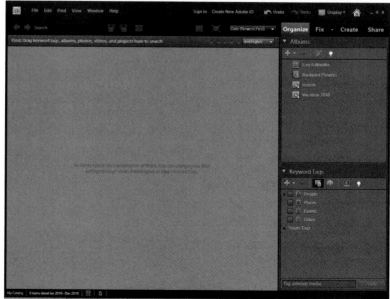

From the Editor

1 Start Photoshop Elements.

2 From the welcome screen that appears, click **Edit** to open the Editor.

3 Click the **Organizer** icon (⊞).

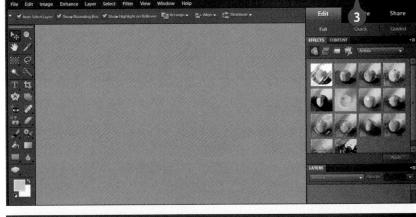

The Organizer opens.

● To return to the Editor, click **Fix** and then click **Full Photo Edit.**

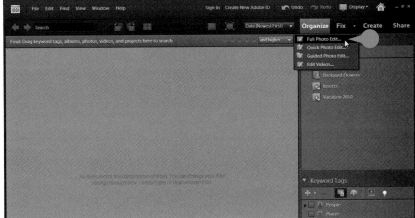

Can I edit photos from within the Organizer?

Yes. The Organizer offers basic editing commands under the Fix tab. The commands can save you from having to switch to the Editor to optimize your photos.

1 In the Organizer, click **Fix**.

The editing buttons appear.

2 Click a thumbnail to select a photo to edit.

3 Click an Auto button to optimize the color or lighting of your photo.

● You can click **Crop** to open an image for cropping. See Chapter 5 for more on cropping.

Create a Catalog

The photos you manage in the Organizer are stored in catalogs. You can keep your photos in one large catalog or separate them into smaller catalogs. When you start the Organizer, Photoshop Elements creates a default catalog for you called My Catalog.

You can organize your photos within a catalog into smaller groups called albums. See the section "Work with Albums" for more. You can also combine similar photos into stacks to save space when viewing your catalog. See Chapter 4 for details. Photoshop Elements 9 can open catalogs created in previous versions of Photoshop Elements and can convert them so you can use all the newest features of the Organizer.

Create a Catalog

1 In the Organizer, click **File**.

2 Click **Catalog**.

● You can restore a catalog you have previously backed up by clicking **Restore Catalog from CD, DVD or Hard Drive**. See Chapter 17 for more on backing up photos.

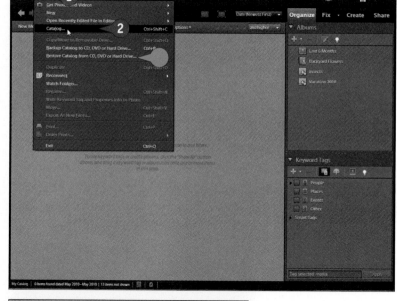

The Catalog Manager dialog box opens.

Photoshop Elements lists the available catalogs.

3 Click **New**.

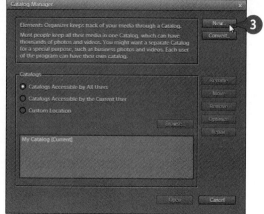

④ Type a name for the new catalog.

● You can click here to import free music (■ changes to ✔), which you can use in the backgrounds of slide shows.

⑤ Click **OK**.

Photoshop Elements creates the new catalog and opens it.

● Photoshop Elements displays the name of the current catalog.

● The number of files in the catalog and the range of dates for the files appear here.

Note: To add photos to your catalog, see Chapter 2.

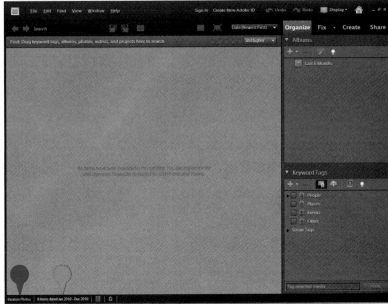

How do I switch to a different catalog in the Organizer?

Open the Catalog Manager by following Steps 1 and 2 in this section. Select the catalog that you want to open in the catalog list and then click **Open**. You can open only one catalog at a time in the Organizer.

How can I protect the photos in the Organizer from viewing by others?

You can change the security settings of a catalog so that only the user currently logged in to your computer can access it.

Open the Catalog Manager by following Steps 1 and 2 in this section. From the list that appears, select the catalog that you want to protect and then click **Move**. A dialog box opens that enables you to change the accessibility of the catalog.

View Photos in the Media Browser

After you add photos to your catalog, you can view them by using the Organizer's Media Browser. The Media Browser displays thumbnails, or miniature versions, of your photos, along with details about those photos.

You can filter, sort, and change the size of the thumbnails. Shrinking the thumbnails enables you to view more of them at once, whereas enlarging the thumbnails lets you examine their details from within the Organizer. Filtering and sorting enables you to find specific photos from thousands very quickly. For more about sorting and filtering using keyword tags, see Chapter 4.

View Photos in the Media Browser

① Open the Organizer.

The Media Browser displays the photos in the Organizer catalog.

● Photos are sorted by their capture date from newest to oldest by default.

② Click and drag the thumbnail size slider (■) to the right.

● The thumbnails enlarge. You can click ▣ to maximize the thumbnails.

Dragging the slider (■) to the left decreases the size of the thumbnails. You can click ⊞ to minimize the thumbnails.

● You can use the scroll bar to browse other available thumbnails in the Media Browser.

③ Click the down arrow (▾) and then click **Date (Oldest First)**.

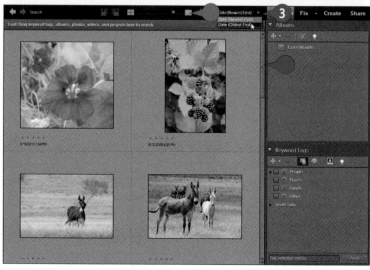

The sorting order reverses in the Media Browser, with the oldest photos at the top.

● The star rating and date details appear below each photo.

Note: See the section "Rate Photos" for more on star ratings.

④ Click the left arrow (◀).

Photoshop Elements returns the Media Browser to the previous view, which was with the images sorted with the newest displayed first.

● You can click the right arrow (▶) to go to the next view.

TIP

How can I hide certain file types in the Media Browser?
The Media Browser can help you organize not only photos but also video files, audio files, creative projects built in Photoshop Elements, and PDF files. You can filter the file types that appear in the Media Browser.

① In the Organizer, click **View**.

② Click **Media Types**.

The shown media types are checked.

③ Click a checked media type.

Photoshop Elements hides the media type in the Media Browser.

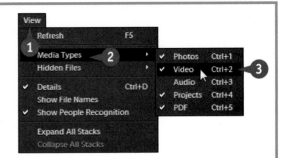

View Photos in Full Screen

You can switch to Full Screen mode in the Organizer to get a clearer view of your photos. Photoshop Elements expands the photos to fill the workspace and displays special panels for applying commands.

Full Screen mode is useful when you want to perform basic edits on a large version of your photo but do not want to switch to the Editor interface. You can access a film strip in Full Screen mode to access image thumbnails from your current catalog. This enables you to switch to another image.

View Photos in Full Screen

① In the Organizer, click the photo you want to view in Full Screen.

② Click ▣.

Photoshop Elements opens the photo in Full Screen.

● A Quick Edit panel for performing image edits is shown.

● A Quick Organize panel for adding images to albums and applying keyword tags is shown.

● The panels automatically hide if not used. You can click **Auto Hide** (▣) to turn this hiding on and off.

● Controls for viewing different photos and managing panels appear here.

③ Click ▣ to go to the next photo in the Organizer, or press the ▣ key.

Photoshop Elements displays the next photo.

④ Click **Toggle Film Strip** (■).

● The Film Strip opens, displaying thumbnail versions of your images.

⑤ Click a thumbnail.

Photoshop Elements displays the photo.

⑥ Click ✕ or press the Esc key to exit Full Screen mode.

TIP

How do I view detailed areas of my photos in Full Screen?

① While in Full Screen mode, roll the mouse wheel forward.

● The image zooms in and displays the zoom percentage.

② Click and drag the image with the mouse.

The image pans.

Display a Slide Show in Full Screen

You can play a slide show in Full Screen mode to cycle through large versions of your images. You can choose background music and transition effects to accompany the slides. This enables you to display photos from a vacation or event to friends and family on a monitor or, if your computer is hooked up to one, on a television screen.

Buttons enable you to play or pause the slide show, or flip through the slides one at a time. You can also create a slide show in Photoshop Elements and turn it into a movie that you can send to others. See Chapter 16 for details.

Display a Slide Show in Full Screen

1 In the Organizer, display the images you want to view as a slide show in the Media Browser.

● You can click an album to display photos from an album as a slide show.

2 Click ▣.

Photoshop Elements displays the first image in Full Screen mode.

3 Click the **Open Settings Dialog** button (▨).

The Full Screen View Options dialog box opens.

4 Click ▾ to choose background music.

● You can click **Browse** to browse for music on your computer to use as background music.

5 Click **OK** to close the dialog box.

⑥ Click the **Transitions** button
().

The Select Transition dialog
box opens.

⑦ Click a transition effect to
display between slides in the
slide show.

● You can position your mouse
pointer over an option to
preview an option.

⑧ Click **OK** to close the dialog
box.

⑨ Click the **Play** button (■) or
press [Spacebar].

Photoshop plays the slide
show, cycling through the
images at full screen.

You can click the **Play** button
(■) again to pause the slide
show.

How can I customize my slide show?

① Click **Open Settings Dialog** (■).

The Full Screen View Options dialog box opens.

● Click and select a slide duration.

● Click to start playing the slide show automatically
(■ changes to ☑).

● Click to include captions (■ changes to ☑).

● Click to repeat the slide show (■ changes to ☑).

② Click **OK** to save the settings.

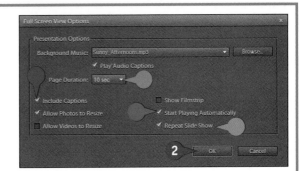

View Photo Properties

You can view the properties for any photo in your catalog. The Properties box displays a photo's general information, which includes the filename, file size, image size, and location.

You can also view any associated tags, file history, and metadata information. Metadata is detailed information about how a digital photo was taken; it includes camera settings, such as exposure time and f-stop. You can automatically organize your photos based on their metadata by creating a Smart Album. For more information, see Chapter 4.

View Photo Properties

1 In the Organizer, right-click a photo.

2 Click **Show Properties**.

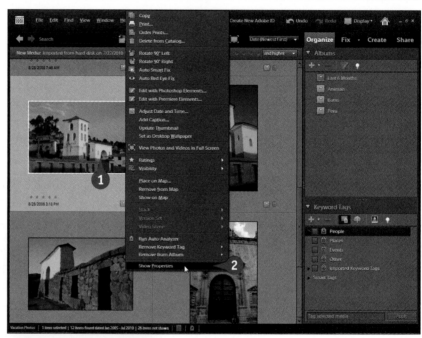

The Properties dialog box opens.

The General properties appear by default.

● You can add or edit a caption for the photo here.

● The rating, size, capture date, and other information for the photo are shown here.

3 Click the **Metadata** button (■).

The Metadata properties appear. This includes the camera model and settings if the photo came from a digital camera.

● You can click here to display the complete metadata for a photo (● changes to ○).

④ Click the **Keyword Tags** button (🏷).

The Keyword Tags properties appear.

Photoshop Elements displays any keyword tags or albums associated with the photo. You can right-click a tag or album to remove it from the photo.

● You can click the **History** button (🔄) to view Organizer statistics for the photo.

⑤ Click ✖ to close the Properties box.

TIP

How do I change the photo's date and time?

❶ Right-click the photo you want to edit.

❷ Click **Adjust Date and Time**.

❸ Click the **Change to a specified date and time** option.

❹ Click **OK**.

❺ Set the new date and time.

❻ Click **OK**.

Add a Caption

I n the Organizer, you can add captions to your photos to help you remember important information about the images you catalog. For example, you may add captions to your vacation pictures with details about the location or subject matter.

Captions appear below a photo when the image is viewed in Single Photo View. You can display captions when viewing a slide show in the Organizer. See "Display a Slide Show in Full Screen" for details. You can also include caption information with photos when you print them. See Chapter 17 for more information.

Add a Caption

1 In the Organizer, right-click the photo you want to caption.

2 Click **Add Caption**.

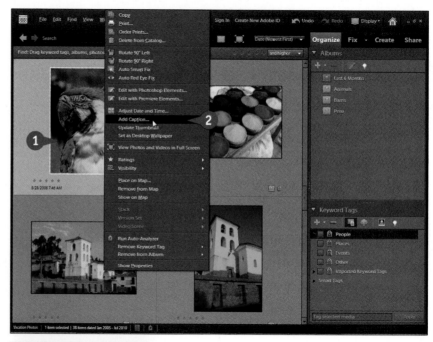

The Add Caption dialog box opens.

3 Type a caption for the photo.

4 Click **OK**.

The Organizer adds the caption to the photo. The caption is added to the metadata of the photo, which is accessible to programs besides Photoshop Elements.

5 Click the **Single Photo View** button (▭).

A large thumbnail of the photo appears.

● The caption appears below the photo.

Are there other ways to add captions to my photos?
Yes. You can also add captions to your photos by using the Properties box. See the section "View Photo Properties" for more.

How do I edit a caption?
To edit a caption, view the photo in Single Photo View in the Media Browser window, click the caption, and make your changes. You can delete the caption completely, type a new caption, or make changes to the existing caption text. Press Enter to save your changes.

Work with Albums

Albums are a way to organize your photos within an Organizer catalog. For example, you can take photos shot at a particular time or place and group them as an album. This makes it easier to find the photos later. Having photos organized in albums is also helpful with projects such as slide shows and photo books. Selecting an album to access a group of interesting photos is often the first step in making these creations.

A Smart Album is a special type of album that Photoshop Elements can automatically add to based on the characteristics of your images. You can also organize photos in a catalog by using keyword tags. See Chapter 4 for more about these features.

Work with Albums

Create a New Album

1 In the Organizer, open the catalog within which you want to create an album.

Note: For more on catalogs, see the section "Create a Catalog."

2 Open the Albums panel in the Panel Bin.

3 Click the plus sign (➕) and then click **New Album**.

The Album Details panel opens.

4 Type a name for the album.

● You can assign the album to an album category.

● If logged in, you can click here to enable Photoshop Elements to back up your album photos by using the Photoshop.com service (■ changes to ☑).

Note: For more on Photoshop.com, see Chapter 17.

5 Click and drag a photo from the Media Browser to the Items list box.

The Organizer adds the photo to the album.

6 Repeat Step **5** for all the photos you want to add to the album.

You can `Ctrl`+click to select multiple photos and then click and drag to add them all to the album.

7 Click **Done** to close the Album Details panel.

View an Album

1 Click the album name in the Albums panel.

The Organizer displays all the photos in the album.

● Photos assigned to an album are marked with an Album icon.

● You can click **Show All** to return to the entire catalog.

● You can click the minus icon (■) to delete the album.

TIP

How do I remove a photo from an album?

1 Under the photo in the Media Browser, right-click the **Album** icon for the album.

2 In the menu that appears, click **Remove from** *name* **Album**.

The Organizer removes the photo from the album. The Album icon under the photo disappears.

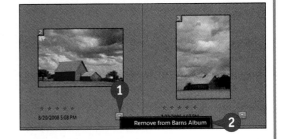

View Photos by Date

To help you keep track of your photos, the Organizer can sort your images by date and display those taken during a specific date range. You can also view the images for a particular date range as a slide show.

When you take a photo with a digital camera, the camera automatically attaches date information to your photo along with other information such as camera model and exposure settings. By accessing your photos' digital time stamps, Photoshop Elements can automatically sort them by the time they were taken. If the date setting of your camera was not set correctly, you can fix the dates associated with your photos. See the tip in the "View Photo Properties" section.

View Photos by Date

1 In the Organizer, click **Display**.

2 Click **Date View**.

The Organizer displays a calendar view of your catalog.

● You can view your photos by year, month, or day. In this example, the Month view is shown.

● To see a different month, click the **Previous Month** (●) or **Next Month** (●) button.

3 Click the date for the photos you want to view.

● The first photo in the group appears here.

4 Click the **Play** button (●).

The Organizer starts a slide show, displaying each photo from the date you selected.

● To pause or stop the sequence, click the **Pause** button (⬤).

To view the previous image again, click the **Previous Item** button (⬤).

To view the next image, click the **Next Item** button (⬤).

⑤ Click the **Find in the Media Browser** button (🎞).

● The Media Browser appears with the photo from the Date View visible.

You can also get to the Media Browser from the Date View by clicking **Display** and then **Media Browser**.

TIP

How can I view the Organizer timeline?
In the Media Browser, you can browse photos by date by clicking and dragging along a timeline.

① Click **Window**.

② Click **Timeline**.

The timeline opens at the top of the Media Browser.

● Click and drag the slider to move to a different photo date.

● Click and drag the endpoints to limit the range of dates.

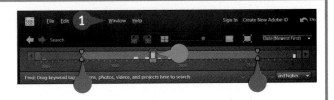

Find Photos

The Organizer offers a variety of methods for finding particular photos in your catalog. You can search for photos by date, filename, tags, text, and more. This can be helpful as your catalogs in the Organizer grow to thousands of photos and span years.

In this example, you search for photos taken during a specific date range and by text. When you search by text, Photoshop Elements examines captions, keyword tags, album names, and other text associated with your Organizer catalog.

Find Photos

Find Photos by Date

1 In the Organizer, click **Find**.

2 Click **Set Date Range**.

The Set Date Range dialog box opens.

3 Select the start date for the date range you want to search.

4 Select the end date for the date range you want to search.

5 Click **OK**.

The Organizer displays any matching photos in the Media Browser.

● A summary appears at the bottom of the Media Browser.

You can reset the date search by clicking **Find** and then **Clear Date Range**.

Find Photos by Text

1 Type one or more keywords in the search box.

Photoshop Elements searches the filenames, captions, keyword tags, album names, and other text associated with your photos.

● Photoshop Elements displays photos associated with the text as you type.

If you type multiple keywords, photos must be associated with all the keywords to match.

2 Click **Show All**.

Photoshop Elements cancels the search and displays all the photos.

TIP

What other search methods can I use to find photos?

You can search the Organizer by way of the Find menu.

Search Option	Function
By Caption or Note	Looks for photos based on the text of the notes and captions you have added to a photo
By Filename	Searches the catalog for a particular filename
By History	Looks up a photo based on when it was printed or e-mailed or by other criteria
By Media Type	Searches for creations, photos, and audio or video files in your catalog

Rate Photos

You can add star ratings to your photos in the Organizer to distinguish which ones are interesting and suitable for editing or projects. Photoshop Elements enables you to give each photo a rating of from one to five stars. After you rate your photos, you can filter them by rating and then add those photos to an album or use them in a slide show.

With the Smart Album feature, you can automatically have all images with a certain rating grouped together in an album. For information about Smart Albums, see Chapter 4.

Rate Photos

Apply a Rating

1 Click a star rating icon (■) below a photo in the Media Browser.

You can add a star rating from 1 to 5 by clicking the icons from left to right. You can also press a number key from 0 to 5. Pressing 0 removes the rating.

● Photoshop Elements assigns the rating and gold stars (■) appear.

You can also apply ratings in the Properties box in the General section. See the section "View Photo Properties" for more.

Filter by Rating

1 Click a star rating (⭐).

2 Click the ▾ and then choose **and higher**, **and lower**, or **only**.

Photoshop Elements displays photos that meet the rating criteria.

● You can click **Show All** to remove the rating filter.

TIP

How do I apply the same rating to multiple photos?

1 Ctrl+click to select the photos you want to rate.

2 Apply a star rating to one of the selected photos.

● The rating is applied to all the selected photos.

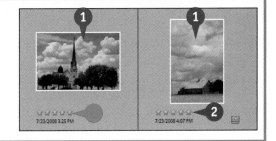

CHAPTER 4

Using Advanced Organizing Tools

Photoshop Elements gives you a number of advanced tools for managing the images in a collection. For example, you can create Smart Albums that automatically group photos that meet certain criteria. You can associate special terms, known as keyword tags, with photos to help you identify their content. You can also locate photos on a geographic map to associate them with the place they were shot.

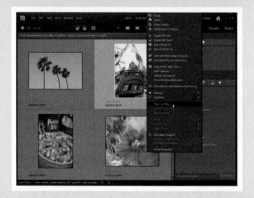
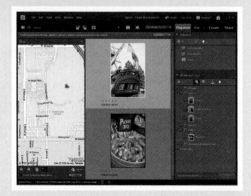

Create a Smart Album

A Smart Album has special criteria that determine what Photoshop Elements adds to the album. You can create Smart Albums for particular dates, tags, camera models, file sizes, and more. When you add a photo to the Organizer that meets the criteria for a Smart Album, Photoshop Elements automatically places that photo in the Smart Album.

If you regularly add keyword tags to family members in your photos, you can create a Smart Album for your family by setting rules that recognize those tags. You can create a date-based Smart Album to collect all the photos taken on your birthday or a holiday. The Organizer starts with a default Smart Album that contains all photos taken in the past six months.

Create a Smart Album

1 Open the Albums panel in the Organizer Bin.

2 Click the plus sign (![]) and then click **New Smart Album**.

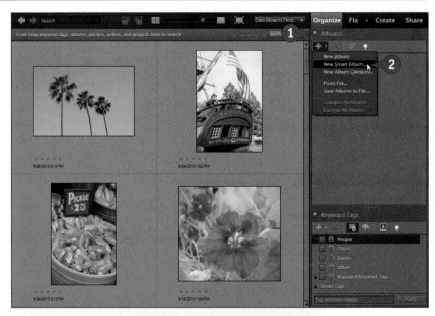

The New Smart Album dialog box opens.

3 Type a name for your Smart Album.

4 Click the down arrow (![]) to choose a photo attribute.

5 Click ![] to choose the criterion for the attribute.

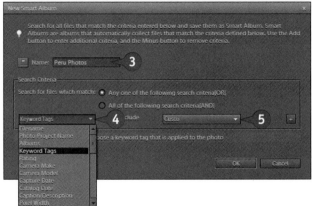

- You can click the plus sign (+) to add additional criteria.

- If your Smart Album includes more than one criterion, you can specify whether the album requires any or all of the criteria to be met.

6 Click **OK**.

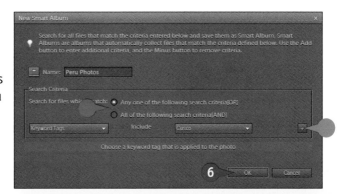

Photoshop Elements automatically adds photos that meet the criteria to the Smart Album and then displays the album in the Photo Browser.

As you add more photos to your catalog, photos that meet the criteria are automatically added to the Smart Album.

- You can click **Options** and then **Modify Search Criteria** to change the Smart Album settings.

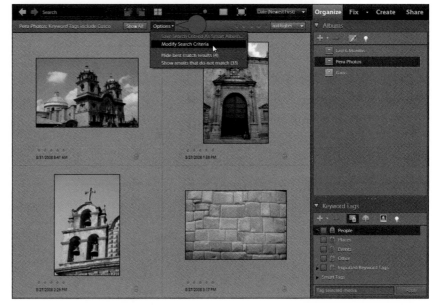

TIP

How can I create an album category?

You can organize similar albums in your Organizer into album categories.

1 Click the plus sign (+) and then click **New Album Category**.

The Create Album Category dialog box opens.

2 Type a name for the album category.

3 Click **OK**.

Photoshop Elements creates a new album category in the Albums panel. You can add albums to the category when you create them.

Work with Keyword Tags

Keyword tags help you categorize and filter your digital photos. For example, you can create a tag called *car* and apply it to all your photos of cars. You can assign the Organizer's preset tags or use tags that you have created. You can also assign more than one tag to a photo. For example, a photo of an automobile could have a *car* tag as well as a *convertible* tag.

Preset tags include those for people, family, friends, places, and events. You can assign tags to categories and subcategories.

Work with Keyword Tags

Create a Keyword Tag

1 In the Organizer, open the **Keyword Tags** panel in the Organizer bin.

2 Click ■ and then click **New Keyword Tag**.

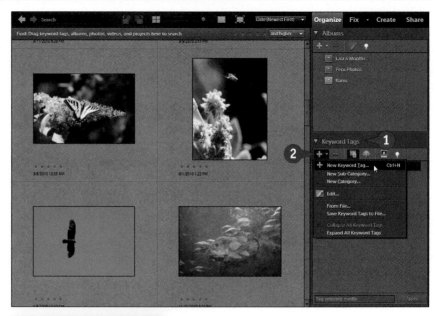

The Create Keyword Tag dialog box opens.

3 Click ■ and choose a category for the new tag.

4 Type a name for the keyword tag.

● You can add a note about the keyword tag here.

5 Click **OK**.

Assign Tags

6 Click and drag the tag from the Keyword Tags panel and then drop it on the photo you want to tag.

● The Organizer assigns the keyword tag. A keyword tag icon indicates that the photo has a tag assigned to it.

You can also drag a thumbnail image from the Media Browser to a keyword tag to assign a tag.

The tag displays a thumbnail image of the first photo it was assigned to.

7 Type text for a tag in the Keyword Tags search box.

Photoshop Elements suggests tags with that text.

8 Click a tag in the list that appears.

9 Ctrl+click to select photos you want to tag.

10 Click **Apply**.

● Photoshop Elements applies the tag to the selected photos.

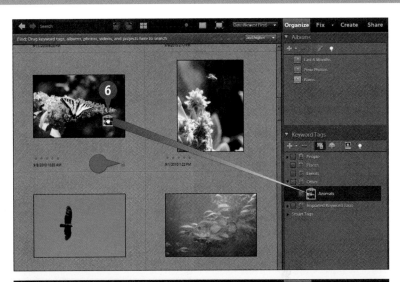

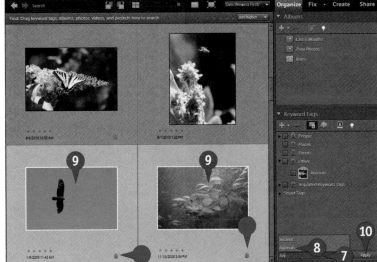

TIP

How do I edit a keyword tag?

1 Right-click the keyword tag and then choose **Edit *name* keyword tag**.

The Edit Keyword Tag dialog box opens.

2 Type a new keyword tag name or make other edits to the tag.

3 Click **OK**.

Photoshop Elements applies the changes. Any images that have the keyword tag applied are updated.

continued ▶

fter you assign keyword tags, you can filter your catalog to show only those photos that have certain tags. For example, you can filter your photos to show only photos of people or events. You can also simultaneously filter multiple keyword tags.

To learn about how to quickly add tags to people in your photos by recognizing their faces, see "Tag Faces." Another way to filter photos in your Organizer catalog is to place them into albums. See "Create a Smart Album" for more about albums.

Work with Keyword Tags (continued)

Filter by Tags

1 Open the Keyword Tags panel if it is not already displayed.

2 Click the check box next to the keyword tag on which you want to filter (■ changes to ☑).

● You can click ▶□ to expand a tag category.

● You can click ▼□ to collapse a tag category.

To filter by more than one keyword tag, you can click additional tags.

● The Organizer displays the photos that share the keyword tag.

If you selected multiple tags, only photos that have all the tags appear.

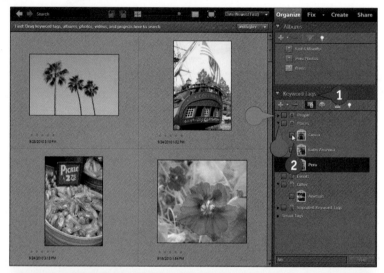

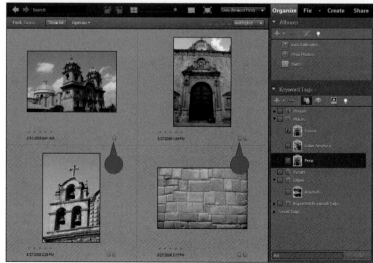

Remove a Tag from a Photo

1 Right-click the photo containing the tag you want to remove.

2 Click **Remove Keyword Tag**.

3 Click the keyword tag you want to remove.

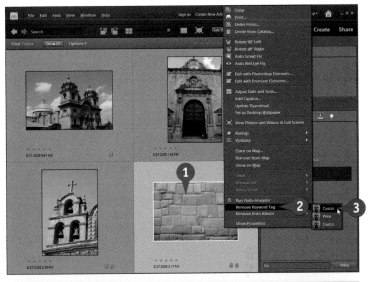

The Organizer removes the keyword tag from the photo.

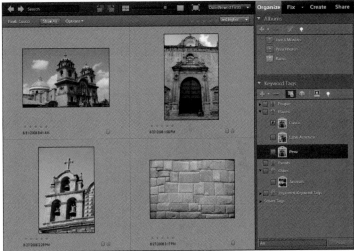

How can I use keyword tags when I use the regular search box?

The regular search box suggests keyword tags as you type search terms.

1 Type text in the search box.

● Photoshop Elements displays any keywords that match that text.

2 Click the keyword tag to display tagged photos with that keyword.

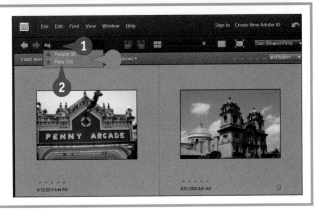

View a Tag Cloud

You can view your keyword tags as a tag cloud, which organizes tags alphabetically and sizes them by the number of times applied. You can click tags in the tag cloud to filter the photos in the Media Browser.

A tag cloud offers an interesting way to assess the keyword tags that categorize your photos in a small amount of space. When you have dozens or hundreds of keyword tags, viewing them as a tag cloud can help you quickly pick out the most popular ones. For information about creating keyword tags, see "Work with Keyword Tags."

View a Tag Cloud

1 In the Organizer, open the Keyword Tags panel if it is not already displayed.

● The default view is Keyword Tag Hierarchy View, which lists tags categorically.

2 Click the **View Keyword Tag Cloud** button ( ).

Photoshop Elements displays a tag cloud.

● A tag cloud displays tags in alphabetical order and sizes the terms according to the number of times they are used.

3 Click a keyword tag.

● Photoshop Elements highlights the term.

● Only the photos tagged with that term are shown in the Media Browser.

Only one tag in the tag cloud may be selected at a time.

④ Click the keyword tag again.

● Photoshop Elements removes the highlighting.

The view in the Media Browser is reset.

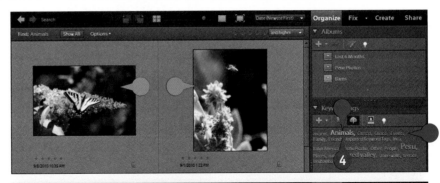

TIP

How can someone else use the keyword tags that I have created?

① In the Keyword Tags panel, click the plus sign (⊞).

② Click **Save Keyword Tag(s) to File**.

● To import tags from a file, click **From File**.

③ In the dialog box, click **Export All Keyword Tags** (● changes to ○).

④ Click **OK**.

A Save dialog box opens, enabling you to save the keyword tags, which you can then send.

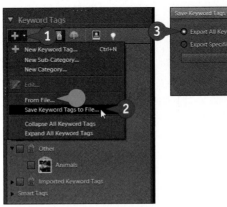

Tag Faces

You can use the Organizer's face-recognition feature to pinpoint the faces in your photos for easy tagging. Photoshop Elements automatically scans photos in the Organizer for the colors and structures characteristic of human faces. It then presents just the faces from the photos for you to classify.

As you label the faces, Photoshop Elements creates custom keyword tags in the People category for the friends and family members whose faces appear often in your photos. You can select the face tags to quickly display photos of specific people from your collection.

Tag Faces

1 In the Organizer, open the Keyword Tags panel if it is not already displayed.

2 Ctrl+click to select the photos in which you want to recognize faces.

If you do not select any photos, Photoshop Elements searches all the photos.

3 Click the **Start People Recognition** button (⬛).

Photoshop Elements searches for faces and displays the results in a People Recognition dialog box.

● Recognized faces are highlighted in boxes.

4 Click a box.

5 Type a descriptive tag, such as a name for the face.

6 Press Enter.

Photoshop Elements tags the face.

7 Repeat Steps **4** to **6** for the other faces.

● You can right-click a box to open a menu that enables you to ignore a face or mark the selection as not a face.

8 When you finish adding tags, click **Save**.

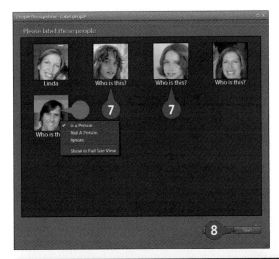

● Photoshop Elements creates tags for the labeled faces under the People tag category.

You can double-click a tag to display only images with that tag.

● Images with labeled faces are marked with tag icons.

Note: For more on using tags to filter photos, see the section "Work with Keyword Tags."

TIP

How can I automatically find visually similar photos?

1 In the Organizer, click to select a photo.

2 Click **Find**.

3 Click **By Visual Similarity with Selected Photo(s) and Video(s)**.

Photoshop Elements displays similar photos in the Organizer.

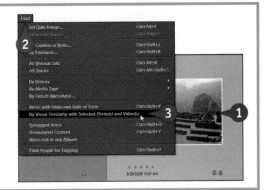

Map a Photo

You can place your Organizer photos on a geographic map to specify where they were taken. The mapping feature in Photoshop Elements uses navigable-map technology from Yahoo, allowing you to pan and zoom on the map and then place your photos with precision. It also has a search feature that enables you to input a street address and then be taken to that location on a map for placing your photo.

Categorizing your photos by location, a process known as *geotagging*, can help you retrieve meaningful photos years later. For example, you can easily pull up photos from where you lived as a child or where you vacationed each summer. You need an active Internet connection for the mapping feature to work in Photoshop Elements.

Map a Photo

① Right-click a photo in the Organizer.

② Click **Place on Map**.

The Photo Location on Map dialog box opens.

③ Type a location for your photo.

In addition to specific addresses, cities, and states, you can type famous locations, such as the Golden Gate Bridge or the Eiffel Tower.

④ Click **Find**.

Photoshop Elements suggests one or more locations from its database.

⑤ Choose a location.

⑥ Click **OK**.

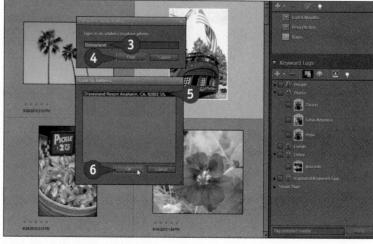

If a dialog box with tips about mapping photos opens, click **OK** to close it.

● Photoshop Elements displays a map with a red pushpin (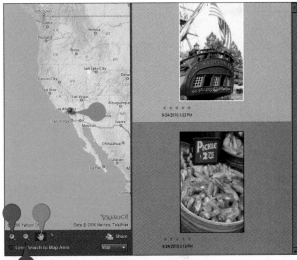) at the selected location.

● You can select the **Zoom In** tool ( ) and then click the map to zoom in.

● You can select the **Zoom Out** tool ( ) and then click the map to zoom out.

● You can select the **Hand** tool ( ) and then click and drag the map to scroll.

7 Click to zoom in to the location.

8 Click the **Move** tool ( ).

9 Click and drag the red pushpin ( ) to a more specific location.

10 To close the map, click .

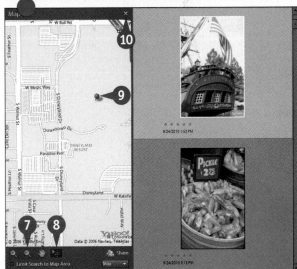

TIP

How else can I add photos to a map?
With the Map window open, you can click and drag thumbnails to place photos on a map.

1 In the Organizer, click **Window**.

2 Click **Show Map**.

If a dialog box about mapping opens, click **OK**.

3 In the Map window, click and drag a thumbnail to the map.

Photoshop Elements maps the photo.

Apply Photo Fixes in Full Screen

You can optimize color, lighting, and other aspects of your photos in the Organizer's Full Screen view. This can be convenient when you want to make simple changes to your photos in the Organizer but do not want to switch to the Editor. You apply commands by using the Quick Edit panel.

Most of the fixes available in the Full Screen view are automatic fixes requiring a single click of a button. You can also add photos to albums and apply keyword tags in Full Screen view. For more on Full Screen view, see Chapter 3. For more on opening the Editor, see Chapter 1.

Apply Photo Fixes in Full Screen

1 In the Organizer, click the photo you want to fix.

2 Click the **Full Screen** button (▣).

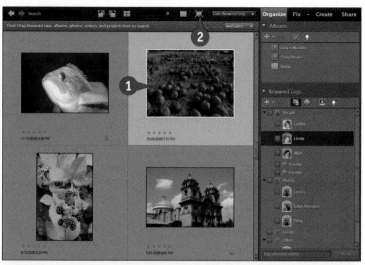

Photoshop Elements opens the photo in Full Screen.

● A Quick Edit panel appears.

● If the panel is hidden, you can click **Toggle Quick Edit Panel** (▣) to open it.

3 Position the mouse cursor over a button.

● A description of the edit command appears.

4 Click the button.

Photoshop Elements applies the edit.

5 Click ✖ or press `Esc`.

Photoshop Elements exits Full Screen view.

● The edited version of the photo is saved in a photo stack with the original version of the photo.

Note: For more on stacks, see the section "Stack Photos."

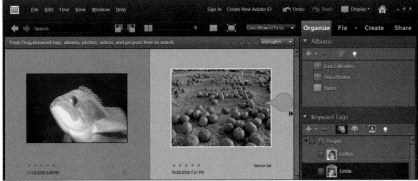

How do I add photos to albums or apply keyword tags while in Full Screen?

1 If the Quick Organize panel is hidden, click **Toggle Quick Organize Panel** (✦) to open it.

2 Click an album name.

Photoshop Elements adds the current photo to the album.

3 Click a keyword tag.

Photoshop Elements assigns the keyword tag to the current photo.

Stack Photos

In the Organizer, you can group similar photos into stacks. This can help you conserve space in the Organizer interface because stacks can be collapsed so that only the top photo on the stack appears.

Stacks can be based on any measure of similarity that you choose. For example, you can stack photos of the same scene or group of people, or photos that have similar lighting, exposure, or colors. In addition to manually stacking your photos, you can have Photoshop Elements suggest stacks based on photographic similarity.

Stack Photos

Create a Stack

1 In the Organizer, **Ctrl**+click to select the photos you want to stack.

2 Right-click one of the selected photos.

3 Click **Stack**.

4 Click **Stack Selected Photos**.

● You can click **Automatically Suggest Photo Stacks** to have Photoshop Elements suggest stacks based on photographic similarity.

● Photoshop Elements creates a stack for the selected photos. The photo that you right-clicked is placed on top of the stack and is shown here.

5 Click the stack button (▶) to expand.

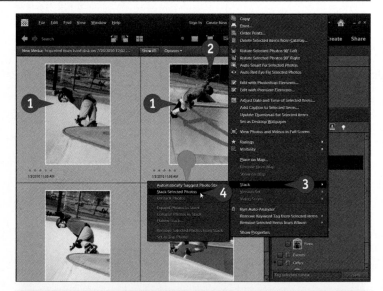

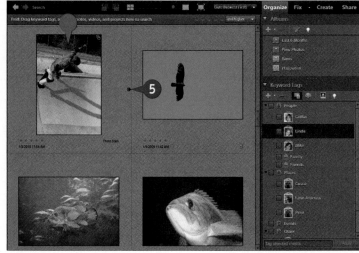

The stack expands to show its contents.

● You can click here to collapse the stack (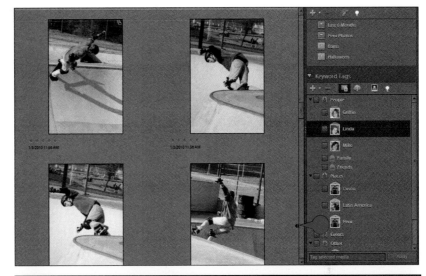).

Unstack Photos

1 Right-click a photo in a stack. If the stack is collapsed, right-click the top photo.

2 Click **Stack**.

3 Click **Unstack Photos**.

Photoshop Elements removes the stack and places photos in the Organizer separately.

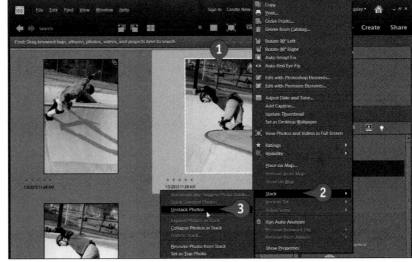

TIP

How do I automatically stack photos as I import them?

1 Click **File**, click **Get Photos and Videos**, and click **From Files and Folders**.

2 In the dialog box that opens, click the **Automatically Suggest Photo Stacks** check box (☐ changes to ☑).

When you import the photos, Photoshop Elements suggests groups of photos to be stacked based on their photographic similarity.

CHAPTER 5

Applying Basic Image Edits

Are you ready to start working with images? This chapter shows you how to fine-tune your workspace to best arrange your open images. You also discover how to change the on-screen image size, set a print size, and change the print resolution.

Manage Open Images

Each image you open in Photoshop Elements appears in its own window, and you can have multiple windows open at once. When viewing one image window at a time, tabs at the top of each window enable you to switch between images. Each tab lists the name of the image file, the current magnification, and the image mode.

Viewing one image at a time gives you the maximum space for viewing and editing an image. You can also use the Project Bin or Image menu to switch between different open images.

Manage Open Images

Using Tabs

1 In the Editor, open two or more images.

Note: For more on opening the Editor, see Chapter 1. For more on opening image files, see Chapter 2.

● The active or current image appears here.

● Each open image has its own tab, which displays its filename and magnification.

2 Click a tab for the image you want to view.

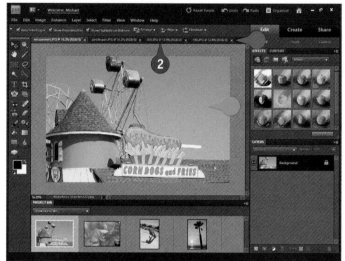

● The image appears as the active image. You can make changes to the active image by applying commands and effects.

Using the Project Bin

● By default, the Project Bin displays smaller versions, or *thumbnails*, of the images.

Note: See the tip on the next page for more on how to display other images in the Project Bin.

If the Project Bin is closed, you can click **Window** and then **Project Bin** to open it.

3 Double-click a thumbnail.

● The image appears as the
active image.

Using the Window Menu

④ Click **Window**.

⑤ Click an image filename.

● The image appears as the
active image.

● You can click ☒ to close an
image.

TIP

How do I display different images in the Project Bin?

In the Project Bin, you can display images from albums created in the Organizer.

① Click the down arrow (▾).

② Click an album name.

● You can click here to display all the
images from the Organizer.

● Photoshop Elements displays the
album images.

continued ▶

You can view multiple image windows at the same time by choosing a layout. Layouts enable you to display images as a grid, in vertical columns, or in horizontal rows. Viewing more than one image window at a time can be helpful when comparing images.

When viewing multiple images at once, only one of the windows is active. You can choose the active window by clicking its tab, clicking inside the window, or selecting the image from the Window menu. When you apply commands in Photoshop Elements, the commands act on the active image.

Manage Open Images (continued)

Using Layouts

6 Click the down arrow (▾).

Photoshop Elements displays a menu of layouts.

● The top row enables you to display images one at a time, as a grid, in vertical columns, or in horizontal rows.

7 Click a layout.

Photoshop Elements displays multiple windows, each with a different image.

8 Click ▣.

● The lower rows enable you to display a specific number of images at a time.

For example, selecting a 3 Up layout displays three windows, with an open image in each one.

9 Click a layout.

Photoshop Elements displays multiple windows at once, each with a different image.

● If you have more open images than windows, you can click tabs to switch between images.

How can I magnify all my visible images at once?
When the Zoom tool (🔍) is selected, you can click the **Zoom All Windows** check box (■ changes to ☑) in the Options bar to make the tool affect all windows. See the section "Magnify with the Zoom Tool" for more on changing magnification.

Where else can I find commands for controlling my image windows?
You can select various commands in the layout menu. If you are comparing several photos on-screen, you can click **Match Location** to view the same area in each open window. You can click **Match Zoom** to view each open window at the same zoom percentage.

Magnify with the Zoom Tool

You can change the magnification of an image with the Zoom tool. This enables you to view small details in an image or view an image at full size. Magnifying has no effect on the size of the actual saved image.

Zooming in on an image can be helpful when you are making detailed selections with a selection tool, searching for imperfections in your image, or aligning layers precisely with one another. For more about making selections, see Chapter 6. For details about layers, see Chapter 8. You can also adjust the magnification of an image to an exact percentage using the field in the lower left corner of the image window.

Magnify with the Zoom Tool

Increase Magnification

1. In the Editor, click the **Zoom** tool (🔍).

   You can also press the **Z** shortcut key.

   Note: For more on opening the Editor, see Chapter 1.

2. Click the image.

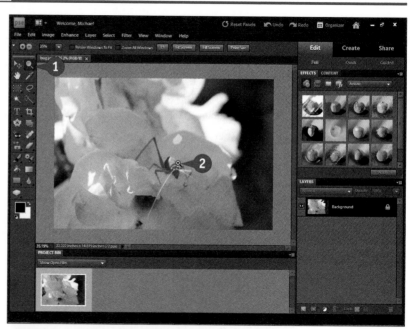

Photoshop Elements increases the magnification of the image. By default, the Zoom tool zooms in when you click the image.

The current magnification shows in the image title bar and Options bar.

● You can select an exact magnification by typing a percentage value in the Options bar or in the lower left corner of the image window.

Decrease Magnification

1 Click the **Zoom Out** button (⊖).

You can also press and hold **Alt** to zoom out.

2 Click the image.

Photoshop Elements decreases the magnification of the image.

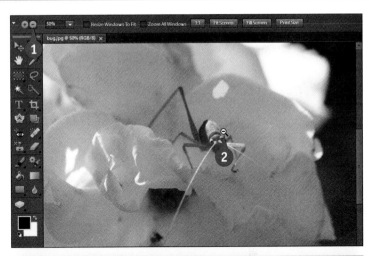

Magnify a Detail

1 Click the **Zoom In** button (⊕).

2 Click and drag with the **Zoom** tool (🔍) to select the detail.

The area appears enlarged on-screen.

The more you zoom in, the larger the pixels appear and the less you see of the image's content.

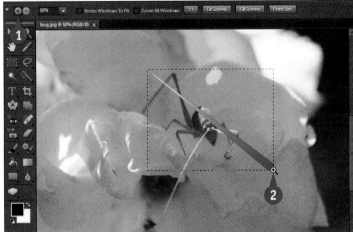

TIP

How do I quickly return an image to 100% magnification?
The following are seven ways to return the image to 100%.

1 Double-click the **Zoom** tool (🔍).

2 Click **1:1** on the Options bar.

3 Click **View** and then **Actual Pixels** from the menu.

4 Type **100%** in the Options bar field.

5 Type **100%** in the lower left corner of the image window.

6 Right-click the image and select **Actual Pixels**.

7 Press **Alt**+**Ctrl**+**0**.

Adjust the Image View

You can move an image within the window by using the Hand tool or scrollbars. The Hand tool helps you navigate to an exact area in the image by dragging freely in two dimensions. The scrollbars enable you to pan an image vertically or horizontally.

Using the Hand tool is helpful when you are working with a high-resolution image and want to examine details throughout the image at high magnification. The tool is also useful when you have a low-resolution monitor, which means there is a smaller area in which to display the Photoshop Elements workspace.

Adjust the Image View

Using the Hand tool

1 In the Editor, click the **Hand** tool (![hand icon]).

You can also press the **H** shortcut key.

Note: For more on opening the Editor, see Chapter 1.

Note: For the Hand tool (![hand icon]) to have an effect, the image must be larger than the image window.

2 Click and drag inside the image window.

The view of the image shifts inside the window.

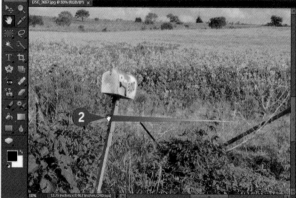

Using the Scroll Bars

1 Click and hold one of the window's scrollbar buttons (■, ■, ■, or ■).

The image scrolls in the direction you select — in this example, down.

How can I quickly adjust the image window to see the entire image at its largest possible magnification on-screen?

The following are five ways to magnify the image.

1 Double-click the **Hand** tool (■).

2 Click **Fit Screen** on the Options bar.

3 Click **View** and then **Fit on Screen** from the menu.

4 Right-click the image and choose **Fit on Screen** from the pop-up menu.

5 Press Ctrl + 0.

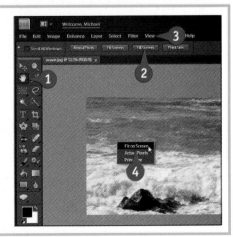

Change the On-Screen Image Size

ou can change the on-screen size of an image you are working with in Photoshop Elements to make it better fit the confines of your monitor when viewed at the same magnification. Shrinking an image can also lower its file size and make it easier to share via e-mail or on the Web.

When you change an image's on-screen size, you need to resample it. Resampling is the process of increasing or decreasing the number of pixels in an image. Enlarging or shrinking an image too much can cause a noticeable decrease in image quality, which you can notice by examining details using the Zoom tool.

Change the On-Screen Image Size

1 In the Editor, click **Image**.

Note: For more on opening the Editor, see Chapter 1.

2 Click **Resize**.

3 Click **Image Size**.

The Image Size dialog box opens, listing the width and height of the image in pixels.

You can also press **Alt** + **Ctrl** + **I** to open the Image Size dialog box.

● To resize by a certain percentage, click the ▼ and change the units to **percent**.

4 Click the **Resample Image** check box (■ changes to ☑).

Note: Of the options in the Resample Image menu, Bicubic Smoother is often better for enlarging, whereas Bicubic Sharper is better for shrinking.

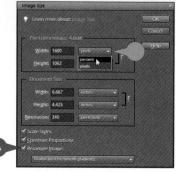

5 Type a size or percentage for a dimension.

● You can click the **Constrain Proportions** check box (■ changes to ☑) to cause the other dimension to change proportionally.

6 Click **OK**.

● You can restore the original dialog box settings without exiting the dialog box by pressing and holding `Alt` and clicking **Cancel**, which changes to Reset.

Photoshop Elements resizes the image.

In this example, the image decreases to 50 percent of the original size.

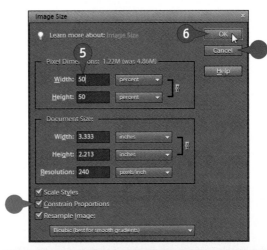

TIP

How do I change the size of an image as I am saving it for the Web?

1 Click **File** and then click **Save For Web**.

The Save For Web dialog box opens.

2 Type a new value in the **Width** or **Height** field to change the dimensions of your image.

● You can also change the size of your image by a percentage.

3 Click **Apply** to resize the image.

4 Click **OK** to save the image.

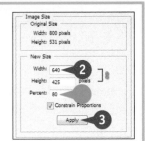

Change the Image Print Size

You can change the printed size of an image to determine how it appears on paper. Print size is also called *document size* in Photoshop Elements.

If you change the print size of an image with the resampling option checked, Photoshop Elements adjusts the number of pixels in the image but keeps the resolution the same. If the resampling option is unchecked, the resolution changes but not the number of pixels.

Photoshop Elements also gives you resizing options when you print your image. You can either print it at actual size or you can choose from a list of common photo print sizes. For more about printing, see Chapter 17.

Change the Image Print Size

1. In the Editor, click **Image**.

Note: For more on opening the Editor, see Chapter 1.

2. Click **Resize**.

3. Click **Image Size**.

The Image Size dialog box opens, listing the current width and height of the printed image.

● You can click ▾ to change the unit of measurement.

● If you click the **Resample Image** check box, Photoshop Elements adjusts the number of pixels in the image to resize. Otherwise, it adjusts the resolution.

Note: For more on resolution, see the section "Change the Image Resolution."

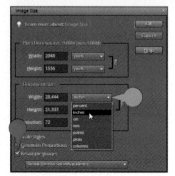

④ Type a size or percentage for a dimension.

● You can click the **Constrain Proportions** check box (■ changes to ☑) to cause the other dimension to change proportionally.

⑤ Click **OK**.

● You can restore the original dialog box settings by pressing and holding **Alt** and clicking **Cancel**, which changes to Reset.

Photoshop Elements resizes the image.

Note: Changing the size of an image, especially enlarging, can add blur. To sharpen a resized image, see Chapter 9.

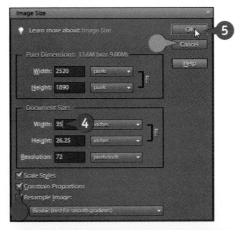

TIP

How do I preview an image's printed size?
① Click **File**.
② Click **Print**.

● The Print Preview dialog box shows how the image will print on the page.

● To select other dimensions, click ▼ and choose a print size.

③ Click **Print** to print the image.

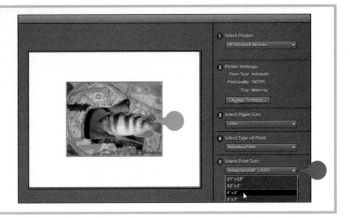

Change the Image Resolution

You can change the print resolution of an image to increase or decrease the print quality. The resolution, combined with the number of pixels in an image, determines the size of a printed image. The greater the resolution, the better the image appears on the printed page — up to a limit, which varies with the type of printer you use and the paper on which you are printing.

For more about how the size of images are determined in Photoshop Elements, see "Change the On-Screen Image Size" and "Change the Image Print Size."

Change the Image Resolution

1 In the Editor, click **Image**.

Note: For more on opening the Editor, see Chapter 1.

2 Click **Resize**.

3 Click **Image Size**.

The Image Size dialog box opens, listing the current resolution of the image.

● You can click the ▾ to change the resolution units.

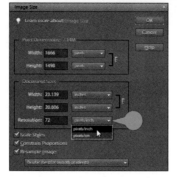

④ Type a new resolution.

● You can deselect the **Resample Image** check box (☑ changes to ■) to keep the number of pixels in your image fixed and change the printed dimensions. The print quality will change.

⑤ Click **OK**.

● You can restore the original dialog box settings by pressing and holding **Alt** and clicking **Cancel**, which changes to Reset.

Photoshop Elements adjusts the image resolution.

If you deselected the Resample Image check box, the number of pixels stays the same, as does the on-screen image size. Increasing the resolution makes the print size smaller, and decreasing the resolution makes it bigger.

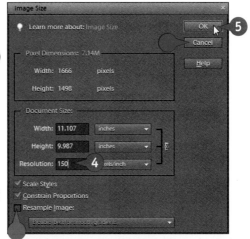

TIPS

What is the relationship between resolution, on-screen size, and print size?

To determine the printed size of a Photoshop Elements image, you can divide the on-screen size by the resolution. If you have an image with an on-screen width of 480 pixels and a resolution of 120 pixels per inch, the printed width is 4 inches.

What resolution should I use for images that I intend to print?

The appropriate resolution depends on a variety of factors, including the type of printer and paper you are using. 300 dpi is standard resolution for offset printing. For most standard inkjet printers, a resolution of 240-280 pixels per inch should be sufficient to produce good-quality prints on photo-quality paper. A resolution of 150 pixels per inch is sufficient for regular copier paper. Printing at lower resolutions may cause elements in your image to appear jagged.

Change the Image Canvas Size

You can alter the canvas size of an image to change its rectangular shape or add space around its borders. The canvas is the area on which an image sits. Changing the canvas size is one way to crop an image or add *matting*, which is blank space, around an image.

Photoshop Elements warns you when you decrease the dimensions of the image canvas because this deletes part of the image. You might want to increase the canvas size if you are making a collage of images and want the images to overlap one another. Increasing the canvas gives you space to add other images.

Change the Image Canvas Size

1 In the Editor, click **Image**.

Note: For more on opening the Editor, see Chapter 1.

2 Click **Resize**.

3 Click **Canvas Size**.

The Canvas Size dialog box opens, listing the current dimensions of the canvas.

● You can click ▾ to change the unit of measurement.

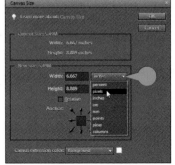

④ Type the new canvas dimensions.

● You can click an arrow (◣) to determine in which directions Photoshop Elements changes the canvas size. Clicking the square in the middle of the arrows crops the image equally on opposite sides.

⑤ Click **OK**.

Note: If you decrease a dimension, Photoshop Elements displays a dialog box asking whether you want to proceed. Click **Proceed**.

Photoshop Elements changes the image's canvas size.

In this example, because the width is increased, Photoshop Elements creates new canvas space on the sides of the image.

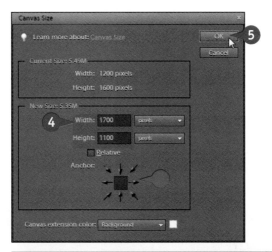

TIP

How do I specify the matte color around my canvas?

❶ In the Canvas Size dialog box, click ▼ to specify the matte color.

● You can click here or select **Other** to select a custom color.

● The color appears when you enlarge a dimension of your image.

Crop an Image

You can use the Crop tool to quickly remove unneeded space on the top, bottom, and sides of an image. Cropping is a great way to edit out unwanted background elements or reposition a subject in your photo. You can also rotate the cropping boundary prior to cropping, which enables you to rotate while you are cropping.

You can also crop an image by changing its canvas size. See the section "Change the Image Canvas Size" for more on setting a new canvas size. Another way is by selecting an area with a selection tool, clicking Image, and then clicking Crop. See Chapter 6 for more on making selections.

Crop an Image

1 In the Editor, click the **Crop** tool (◩).

Note: For more on opening the Editor, see Chapter 1.

2 Click and drag to select the area of the image you want to keep.

Another way to crop an image is by changing its canvas size; you do this by clicking **Image**, **Resize**, and then **Canvas Size**, and then you can type new dimensions for the image.

● You can set specific dimensions for a crop by using the Width and Height boxes in the Options bar.

3 Click and drag the side and corner handles (✥) to adjust the size of the cropping boundary.

You can click and drag inside the cropping boundary to move it without adjusting its size.

You can click and drag outside the cropping boundary to rotate the tool prior to executing the crop.

4 Click ☑ or press **Enter** to accept the crop.

You can also double-click inside the crop area to crop the photo.

● To exit the cropping process, you can click ⊘ or press **Esc** to reject.

Photoshop Elements crops the image, deleting the pixels outside the cropping boundary.

How do I crop my image into an interesting shape?

1 Click the **Cookie Cutter** tool (☆).

2 Click ▾ and then click a shape for the crop.

● You can click here to access additional shapes.

3 Adjust the cropping boundary and then perform the crop similar to using the regular Crop tool.

Photoshop Elements crops the selected content as a shape. Unlike with the Crop tool, the dimensions of the image canvas remain unchanged.

Rotate an Image

You can use the rotate actions on an image to turn it within the image canvas. If you import or scan a horizontal image vertically, you can rotate it so that it appears in the correct orientation.

You can also flip a photo to change the direction of the subject matter. Flipping it horizontally, for example, creates a mirror image of the photo.

Rotating an image can add blank space around the sides. You can crop the image to remove this extra space. Note that rotating an image by something other than 90-degree multiples can decrease image quality slightly.

Rotate an Image

Rotate 90 Degrees

1 In the Editor, click **Image**.

Note: For more on opening the Editor, see Chapter 1.

2 Click **Rotate**.

3 Click **90° Left** or **90° Right** to rotate an image.

● To change subject direction, click **Flip Horizontal** or **Flip Vertical**.

Photoshop Elements rotates the image.

Rotate Precisely

1 Click **Image**.

2 Click **Rotate**.

3 Click **Custom**.

The Rotate Canvas dialog box opens.

4 Type an angle from -359.99 to 359.99.

5 Click a direction to rotate.

6 Click **OK**.

Photoshop Elements rotates the image to your exact specifications.

TIP

How can I automatically straighten a crooked image?
The Straighten Image command is useful for fixing photos that have been scanned crookedly.

1 Click **Image**.

2 Click **Rotate**.

3 Click **Straighten Image**.

● You can click **Straighten and Crop Image** to automatically crop any space left after straightening.

Photoshop Elements straightens the image.

Undo Changes to an Image

You can undo commands by using the Undo History panel. This enables you to correct mistakes or change your mind about operations you have performed on your image. The Undo History panel lists recently executed commands, with the most recent command at the bottom. In the Preferences dialog box, you can control how many commands Photoshop Elements remembers in the Undo History panel. Up to 1000 commands can be remembered. To change preferences in Photoshop Elements, see Chapter 1.

To undo just a single command, you can use the Undo button located at the top of the Photoshop Elements interface or press ctrl+Z. After you undo a command, you can execute the same command again using the Redo command.

Undo Changes to an Image

1 In the Editor, click **Window**.

Note: For more on opening the Editor, see Chapter 1.

2 Click **Undo History**.

The Undo History panel opens, listing recently executed commands.

3 Click the **History** slider (■) and then drag it upward.

● Alternatively, you can click a previous command in the Undo History panel.

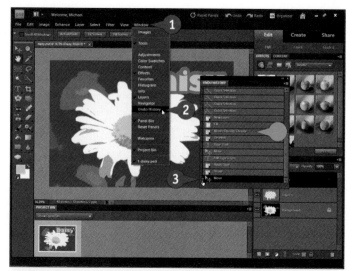

● Photoshop Elements undoes the previous commands.

● You can click and drag the slider down to redo the commands.

108

Revert an Image

You can revert an image to the previously saved state. This enables you to start your image editing over. After you revert an image, you can still change your mind and switch back to the unreverted state by clicking Edit and then Undo Revert.

An alternative to reverting all at once is undoing commands. The Undo History panel enables you to roll back your image-editing work by undoing a set number of commands. See "Undo Changes to an Image" for details.

Revert an Image

1️⃣ In the Editor, click **Edit**.

Note: For more on opening the Editor, see Chapter 1.

2️⃣ Click **Revert**.

Photoshop Elements reverts the image to its previously saved state.

● To return to the unreverted state, click **Undo** (🔄).

CHAPTER 6

Making Selections

Do you want to move, color, or transform parts of your image independently from the rest of the image? The first step is to make a selection. This chapter shows you how to use the Photoshop Elements selection tools to isolate portions of your images for editing. You can use different tools to select objects in your image or areas of similar color. You can even save your selections for loading later.

Select an Area with the Marquee

You can select parts of an image for editing by using a marquee. You can then make changes to the selected area by using other Photoshop Elements commands.

Two marquee tools are available: The Rectangular Marquee enables you to select rectangular shapes, including squares, and the Elliptical Marquee enables you to select elliptical shapes, including circles. You click and drag diagonally in your image to apply both tools. You can also use settings in the Options bar to define specific dimensions for your marquees such as a fixed size or ratio.

Select an Area with the Marquee

Select with the Rectangular Marquee

1 In the Editor, click the **Rectangular Marquee** tool ( ) or press the M shortcut key.

Note: For more on opening the Editor, see Chapter 1.

2 Click and drag diagonally inside the image window.

You can press and hold Shift while you click and drag to create a square selection.

● Photoshop Elements selects a rectangular portion of your image.

You can reposition selections by pressing the keyboard arrow keys: ↑, ↓, ←, and →. You can also click and drag inside the selection while a marquee tool is active.

● You can deselect a selection by clicking **Select** and then **Deselect**, pressing Ctrl+D, or by clicking outside the selection area.

Select with the Elliptical Marquee

1 Right-click the **Rectangular Marquee** tool (▦). Pressing the **M** shortcut key also toggles between the Rectangular and Elliptical marquee tools.

2 Click the **Elliptical Marquee** tool (▢).

3 Click and drag diagonally inside the image window.

You can press and hold (Shift) while you click and drag to create a circular selection, or you can press and hold (Shift) and (Alt) to draw the circle directly out from the center.

● Photoshop Elements selects an elliptical portion of your image.

You can reposition selections by pressing the keyboard arrow keys: ⬆, ⬇, ⬅, and ➡.

● You can deselect a selection by clicking **Select** and then **Deselect** or by clicking outside the selection area.

TIP

How do I customize the marquee tools?

You can customize the marquee tools (▦ and ▢) by using the boxes and menus in the Options bar. Marquee options appear only when you click a marquee tool.

● **Feather:** Typing a value softens and blends selection edges that you move, cut, or copy.

● **Mode:** Selecting an option from the Mode list defines the operation of the marquee tool as Normal (no restrictions), Fixed Ratio, or a Fixed Size.

● **Width and Height:** Entering values enable you to set an exact width and height for a selection.

Select an Area with the Lasso

You can outline irregularly shaped selections with the lasso tools. You can then make changes to the selected area by using other Photoshop Elements commands. You can use three types of lasso tools: the regular Lasso, the Polygonal Lasso, and the Magnetic Lasso. Which lasso you use depends on the objects in your image that you want to select.

You can use the regular Lasso tool to create freehand selections. The Polygonal Lasso tool enables you to easily create a selection composed of many straight lines. The Magnetic Lasso tool automatically applies a selection border to edges as you drag.

Select an Area with the Lasso

Select with the Regular Lasso

1 In the Editor, click the **Lasso** tool ( ).

Note: For more on opening the Editor, see Chapter 1.

2 Click and drag with your mouse pointer ( ) to make a selection.

● To accurately trace a complicated edge, you can initially magnify that part of the image with the Zoom tool ( ).

Note: See Chapter 5 for more on the Zoom tool.

3 Drag to the beginning point and then release the mouse button.

Photoshop Elements completes the selection.

If you release the mouse button before completing the selection, Photoshop Elements completes the selection for you with a straight line.

Select with the Polygonal Lasso

1 Right-click on the **Lasso** tool (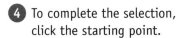).

2 Click the **Polygonal Lasso** tool (⬚).

3 Click multiple times along the border of the area you want to select.

4 To complete the selection, click the starting point.

You can also double-click anywhere in the image. Photoshop Elements adds a final straight line that connects to the starting point.

Photoshop Elements completes the selection.

TIPS

How do I select all the pixels in my image?
For a single-layer image, you can use the Select All command to select everything in your image. Click **Select** and then click **All**. You can also press `Ctrl` + `A` on the keyboard. You can select all the pixels to perform an action on the entire image, such as copying the image. For multilayer images, Select All selects all the pixels in the currently selected layer.

What if my selection is not as precise as I want it to be?
You can deselect your selection by clicking **Select** and then **Deselect**. You can then try to fix your selection. Or you can switch to the Magnetic Lasso tool (⬚).

continued ▶

You can quickly and easily select elements of your image that have well-defined edges by using the Magnetic Lasso tool. The Magnetic Lasso works best when the element you are trying to select contrasts sharply with its background. Some examples of good candidates for the tool include a bird in flight against a clear blue sky or a dark object against a light-colored wall.

As you drag the Magnetic Lasso along an edge, Photoshop Elements places anchor points along the edge that fix the selection outline. You can click the Backspace key to remove the anchor points as you draw to redraw the selection.

Select an Area with the Lasso (continued)

Select with the Magnetic Lasso

1. In the Editor, right-click on the **Lasso** tool ().

Note: For more on opening the Editor, see Chapter 1.

2. Click the **Magnetic Lasso** tool (■).

3. Click the edge of the object you want to select.

   This creates a beginning anchor point, which is a fixed point on the lasso path.

4. Drag your mouse pointer (✎) along the edge of the object.

   The Magnetic Lasso's path snaps to the edge of the element as you drag.

   To help guide the lasso, you can click to add anchor points as you go along the path.

   You can press **Del** to remove the most recently added anchor point. This enables you to restructure the incorrect lasso path.

⑤ Click the beginning anchor point to finish your selection.

Alternatively, you can double-click anywhere in the image and Photoshop Elements completes the selection for you with a straight line.

The path is complete, and the object is selected.

● This example shows that the Magnetic Lasso is less useful for selecting areas where you find little contrast between the image and its background.

TIP

How can I adjust the precision of the Magnetic Lasso tool?
You can use the Options bar to adjust the Magnetic Lasso tool's precision:

● **Width:** The number of nearby pixels the lasso considers when creating a selection.

● **Contrast:** How much contrast is required for the lasso to consider something an edge.

● **Frequency:** How often anchor points appear.

Select an Area with the Magic Wand

You can select groups of similarly colored pixels with the Magic Wand tool. You may find this useful if you want to remove an object from a background. The tool is especially handy for selecting a clear sky, a green lawn, or white sand at a beach.

By specifying an appropriate tolerance value, you can control how similar a pixel needs to be for Photoshop Elements to select it. The tolerance value for the tool can range from 0 to 255, with smaller numbers causing the tool to select a narrower range of colors.

Select an Area with the Magic Wand

1 In the Editor, click the **Magic Wand** tool (▨).

Note: For more on opening the Editor, see Chapter 1.

The mouse pointer (↳) changes to a magic wand (✳).

2 Type a number from 0 to 255 in the Tolerance field. The default value of 32 will often produce good results.

To select a narrow range of colors, type a small number; to select a wide range of colors, type a large number.

3 Click the area you want to select inside the image.

● Photoshop Elements selects the pixel you clicked, plus any similarly colored pixels near it.

● To select all the similar pixels in the image, not just the contiguous pixels, deselect the **Contiguous** check box (☑ changes to ■). See the Tip for more.

● This example shows a higher-tolerance value, resulting in a greater number of similarly colored pixels selected in the image.

④ To add to your selection, press Shift and then click elsewhere in the image.

Photoshop Elements adds to your selection.

● You can also click one of three selection buttons in the Options bar to grow or decrease the selection.

Note: For more details on adding to or subtracting from a selection, see Chapter 7.

TIP

How can I ensure that the Magic Wand tool selects all the instances of a color in an image?
You can deselect **Contiguous** (☑ changes to ■) in the Options bar so the Magic Wand tool selects similar colors, even when they are not contiguous with the pixel you click with the tool. This can be useful when objects intersect the solid-color areas of your image. You can also select **Sample All Layers** (■ changes to ☑) to select similar colors in all layers in the image, not just in the currently selected layer.

Select an Area with the Quick Selection Tool

You can paint selections onto your images by using the Quick Selection tool. The tool automatically expands the area you paint over to include similar colors and textures. This tool offers a quick way to select objects that have solid colors and well-defined edges. You can control the size and hardness of the tool, similar to how you define the characteristics of the Brush tool. This determines how much area the tool selects as well as the softness of the selection edges.

To paint a selection onto your image without automatically selecting similar, nearby colors, you can use the Selection Brush tool. See "Select an Area with the Selection Brush" for details. You can adjust the brush size of the tool to fine-tune your selections.

Select an Area with the Quick Selection Tool

① In the Editor, click the **Quick Selection** tool (▨).

Note: For more on opening the Editor, see Chapter 1.

② Click ▾ to open the Brush menu.

The Brush menu opens.

In the Brush menu, you can specify the tool's size and other characteristics. Decreasing the tool's hardness causes it to partially select pixels at the perimeter.

③ Click and drag inside the object you want to select.

● Photoshop Elements selects parts of the object based on its coloring and the contrast of its edges.

● After you make a selection, the Add to Selection button () becomes active.

4 Click and drag to select more of the object.

Note: You can select an object and apply color and tonal adjustments at the same time with the Smart Brush. See Chapter 12 for more.

● Photoshop adds to the selection.

TIP

How can I adjust my selection?
1 In the Options bar, click **Refine Edge** to open the Refine Edge dialog opens.

● Increase **Smooth** to lessen the sharpness of any corners.

● Increase **Feather** to make the edges partially transparent.

● Use **Contract/Expand** to decrease or increase the selection slightly.

● Click here to define your selection with a custom overlay color.

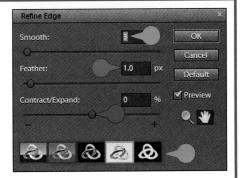

Select an Area with the Selection Brush

Using the Selection Brush, you can select objects in your image by painting over them. By customizing the size and hardness of the brush, you can accurately select objects with edges that are curved or not well-defined. Painting on a selection with a the Selection Brush tool can often be faster than using a lasso tool if the object being selected has smooth edges and no sharp corners.

The Selection Brush differs from the Quick Selection tool in that it selects only the area you paint over and does not automatically select similar pixels. For more information, see "Select an Area with the Quick Selection Tool."

Select an Area with the Selection Brush

Select with the Selection Brush

1 Right-click the **Quick Selection** tool ().

2 In the Editor, click the **Selection Brush** tool (■).

Note: For more on opening the Editor, see Chapter 1.

3 Click ■ to specify a size for the tool.

You can also type a size.

4 Type a hardness from 0% to 100%.

A smaller value produces a softer selection edge.

5 Click here and then click **Selection**.

6 Click and drag to paint a selection.

7 Click and drag multiple times to paint a selection over the area you want to select.

Photoshop Elements creates a selection.

You can change the brush settings as you paint to select different types of edges in your object.

Deselect with the Selection Brush

1 Click the **Selection Brush** tool (■).

2 Click the **Subtract from Selection** button (■).

3 Click and drag where you want to remove the selection area.

Photoshop Elements removes the selection.

TIP

How do I paint a mask with the Selection Brush?

1 Click the **Mode** ■ in the Options bar and then select **Mask**.

2 Click and drag to define the mask.

By default, the masked area appears as a see-through red color called a *rubylith*.

To turn a painted mask into a selection, click the **Mode** ■ in the Options bar and then click **Selection**.

Save and Load a Selection

You can save a selected area in your image to reuse later. This can be useful if you anticipate future edits to the same part of your image and have complicated and difficult-to-select objects in your image. You can load the saved selection instead of having to reselect it.

If you save your image project as a Photoshop file, any stored selections are saved with the image and are available if you close the image and open it again. See Chapter 17 for more about saving image files. See the previous sections in this chapter to learn about choosing the appropriate tool for selecting areas in your image.

Save and Load a Selection

Save a Selection

1 In the Editor, make a selection by using one of the selection tools.

Note: For more on opening the Editor, see Chapter 1.

2 Click **Select**.

3 Click **Save Selection**.

The Save Selection dialog box opens.

4 Make sure New is chosen in the Selection field.

New is the default setting.

5 Type a name for the selection.

6 Click **OK**.

Photoshop Elements saves the selection.

Load a Selection

1 Click **Select**.

2 Click **Load Selection**.

Note: See the section "Save a Selection" to learn how to save your selection.

The Load Selection dialog box opens.

3 Click here and then choose the saved selection you want to load.

4 Click **OK**.

● The selection appears in the image.

TIP

How can I modify a saved selection?
You can modify a saved selection by making a new selection in your image window, completing Steps **2** and **3** of "Save a Selection" to open the Save Selection dialog box, and then choosing the selection you want to modify from the Selection menu. Selecting the **Intersect with Selection** option keeps any area where the new selection and the saved selection overlap. Click **OK** to modify your saved selection.

Invert a Selection

You can invert a selection to deselect what is currently selected and select everything else. This is useful when you want to select the background around an object. You can select the object with one of the Photoshop Elements selection tools and then perform the invert command to switch the selection to the background.

The inverted selection has the same characteristics as your initial selection. For example, if the initial selection has a feather edge, the inverted result will also have a feathered edge. For more information about selecting objects, see the other sections in this chapter.

Invert a Selection

1 In the Editor, make a selection by using one of the selection tools.

Note: For more on the various selection tools, see the previous sections in this chapter. For more on opening the Editor, see Chapter 1.

2 Click **Select**.

3 Click **Inverse**.

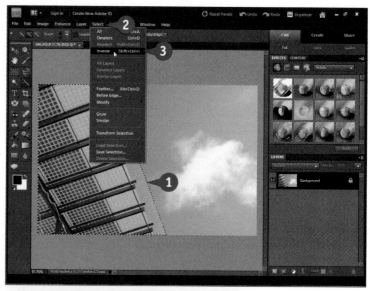

● Photoshop Elements inverts the selection.

Note: You can also press Shift + Ctrl + I to invert a selection.

Deselect a Selection

You can deselect a selection when you are done manipulating what is inside it or if you make a mistake and want to try selecting again.

If you want to keep your selection but temporarily hide it, you can use the Hide command, which is located under the View menu. You can undo a deselect command that you have just performed by clicking Edit and then Undo Deselect. This is useful if you want to reselect an object after accidentally deselecting it.

Deselect a Selection

1 In the Editor, make a selection by using one of the selection tools.

Note: For more on the various selection tools, see the previous sections in this chapter. For more on opening the Editor, see Chapter 1.

In this example, a leaf is selected.

2 Click **Select**.

3 Click **Deselect**.

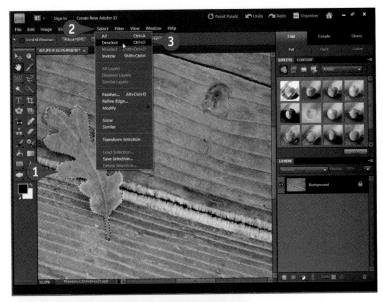

Photoshop Elements deselects the selection.

Note: You can also press Ctrl+D or Esc to deselect a selection.

CHAPTER 7

Manipulating Selections

Making a selection in Photoshop Elements isolates a specific area of your image. This chapter shows you how to move, stretch, erase, and manipulate your selection in a variety of ways. You can use these techniques to rearrange people and objects in your image, enlarge elements to give them prominence, or delete things altogether.

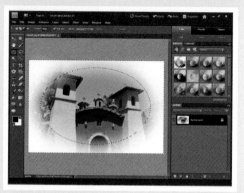

Add to or Subtract from a Selection

You can add to or subtract from your selection by using various selection tool options. Adding enables you to select a large object in your image by making multiple selections. By subtracting, you can fix a selection that includes extraneous pixels.

Most selection tools have add and subtract settings in the Options bar. You can also create a selection using one selection tool and then add to or subtract from the selection using other tools. See Chapter 6 to learn how to choose the appropriate tool for selecting elements in your photo.

Add to or Subtract from a Selection

Add to Your Selection

1 In the Editor, make a selection by using one of the selection tools.

Note: For more on opening the Editor, see Chapter 1.

2 Click a selection tool.

This example uses the Magnetic Lasso tool ().

3 Click the **Add to Selection** button (■).

4 Select the area you want to add.

5 Complete the selection. In this example, the starting point is clicked to complete the selection.

Photoshop Elements adds to the selection.

You can enlarge the selection further by repeating Steps **2** to **5**.

You can also add to a selection by pressing Shift as you select an area.

Subtract From Your Selection

1 Make a selection by using one of the selection tools.

2 Click a selection tool.

This example uses the Elliptical Marquee tool (▦).

3 Click the **Subtract from Selection** button (▣).

4 Select the area you want to subtract.

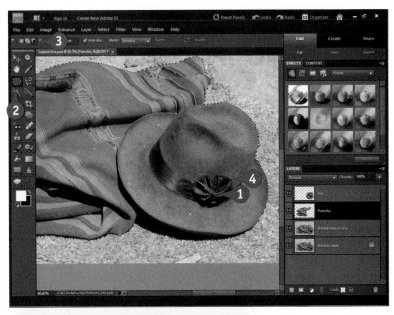

● Photoshop Elements deselects, or subtracts, the selected area.

You can subtract other parts of the selection by repeating Steps **2** to **4**.

You can also subtract from a selection by pressing **Alt** as you select an area.

How do I add to or subtract from a selection by using the Quick Selection tool?

The Quick Selection tool (▨) features buttons for adding to or subtracting from a selection. In the Options bar, you can click the **Add to Quick Selection** button (▨) to add to a selection and the **Subtract from Quick Selection** (▨) button to subtract from a selection. You can also press and hold **Alt** to switch to the subtraction mode.

Can I move the selection marquee without moving the item selected?

Yes. Use any of the selection tools to select an area and then press an arrow key — ⬆, ⬇, ⬅, ➡ — to move the selection in 1-pixel increments. Press and hold **Shift** while pressing an arrow key to move the selection in 10-pixel increments. This technique is handy when you need to slightly nudge the marquee across your image.

Move a Selection

You can rearrange elements of your image by moving selections with the Move tool. This enables you to change the composition of you image to emphasize or de-emphasize certain elements. You can move elements of your image either in the default Background layer or in other layers you create for your image.

If you move elements in the Background layer, Photoshop Elements fills the original location with the current background color. If you move elements in another layer, Photoshop Elements makes the original location transparent, revealing any underlying layers. See Chapter 8 for more on layers.

Move a Selection

Move a Selection in the Background

1 In the Editor, display the Layers panel.

Note: For more on opening the Editor or opening panels, see Chapter 1.

2 Click the Background layer.

A newly imported image has only a Background layer.

3 Make a selection with a selection tool.

Note: For more on selecting elements, see Chapter 6.

4 Click the **Move** tool (⊞).

5 Click inside the selection and then drag.

● Photoshop Elements fills the original location of the selection with the current background color.

● In this example, white is the default background color.

If you press Alt while you drag, copy of the selection is created.

Move a Selection in a Layer

1 Click a layer in the Layers panel.

Note: See Chapter 8 for more on layers.

2 Make a selection with a selection tool.

Note: See Chapter 6 for more on making selections.

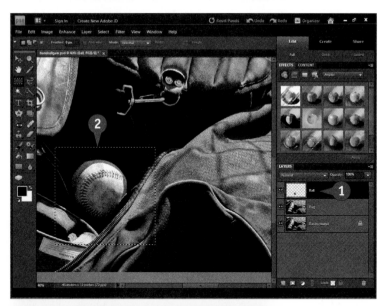

3 Click the **Move** tool (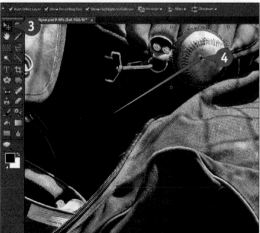).

4 Click inside the selection and then drag.

Photoshop Elements moves the selection and fills the original location of the selection with transparent pixels.

Note: Unlike the Background — the opaque default layer in Photoshop Elements — other layers can include transparent pixels.

TIPS

How do I move a selection in a straight line?
Press and hold `Shift` while you drag with the **Move** tool (). Doing so constrains the movement of your selection horizontally, vertically, or diagonally, depending on the direction you drag.

How do I move several layers at a time?
You can link the layers you want to move, select one of the linked layers, and then move them all with the Move tool. For more, see Chapter 8. You can also `Ctrl`+click to select multiple layers in the Layers panel. Using the Move tool moves the selected layers.

Duplicate a Selection

You can copy a selection and make a duplicate of it somewhere else in the image. You may use this technique to retouch an element in your photo by placing good content over bad. When you perform the copy using the Move tool and **Alt**, Photoshop keeps the duplicate in the same layer as the original.

You can also use the Copy and Paste commands to duplicate content in your image. This places the duplicate content in a new layer, which you can then freely move and transform independent of the rest of the image. For more using the Copy and Paste commands with layers, see Chapter 8.

Duplicate a Selection

1 In the Editor, make a selection with a selection tool.

Note: For more on opening the Editor, see Chapter 1. For more on using selection tools, see Chapter 6.

2 Click the **Move** tool (⊹).

● You can also click **Copy** and **Paste** in the Edit menu to copy and paste selections or press **Ctrl**+**J**.

3 Press **Alt** while you click and drag the selection.

4 Release the mouse button to drop the selection into place.

Photoshop Elements creates a duplicate of the selection and then places it in the new location.

5 Press **Esc** to deselect the selection.

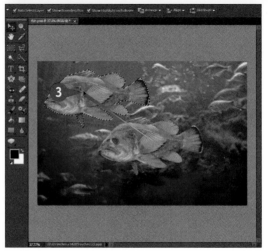

Delete a Selection

You can delete a selection to remove unwanted elements from an image. If you are working in the Background layer, Photoshop Elements turns deleted pixels the current background color. For more about specifying the background color, see Chapter 12. If you are working in a layer other than the Background layer, deleting a selection turns the selected pixels transparent, and layers below it show through.

Another way to remove content from your image is to place that content in a layer and then hide the layer. You can reveal the layer to make the content reappear. For more about hiding layers, see Chapter 8.

Delete a Selection

1 In the Editor, make a selection with a selection tool.

Note: For more on opening the Editor, see Chapter 1. For more on using selection tools, see Chapter 6.

2 Press Del.

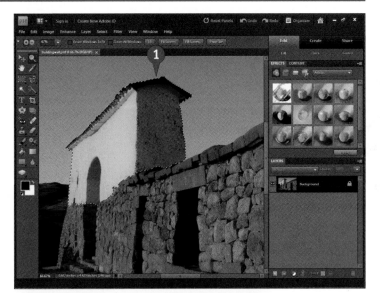

● Photoshop Elements deletes the contents of the selection.

● If you are working in the Background layer, the original location fills with the background color — in this example, white.

If you are working in a layer other than the Background layer, deleting a selection turns the selected pixels transparent, and layers below it show through.

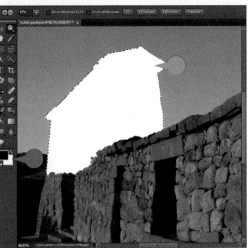

Rotate a Selection

You can rotate a selection to tilt an element or turn it upside down in your image. You may rotate an element to create a better composition or to correct the appearance of an element. The Free Rotate Selection command, located under the Rotate submenu, enables you to rotate a selection an arbitrary amount. Other rotate commands let you rotate a selection a fixed number of degrees.

When you rotate a selection in the Background layer, Photoshop Elements replaces the exposed areas that the rotation creates with the current background color. If you rotate a selection in another layer, the underlying layers appear in the exposed areas. See Chapter 8 for more on layers.

Rotate a Selection

1 In the Editor, make a selection with a selection tool.

In this example, content in a layer is selected.

Note: See Chapter 6 for more on using selection tools. See Chapter 8 for more on layers.

2 Click **Image**.

3 Click **Rotate**.

4 Click **Free Rotate Selection**.

You can click other commands under the Rotate menu to rotate your selection in a more constrained way.

5 Click and drag outside the selection.

● You can precisely rotate your selection by typing percentage values in the W and H fields in the Options bar.

The selection rotates.

6 Click ✔ or press Enter to commit the rotation.

● You can click ⊘ or press Esc to cancel.

Scale a Selection

You can scale a selection to make it larger or smaller. Scaling enables you to adjust or emphasize parts of your image.

When you scale a selection in the Background layer, Photoshop Elements replaces the exposed areas that scaling to a smaller size creates with the current background color. If you scale a selection in another layer, the underlying layers appear in the exposed areas. See Chapter 8 for more on layers.

Scaling image content to a much larger size can decrease to quality of the content, making it blurry. You can correct blurriness using the Sharpen filter. See Chapter 9 for details.

Scale a Selection

① In the Editor, make a selection with a selection tool.

In this example, content in a layer is selected.

Note: See Chapter 6 for more on using selection tools. See Chapter 8 for more on layers.

② Click **Image**.

③ Click **Resize**.

④ Click **Scale**.

A box with handles on the sides and corners surrounds the selection.

⑤ Click and drag a handle to scale the selection.

Drag a corner handle to scale both the horizontal and vertical axes.

● You can precisely scale your selection by typing percentage values in the W and H fields in the Options bar.

● With Constrain Proportions selected, the height and width change proportionally.

⑥ Click ✔ or press Enter to apply the scale effect.

● You can click ⊘ or press Esc to cancel.

Photoshop Elements scales the selection.

Skew or Distort a Selection

You can transform a selection by using the Skew or Distort commands. This enables you to stretch elements in your image into interesting shapes. You can also use skewing and distortion to make changes to perspective in your image. You can make an object appear as if it recedes into the distance.

When you skew or distort a selection in the Background layer, Photoshop Elements replaces the exposed areas that the skewing or distorting creates with the current background color. If you skew or distort a selection in another layer, the underlying layers appear in the exposed areas. See Chapter 8 for more on layers.

Skew or Distort a Selection

Skew a Selection

1 In the Editor, make a selection with a selection tool.

Note: For more on opening the Editor, see Chapter 1. See Chapter 6 for more on using selection tools.

2 Click **Image**.

3 Click **Transform**.

4 Click **Skew**.

A rectangular box with handles on the sides and corners surrounds the selection.

5 Click and drag a handle.

Photoshop Elements skews the selection. Because the Skew command works along a single axis, you can drag either horizontally or vertically.

Note: You can precisely skew your selection by typing percentage values in the W and H fields in the Options bar.

6 Click ✔ or press `Enter` to apply the skewing.

● You can click ⊘ or press `Esc` to cancel.

Distort a Selection

1 Make a selection with a selection tool.

Note: See Chapter 6 for more on using selection tools.

2 Click **Image**.

3 Click **Transform**.

4 Click **Distort**.

A rectangular box with handles on the sides and corners surrounds the selection.

5 Click and drag a handle.

Photoshop Elements distorts the selection. The Distort command works independently of the selection's axes; you can drag a handle both vertically and horizontally.

6 Click ☑ or press Enter to apply the distortion.

● You can click ⊘ or press Esc to cancel.

TIP

How can I perform several transforming effects at once on a selection?

1 Click **Image**.

2 Click **Transform**.

3 Click **Free Transform**.

4 Click and drag a handle on the box that surrounds the selection to transform it.

5 Click ☑ or press Enter to apply the effect.

Feather the Border of a Selection

You can feather a selection's border to create soft edges. Feathering enables you to control the sharpness of the edges in a selection. You can use this technique with other layers to create a blending effect between the selected area and any underlying layers. Soft edges around content can add a sentimental or romantic feel to your image.

To create a soft edge around an object, you must first select the object, feather the selection border, and then delete the part of the image that surrounds your selection. You can change the final effect achieved by changing the applied background color.

Feather the Border of a Selection

Feather a Selection

1. In the Editor, make a selection with a selection tool.

Note: For more on opening the Editor, see Chapter 1. For more on using selection tools, see Chapter 6.

2. Click **Select**.

3. Click **Refine Edge**.

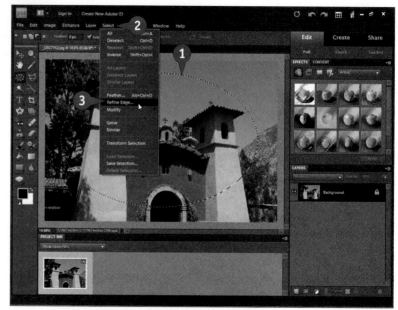

The Refine Edge dialog box opens.

4. Click and drag the Feather slider (■) to determine the softness of the edge.

● Photoshop Elements shows a preview of the feathering.

● You can click and drag the Contract/Expand slider (■) to adjust the selection inward or outward.

5. Click **OK**.

Delete the Surrounding Background

1 Click **Select**.

2 Click **Inverse**.

You can also press Shift + Ctrl + I to apply the Inverse command.

The selection inverts but remains feathered.

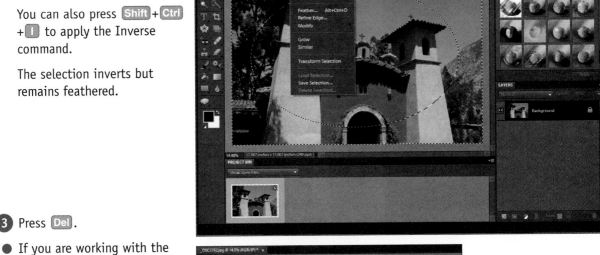

3 Press Del .

● If you are working with the Background layer, the deleted area is filled with the current background color.

If you are working with a layer other than the Background layer, the deleted area becomes transparent, and the layers below show through.

You can now see the effect of the feathering.

TIPS

How do I feather my selection into a colored background?

You can add a solid-color fill layer behind your photo and then blend the feathered selection into the new layer. The layer containing the selection appears on top of the solid-color fill layer, and the feathering technique creates a softened blend between the two layers. For more on creating a fill layer, see Chapter 8.

What happens if I feather a selection and then apply a command to it?

Photoshop Elements applies the command only partially to pixels near the edge of the selection. For example, if you are removing color from a selection by using the Hue/Saturation command, color at the feathered edge of the selection is only partially removed. For more on the Hue/Saturation command, see Chapter 11.

CHAPTER 8

Working with Layers

You can separate the elements in your image so you can move and transform them independently of one another. You can accomplish this by placing them in different layers. To determine what layer elements are visible, you can rearrange the stacking order of layers or change their opacity. You can also add special layers known as adjustment layers to control the lighting, color, and other aspects of your image.

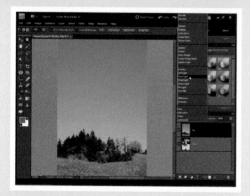

Introducing Layers

A Photoshop Elements image can consist of multiple layers, with each layer containing different objects in the image. This enables you to edit and adjust parts of the image independently. You can select different layers in an image or change their stacking order using the Layers panel.

When you open a digital camera photo or a newly scanned image in Photoshop Elements, it exists as a single layer known as the Background layer. You can add new layers on top of the Background layer as you work.

Layer Independence

Layered Photoshop Elements files act like several images combined into one. Each layer of an image has its own set of pixels that you can move and transform independently of the pixels in other layers. The content of a layer can take up the entire image canvas or include just a small object within a larger image. You can select every distinct object in your image in its own layer. An image can have dozens or even hundreds of layers.

Layer Independence
Layered Photoshop Elements files act like several images combined into one. Each layer of an image has its own set of pixels that you can move and transform independently of the pixels in other layers. The content of a layer can take up the entire image canvas or include just a small object within a larger image.

Apply Commands to Layers

Most Photoshop commands affect only the layer that you select in the Layers panel. For example, if you click and drag by using the Move tool (![icon]), the selected layer moves, but the other layers stay in place. If you apply a color adjustment, only colors in the selected layer change. Putting content into layers offers a useful way to isolate the effects that you apply to you image projects. For example, by placing a fish in its own layer, you can change the color of the fish without change the colors of the other sea creatures in your image.

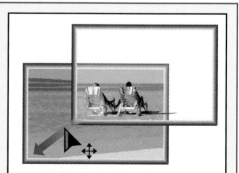

Apply Commands to Layers

Most Photoshop commands affect only the layer that you select. For example, if you click and drag by using the Move tool (@@ma005), the selected layer moves, but the other layers stay in place. If you apply a color adjustment, only colors in the selected layer change.

Manipulate Layers

You can combine, duplicate, and hide layers in an image and also shuffle their order. You can also link particular layers so they move in unison, or you can blend content from different layers in creative ways. You manage all this in the Layers panel.

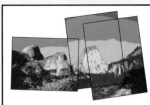

Manipulate Layers

You can combine, duplicate, and hide layers in an image and also shuffle their order. You can also link particular layers so they move in unison or you can blend content from different layers in creative ways. You manage all this in the Layers panel.

Transparency

Layers can have transparent areas, where the elements in the layers below can show through. When you perform a cut or erase command on a layer, the affected pixels become transparent. You can also make a layer partially transparent by decreasing its opacity.

Transparency
Layers can have transparent areas, where the elements in the layers below can show through. When you perform a cut or erase command on a layer, the affected pixels become transparent. You can also make a layer partially transparent by decreasing its opacity.

Adjustment Layers

Adjustment layers are special layers that contain information about color or tonal adjustments. An adjustment layer affects the pixels in all the layers below it. You can increase or decrease an adjustment layer's intensity to get precisely the effect you want.

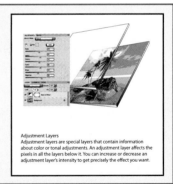

Adjustment Layers
Adjustment layers are special layers that contain information about color or tonal adjustments. An adjustment layer affects the pixels in all the layers below it. You can increase or decrease an adjustment layer's intensity to get precisely the effect you want.

Save Layered Files

You can save multilayered images only in the Photoshop, PDF, and TIFF file formats. To save a layered image in another file format — for example, PNG, BMP, GIF, or JPEG — you must combine the image's layers into a single layer, a process known as *flattening*. For more on saving files, see Chapter 17.

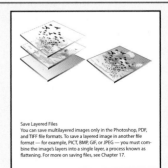

Save Layered Files
You can save multilayered images only in the Photoshop, PDF, and TIFF file formats. To save a layered image in another file format — for example, PICT, BMP, GIF, or JPEG — you must combine the image's layers into a single layer, a process known as flattening. For more on saving files, see Chapter 17.

Create and Add to a Layer

To keep elements in your image independent of one another, you can create separate layers and add objects to them. Typically, you copy and paste elements from one part of your image, or from a different image, and paste them to place them into new layers.

When you create a new layer, the layer appears in a list in the Layers panel. Layers higher in the list appear above and can cover layers lower in the list. To rearrange layers that you have created, see "Reorder Layers." To get rid of layers in your image, see "Delete a Layer."

Create and Add to a Layer

Create a Layer

1 In the Editor, open the Layers panel.

Note: For more on opening the Editor or panels, see Chapter 1.

2 Click the layer above which you want to add the new layer.

3 In the Layers panel, click the **Create a New Layer** icon (⬚).

Alternatively, you can click **Layer**, **New**, and then **Layer**.

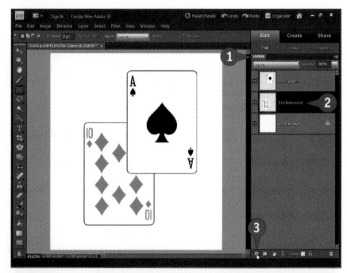

● Photoshop Elements creates a new, transparent layer.

Note: To change the name of a layer, see the section "Rename a Layer."

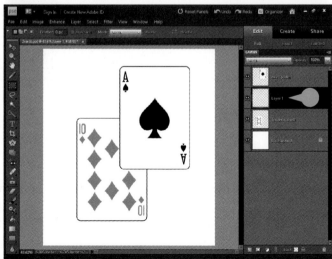

Copy and Paste into a Layer

Note: This example shows how to add content to the new layer by copying and pasting from another image file.

1 Open another image.

2 Using a selection tool, select the content you want to copy into the other image.

Note: See Chapter 1 for more on opening an image. See Chapter 6 for more on the selection tools.

3 Click **Edit**.

4 Click **Copy**.

5 Click the tab for the image window where you created the new layer.

Note: See Chapter 1 for more on using tabs to select open images.

6 Click the new layer in the Layers panel.

7 Click **Edit**.

8 Click **Paste**.

● The selected content from the other image appears in the new layer.

Note: You can also click and drag selections between image windows by using the Move tool to add content to a new layer. See Chapter 5 to manage image windows, and see Chapter 7 for more on the Move tool.

TIPS

What is the Background layer?
The Background layer is the default bottom layer. It appears when you create a new image that has a nontransparent background color or when you import an image from a scanner or digital camera. You can create new layers on top of a Background layer but not below it. Unlike other layers, a Background layer cannot contain transparent pixels.

How do I turn the Background layer into a regular layer?
If you have the Background layer selected, you can click **Layer**, **New**, and then **Background from Layer** to turn it into a regular layer. You can also press Ctrl + J to achieve the same result. The converted layer can be edited just like any other layer.

Hide a Layer

You can hide a layer to temporarily remove elements in that layer from view. Hiding a layer can be useful if you want to view or edit objects that appear in layers underneath.

Hidden layers do not appear when you print or use the Save for Web command.

You can remove a layer altogether by deleting it. See "Delete a Layer" for details. Hiding a layer is different than deleting a layer because you can always make a hidden layer visible again by clicking the visibility icon in the Layers panel.

Hide a Layer

1 In the Editor, open the Layers panel.

Note: For more on opening the Editor or panels, see Chapter 1.

2 Click a layer.

3 Click the **Visibility** icon (👁) for the layer.

The icon disappears.

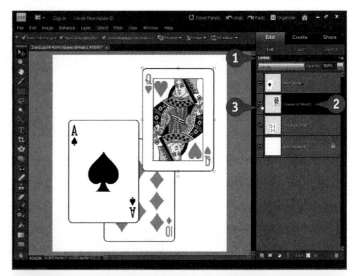

Photoshop Elements hides the layer.

To show one layer and hide all the others, you can press **Alt** and then click the **Visibility** icon (👁) for the layer you want to show.

Note: You can also delete a layer. See the section "Delete a Layer" for more.

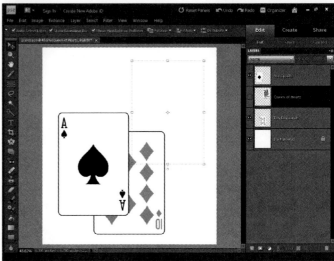

Move a Layer

You can use the Move tool to reposition the elements in one layer without moving those in others. You determine what layer elements move by selecting a layer in the Layers panel. Then you click and drag with the Move tool inside your image.

If you make a selection with a selection tool before using the move command, Photoshop Elements moves only the selected objects in the layer. For more about using selection tools, see Chapter 6.

To undo a move command, you can click Edit and then Undo or press Ctrl+Z. For more about undoing commands, see Chapter 5.

Move a Layer

1 In the Editor, open the Layers panel.

Note: For more on opening the Editor or panels, see Chapter 1.

2 Click a layer.

3 Click the **Move** tool (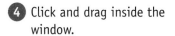).

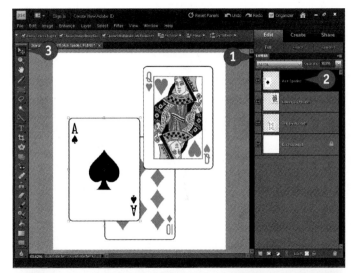

4 Click and drag inside the window.

Content in the selected layer moves.

Content in the other layers does not move.

Note: To move several layers at the same time, see the section "Link Layers."

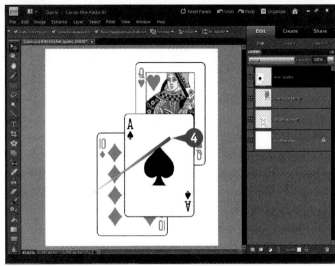

Duplicate a Layer

By duplicating a layer, you can manipulate elements in an image while keeping a copy of their original state. Duplicating a layer creates a new layer in the Layers panel.

You can repeat the duplicate command to create many copies of objects in your image, and then use the move command to arrange the copies. For more about moving elements in layers, see "Move a Layer."

When you duplicate a layer, the elements in that layer appear in exactly the same position as in the original layer. Unless you change the position of elements in one of the two layers, one layer covers the content in the other layer.

Duplicate a Layer

1 In the Editor, open the Layers panel.

Note: For more on opening the Editor or panels, see Chapter 1.

2 Click a layer.

3 Click and drag the layer to the **Create a New Layer** icon (⬛).

Alternatively, you can click **Layer** and then **Duplicate Layer**; a dialog box opens, asking you to name the layer you want to duplicate.

You can also press Ctrl + J to duplicate a selected layer in the Layers panel.

● Photoshop Elements duplicates the selected layer.

Note: To rename the duplicate layer, see the section "Rename a Layer."

● You can test that Photoshop Elements has duplicated the layer by selecting the new layer, clicking the **Move** tool (⬛), and clicking and dragging the layer.

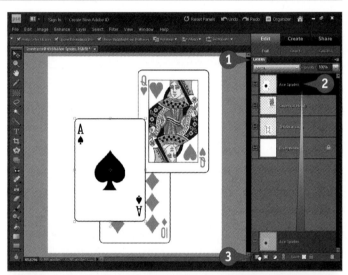

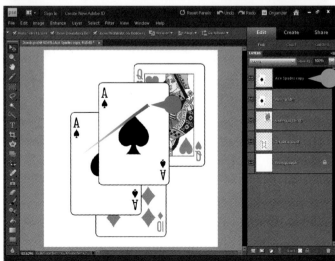

Delete a Layer

Y ou can delete a layer when you no longer have a use for its contents. After deleting a layer, the layer no longer appears in the Layers panel and its content disappears from your image.

An alternative to deleting a layer is to hide it. Hiding a layer keeps the layer content in your image but does not display it in the image window. For more details, see "Hide a Layer."

To undo the deletion of a layer, you can click Edit and then Undo or press Ctrl+Z. For more about undoing commands, see Chapter 5.

Delete a Layer

① In the Editor, open the Layers panel.

Note: For more on opening the Editor or panels, see Chapter 1.

② Click a layer.

③ Click and drag the layer to the **Trash Can** icon (🗑).

Alternatively, you can click **Layer** and then **Delete Layer**, or you can select a layer and then click the **Trash Can** icon (🗑). In both cases, a confirmation dialog box opens.

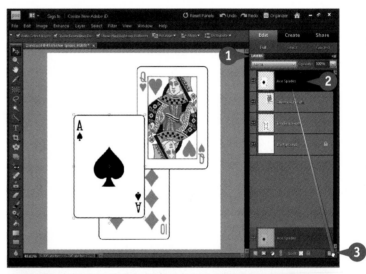

Photoshop Elements deletes the selected layer, and the content in the layer disappears from the image window.

Note: You can also hide a layer. See the section "Hide a Layer" for more.

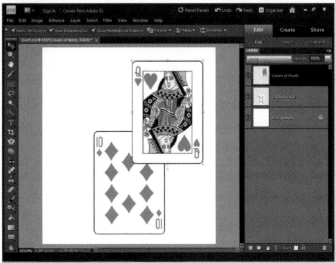

Reorder Layers

Layers listed in the Layers panel overlap one another depending on their stacking order. Layers higher in the list appear above layers lower in the list. You can change the stacking order of layers to move elements up or down in your image.

You can move a layer up in the Layers panel to display objects currently covered by content in layers above. If you have a layer in your image that you want to use as a background, you can move it down in the Layers panel to make it appear behind everything else.

Reorder Layers

Using the Layers Panel

1 In the Editor, open the Layers panel.

Note: For more on opening the Editor or panels, see Chapter 1.

2 Click a layer.

3 Click and drag the layer to change its arrangement in the stack.

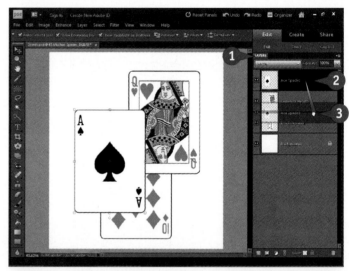

- The layer assumes its new position in the stack.

- In this example, the Ace Spades layer moves down in the stack.

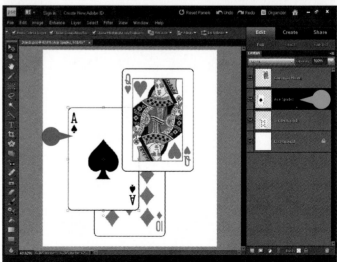

Using the Arrange Commands

1 Click a layer.

2 Click **Layer**.

3 Click **Arrange**.

4 Click the command for how you want to move the layer.

You can choose Bring to Front, Bring Forward, Send Backward, Send to Back, or Reverse.

Note: Reverse is available only if more than one layer is selected. You can Ctrl+ click in the Layers panel to select multiple layers.

In this example, Bring Forward is chosen.

● The layer assumes its new position in the stack.

● In this example, the Ace Spades layer moves to the top of the stack.

Note: You cannot move a layer in back of the default Background layer.

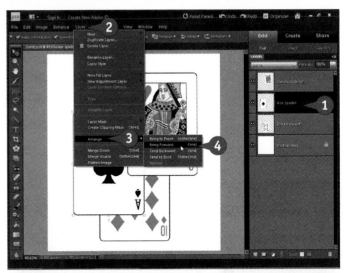

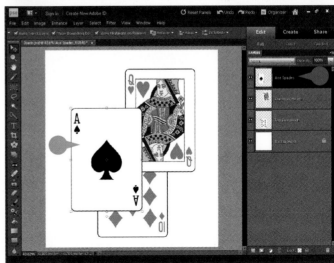

TIP

Are there shortcuts for changing the order of layers?
You can shift layers forward and backward in the stack by pressing the following shortcut keys:

Move	Shortcut
Forward one step	Ctrl +]
Backward one step	Ctrl + [
To the very front	Shift + Ctrl +]
To the very back	Shift + Ctrl + [

Change the Opacity of a Layer

You can adjust the opacity of a layer to let elements in the layers below show through. Opacity is the opposite of transparency — decreasing the opacity of a layer increases its transparency.

Layers can have opacities from 0 to 100 percent. A layer with an opacity of 100 percent is completely visible and obscures content that exists below it. A layer with an opacity of 0 percent is completely transparent and will not be visible in your image. Another way to make a layer disappear in your image is to hide it. For details, see "Hide a Layer."

Change the Opacity of a Layer

1 In the Editor, open the Layers panel.

Note: For more on opening the Editor or panels, see Chapter 1.

2 Click the layer whose opacity you want to change.

Note: You cannot change the opacity of the Background layer.

● The default opacity is 100%, which is completely opaque.

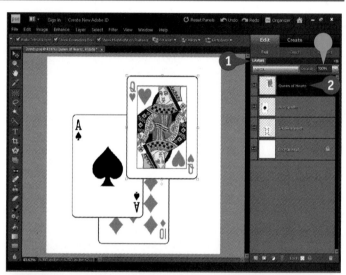

3 Type a new value in the Opacity field.

● Alternatively, you can click the ▼ and then drag the selection slider (⬚).

A layer's opacity can range from 0% to 100%.

● The layer changes in opacity.

Changing the opacity of a layer also affects any layer styles applied to the layer. For more on layer styles, see Chapter 15.

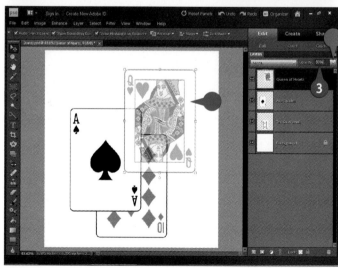

Link Layers

Linking causes different layers to move in unison when you drag them with the Move tool. You may find linking useful when you want to keep elements of an image aligned with one another but do not want to merge their layers. Keeping layers unmerged enables you to apply effects to each layer independently.

See the section "Merge Layers" for more on merging. For more on moving a layer, see the section "Move a Layer." When you select a layer in the Layers panel, any other layers linked to that layer are indicated by a link icon.

Link Layers

① In the Editor, open the Layers panel.

Note: For more on opening the Editor or panels, see Chapter 1.

② Click one of the layers you want to link.

③ Press **Ctrl** and then click one or more other layers that you want to link.

④ Click the **Link Layers** tool (■) in the Layers panel.

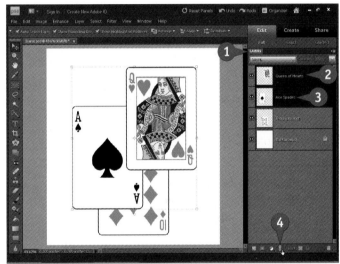

● A linking icon (■) appears next to each linked layer.

● To see that Photoshop Elements has linked the layers, select one of the layers, click the **Move** tool (■), and then click and drag the layer.

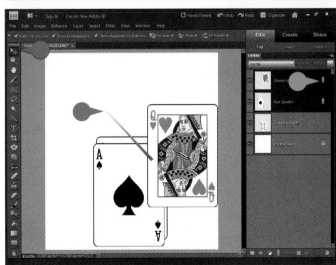

Merge Layers

Merging layers lets you permanently combine information from two or more separate layers. The different layers become a single layer in the Layers panel. After merging layers, you can no longer move them independently of one another.

For more on moving a layer, see the section "Move a Layer." To move content in multiple layers in unison without merging the layers, you can link the layers. For details, see "Link Layers."

To undo a merge, you can click Edit and then Undo or press Ctrl+Z. For more about undoing commands, see Chapter 5.

Merge Layers

1 In the Editor, open the Layers panel.

2 Place the two layers you want to merge next to each other.

3 Click the topmost of the two layers.

4 Click **Layer**.

5 Click **Merge Down**.

You can merge all the layers together by clicking **Flatten Image** or just the visible layers by clicking **Merge Visible**.

You can also Ctrl +click to select multiple layers in the Layers panel and then click **Merge Selected** to merge them.

● The two layers merge.

Photoshop Elements keeps the name of the lower layer.

In this example, the Ace Spades layer has merged with the Queen of Hearts layer.

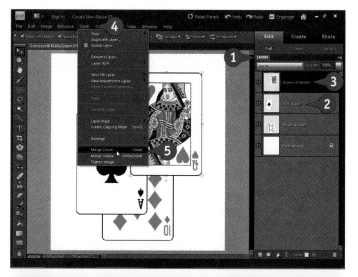

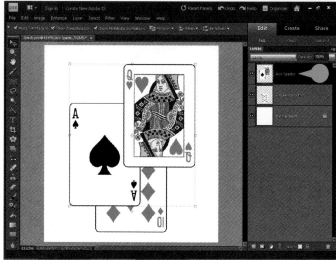

Rename a Layer

You can rename a layer to give it a name that describes its content. For example, in a multilayered image of flowers, you can give one layer the name "red rose" and another the name "white lily."

When you create a new layer in the Layers panel, Photoshop Elements gives it a generic name such as "Layer 1." When you duplicate a layer in the Layers panel, the duplicate layer is given the same name as the original layer with a "copy" suffix. After you create a layer or duplicate a layer, you can rename the new layer to make the name more specific.

Rename a Layer

1 In the Editor, open the Layers panel.

Note: For more on opening the Editor or panels, see Chapter 1.

2 Click a layer.

3 Click **Layer**.

4 Click **Rename Layer**.

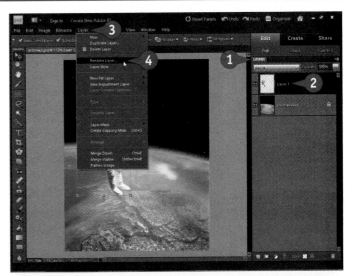

The Layer Properties dialog box opens.

5 Type a new name for the layer.

6 Click **OK**.

● The name of the layer changes in the Layers panel.

You can also double-click the name of the layer in the Layers panel to edit the name.

157

Create a Fill Layer

You can create a solid fill layer to place an opaque layer of color throughout your image. You can use fill layers behind layers containing objects to create all kinds of color effects in your photos.

When you create a solid fill layer, a Color Picker dialog box appears, enabling you to select a color for the fill layer. The dialog also allows you to select a blend mode and opacity. For more about these settings, see "Blend Layers" and "Change the Opacity of a Layer."

You can rearrange the stacking order of a fill layer just as you can any other layer. For more information, see "Reorder Layers."

Create a Fill Layer

1 In the Editor, open the Layers panel.

Note: For more on opening the Editor or panels, see Chapter 1.

2 Click the layer you want to appear below the solid color layer.

3 Click **Layer**.

4 Click **New Fill Layer**.

5 Click **Solid Color**.

The New Layer dialog box opens.

6 Type a name for the layer or use the default name.

● You can click the **Mode** ▾ to specify a type of blend or opacity setting for the layer.

Note: See the sections "Blend Layers" or "Change the Opacity of a Layer" for more.

7 Click **OK**.

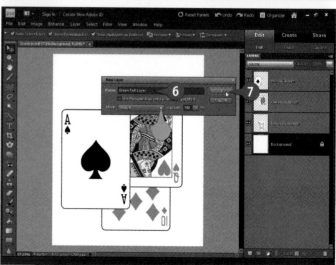

The Color Picker dialog box opens.

8 To change the range of colors that appears in the window, click and drag the slider (◀).

9 To select a fill color, click in the color window.

10 Click **OK**.

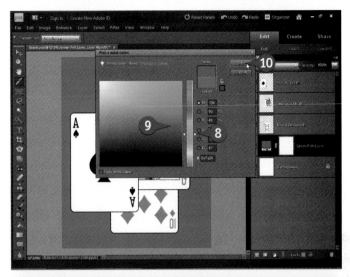

● Photoshop Elements creates a new layer filled with a solid color.

In this example, a solid green layer appears below the card layers.

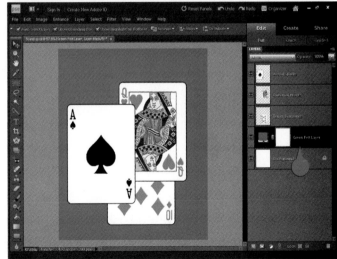

TIPS

How do I add solid color to just part of a layer?
To add color to a specific part of a layer, make a selection with a selection tool before creating the solid fill layer and then apply a color fill as outlined in the previous steps. Photoshop Elements adds color only inside the selection.

What other types of fill layers can I add?
In the New Fill Layer menu, you can create gradient fill layers, which apply bands of colors rather than a solid fill. Or you can create a pattern fill layer, which applies a repeating pattern as a fill instead of a solid color. You can select from a variety of preset gradient effects and patterns.

Create an Adjustment Layer

Adjustment layers enable you to store color and tonal changes in a layer instead of having them permanently applied to your image. The information in an adjustment layer is applied to the pixels in the layers below it. By changing the opacity of an adjustment layer, you can control the amount of changes applied. You can also hide an adjustment layer to turn the changes off completely.

You can use adjustment layers to test an editing technique without applying it to the original layer. Adjustment layers are especially handy for experimenting with colors, tones, and brightness settings.

For more about the effects you can apply with adjustment layers, such as levels and curves adjustments, see Chapters 10 and 11.

Create an Adjustment Layer

1 In the Editor, open the Layers panel.

Note: For more on opening the Editor or panels, see Chapter 1.

2 Click the layer you want to appear below the adjustment layer.

3 Click **Layer**.

4 Click **New Adjustment Layer**.

5 Click an adjustment command.

The New Layer dialog box opens.

6 Type a name for the adjustment layer or use the default name.

● You can specify a type of blend or opacity setting for the layer.

Note: See the sections "Blend Layers" or "Change the Opacity of a Layer" for more.

7 Click **OK**.

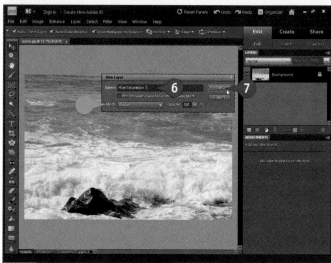

160

● Photoshop Elements adds an adjustment layer to the image.

The panel for the adjustment command appears.

Note: Depending on the type of adjustment layer you create, different settings appear.

In this example, an adjustment layer is created that changes the hue and saturation.

⑧ Click and drag the sliders () or type values to adjust the settings.

You can see the adjustments take effect in the workspace.

● Photoshop Elements applies the effect to the layers below the adjustment layer.

You can double-click the adjustment layer to make changes to the settings.

TIPS

How do I apply an adjustment layer to only part of my image canvas?
Make a selection with a selection tool before creating the adjustment layer. Photoshop Elements applies an adjustment layer to the selected content by creating a layer mask. See "Add a Layer Mask" for more about masks. You can experiment with edits to the adjustment layer; any changes you make to the selection affect the underlying layers. See Chapter 6 for more on the kinds of selections you can make with the selection tools in Photoshop Elements.

Is there a shortcut for creating an adjustment layer?
Yes. You can click the **Create Adjustment Layer** icon (⬛) in the Layers panel and then click the type of adjustment layer you want to create.

Blend Layers

You can use the blending modes in Photoshop Elements to specify how pixels in a layer should blend with the layers below. You can blend layers to create all kinds of visual effects in your photos.

In the following example, two photos are combined in one image file as two separate layers and then the layers are blended together. To copy a photo into a layer, see the section "Create and Add to a Layer."

When you create a new layer, the default blending mode is Normal, which applies no special blending to the layer. If you make changes to the Blending mode, switching back to Normal removes any blending effects.

Blend Layers

Blend a Regular Layer

1 In the Editor, open the Layers panel.

Note: For more on opening the Editor or panels, see Chapter 1.

2 Click the layer that you want to blend.

3 Click the down arrow (▼) and choose a blend mode.

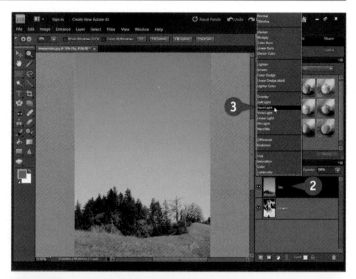

Photoshop Elements blends the selected layer with the layers below it.

This example blends a sky image with the image of a flower by using the Hard Light mode.

Blend an Adjustment Layer

1 Open the Layers panel.

Note: For more on opening panels, see Chapter 1.

2 Click an adjustment layer that you want to blend.

3 Click the ▼ and choose a blend mode.

Photoshop Elements blends the selected layer with the layers below it.

This example shows the Exclusion mode applied to a Hue and Saturation adjustment layer, which creates a photonegative effect where the layers overlap.

TIP

What effects do some of the different blending modes have?
- **Multiply:** Darkens the colors where the selected layer overlaps layers below it.
- **Screen:** The opposite of Multiply. It lightens colors where layers overlap.
- **Color:** Takes the selected layer's colors and blends them with the details in the layers below it.
- **Luminosity:** The opposite of Color. It takes the selected layer's details and mixes them with the colors below it.

Add a Layer Mask

You can apply a layer mask to a layer to precisely control what pixels in the layer are shown and what pixels are hidden. This is a new feature in Photoshop Elements 9.

You define the mask by applying colors using Photoshop Elements tools. A white color in the mask defines what in the layer is visible. Applying black to the layer mask with a brush or other tool specifies what parts of the layer are hidden. You can also apply shades of gray to partially show content in the layer.

When you add a layer mask to a layer, Photoshop Elements adds a mask icon next to the regular layer icon in the Layers panel.

Add a Layer Mask

1 In the Editor, open the Layers panel.

Note: For details about opening the Editor or panels, see Chapter 1.

2 Click to select the layer to which you want to apply the mask.

3 Click **Add Layer Mask** (▣).

You can alternatively click **Layer**, **Layer Mask**, and then **Reveal All** or **Hide All**. This creates an all white or all black layer mask, respectively.

● Photoshop Elements adds a layer mask icon to the layer.

The new layer mask is completely white, which means none of the layer is hidden by the mask.

● The foreground and background colors change to black and white, respectively.

4 Click the **Brush** tool (▨).

5 Set the brush size and shape using the settings in the Options bar.

Note: For more about using the Brush tool, see Chapter 12.

6 Click and drag the part of the layer you want to hide.

● The brush applies a black color to the mask.

● Photoshop Elements hides the pixels where the mask is black in color.

7 Click the foreground color (■) and select a shade of gray in the Color Picker that appears.

Note: See Chapter 12 for more about selecting colors.

8 Click and drag the part of the layer you want to hide partially.

● The brush applies a gray color to the mask.

● Photoshop Elements turns the masked pixels partially transparent.

Darker gray colors result in more of the layer being hidden.

TIPS

How do I paint colors onto layer content that has a mask?

To apply color normally to a layer that has a layer mask, click the regular layer icon in the Layers panel, then apply color with the Brush or other tool. If the layer mask icon is selected instead of the regular layer icon, the painted colors are applied to the mask.

After I have my layer mask exactly how I want it, how do I apply it permanently to the layer?

Right-click the layer mask icon in the Layers panel and select **Apply Layer Mask** from the menu that appears. Photoshop Elements applies the mask to the layer, permanently removing the pixels that have been hidden by the mask. The layer mask is removed from the layer.

Edit a Layer Mask

A layer mask offers a convenient way for editing images because it hides pixels in your image instead of deleting them. You can reveal pixels that were previously hidden, or hide more pixels, by editing the colors in the mask.

To unhide a masked part of an image, you can paint a white color on the mask using the Brush tool. To hide more of your layer, you can paint on the mask using a black color. By zooming in to edges in your image, you can carefully edit the mask and display just the layer content that you want shown.

Edit a Layer Mask

① Add a layer mask to a layer in your image.

Note: See "Add a Layer Mask" for details.

② Click the layer mask icon for the layer you want to edit.

③ Click the foreground color and set it to white using the Color Picker that appears.

Note: See Chapter 12 for more on setting the foreground color.

④ Click to select the **Brush** tool (🖌) or press the Ⓑ shortcut key.

⑤ Click and drag the hidden part of the layer you want displayed.

● The brush applies a white color to the mask.

● Photoshop Elements reveals the pixels where the mask is painted white.

6 Click the **Zoom** tool (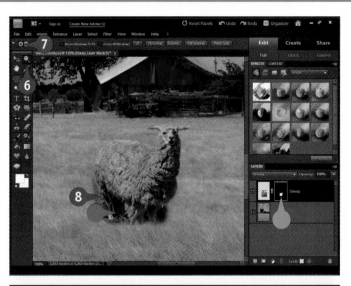).

7 Click **Zoom In** ().

8 Click to magnify the part of the masked layer that you want to edit.

9 Click the **Brush** tool ().

10 Click the foreground color () and set it to black using the Color Picker that appears.

11 Click and drag the visible part of the layer that you want hidden.

The brush applies a black color to the mask and hides content in that area of the mask.

Note: When applying colors to the layer mask, remember that white reveals and black conceals.

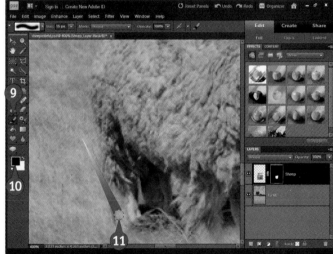

TIP

Are there other ways to view the layer masks that I apply?
With the masked layer selected in the Layers panel, press , which is located above `Enter` on most keyboards. Photoshop Elements displays the mask as a transparent red color, called a rubylith, over your image. To turn off the rubylith, press again. You can display the mask as a black-and-white image by pressing and holding `Alt` and clicking the layer mask icon for the layer. To turn off the black-and-white view, click the regular layer icon. You can edit your mask while in the rubylith or black-and-white modes by painting on the mask.

CHAPTER 9

Enhancing and Retouching Photos

Do you need to fix a photo fast? This chapter offers you all kinds of techniques for retouching your digital photos, including correcting common color problems, making flaws disappear, and rearranging objects.

Retouch with Guided Edit

You can remove unwanted objects by using the step-by-step instructions and adjustments in the Guided Edit view of Photoshop Elements. With the Spot Healing Brush and Healing Brush, you can remove imperfections by copying from unblemished areas of your photo. The Spot Healing brush is good for removing small elements such as skin blemishes; the Healing Brush is better for eliminating larger objects like the Clone Stamp tool.

In addition to retouching a photo in Guided Edit, you can access adjustments that enable you to merge content from multiple photos into a single image, correct lighting, and more. For more about merging content, see the sections "Merge Group Shots" and "Combine Faces" later in this chapter. For more about correcting lighting, see Chapter 10.

Retouch with Guided Edit

1 In the Editor, click **Edit**.

2 Click **Guided**.

Note: For more on opening the Editor, see Chapter 1.

The Guided Edit view opens.

● Make sure the Guided Activities list is open. You can click the ▶ to open it (▶ changes to ▼).

3 Click **Touch Up Scratches and Blemishes**.

4 Click the **Spot Healing Brush** (▨).

5 Click and drag the slider (▤) to select a brush size between 1 and 1000.

Select a brush size that will cover the area you plan to correct.

You can also type a value for the brush size.

6 Click an object in your image.

Photoshop Elements patches and blends the object with the color and texture of nearby pixels.

7 Click the **Healing Brush** (■).

8 Click and drag the slider (■) to select a brush size between 1 and 1000.

Select a brush size slightly smaller than the area you plan to touch up. You can also type a value for the brush size.

9 Press Alt and then click an unblemished area of your image that has a similar color and texture.

10 Click and drag across an object or blemish in your image.

Photoshop Elements covers the object with pixels from the unblemished area.

11 Click **Done** to return to the main Guided Edit view.

TIP

When retouching in Guided Edit, how can I accurately view the objects I want to remove?

1 Click the **Zoom** tool (■) or press the Z shortcut key..

2 Click inside your image to zoom in.

3 Click the **Hand** tool (■) or press the H shortcut key.

4 Click and drag to move your image horizontally and vertically.

Note: For more on the Zoom and Hand tools, see Chapter 5.

Quick Fix a Photo

You can use the Quick Fix view in Photoshop Elements to make fast corrections to your photos in one convenient window. You can adjust lighting, contrast, color, and focus as well as compare Before and After views of your adjustments.

The Quick Fix pane consists of a variety of panels. The General Fixes panel includes Red Eye Fix and Smart Fix, which automatically corrects lighting, color, and contrast. The Lighting panel fixes contrast and exposure problems; the Color panel fixes color problems; and the Sharpen panel sharpens photos. For more about fixing light and color issues, see Chapter 10 and Chapter 11.

Quick Fix a Photo

1 In the Editor, click **Edit**.

2 Click **Quick**.

Note: For more on opening the Editor, see Chapter 1.

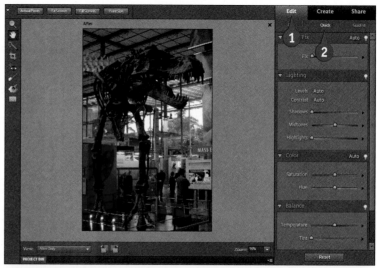

The Quick Fix pane opens.

● You can zoom, pan, select objects, or crop the image with this tool.

3 Click the down arrow (⬛) and then a view mode.

The After Only view shows the results of your changes.

The Before Only view shows the original unedited photo.

The Before and After views show both the original image and the image with changes applied.

④ Click and drag the **Fix** slider (▓).

● You can also click **Auto** to have Photoshop Elements automatically adjust your image.

● Photoshop Elements makes immediate adjustments to the lighting, contrast, and colors in the image.

● You can click **Reset** to return to the original settings.

⑤ Click ✔ or press Enter to accept.

● To make different types of adjustments automatically, click **Auto** for the type of correction you want to make.

● You can also click and drag a slider (▤) to adjust a setting.

● In this example, the shadows in the image are lightened.

⑥ Click ✔ or press Enter to accept.

⑦ Click **Full**.

Photoshop Elements applies the changes and returns to the Full Edit interface.

TIPS

Must I always use the Quick Fix view to correct brightness, color, focus, and rotation problems?
No. You can make these corrections by using other tools in Photoshop Elements. The Enhance menu contains these same corrections, some of which open dialog boxes that enable you to fine-tune the adjustment.

What exactly does the Smart Fix feature do?
Smart Fix analyzes your image and attempts to correct lighting, contrast, and color based on preset algorithms. Depending on the condition of the photo, the changes may be quite pronounced or barely noticeable. You can click and drag the slider (▤) in the Smart Fix panel to control the percentage amount of change made to the color, shadows, and highlights in the image.

Improve Colors with Quick Fix

Yyou can use the tools in the Quick Fix view to correct common color problems in your photos. The tools enable you to whiten teeth and boost the blue in a washed-out sky. These tools give you an easy way to fix common, specific problems in photos. You can perform the same tasks with color and lighting tools in the Full Edit interface, but the settings are more complex.

You can also access the Black and White – High Contrast tool, which is covered in the Tip, and the Red Eye Removal tool in the Quick Fix view. With the exception of the Red Eye Removal tool, the tools in the Quick Fix view apply their changes as adjustment layers, which means you can fine tune their effects later. See Chapter 8 for more about adjustment layers.

Improve Colors with Quick Fix

Add Blue to Skies

1 In the Editor, open a photo that includes a dull-colored sky.

Note: For more on opening the Editor, see Chapter 1. For more on opening a photo, see Chapter 2.

2 Click **Quick**.

The Quick Fix view opens.

3 Click the **Make Dull Skies Blue** tool ().

- You can click the ▼ to adjust the brush size.

4 Click and drag over the sky.

Photoshop Elements selects the sky and boosts the blue color.

- You can click **Reset** to revert the photo to its previous state.

Whiten Teeth

1 Open a photo that includes teeth.

2 Click the **Whiten Teeth** tool (⬚).

● You can click the ▾ to adjust the brush size.

3 Click and drag over teeth in the photo.

Photoshop Elements whitens the teeth, decreasing any colorcast they may have.

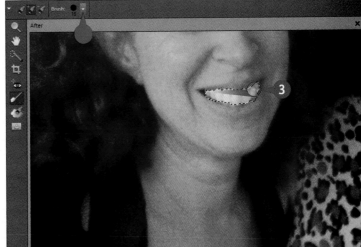

TIP

How can I easily turn an area of my photo to black and white?

1 In the Quick Fix view, click the **Black And White – High Contrast** tool (⬚).

2 Click and drag across an object in your photo.

● You can click the ▾ to adjust the brush size.

Photoshop Elements selects the object and converts it to high-contrast black and white.

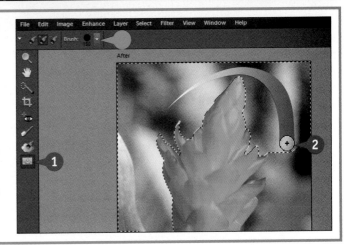

Remove Red Eye

You can use the Red Eye Removal tool to remove the red eye color that a camera flash can cause. Red eye is a common problem in snapshots taken indoors with a flash. The light from the flash reflects off the back of the subject's eyes, creating the red eye appearance. Using the Red Eye Removal tool, you can edit the eye to change its color without changing image details. You can experience a similar problem with animals, but their eyes can turn yellow or green. See the tip for details about how to fix that.

Remove Red Eye

1 In the Editor, click the **Red Eye Removal** tool ( ).

Note: For more on the Editor, see Chapter 1.

2 Click the and then drag the slider ( ) to control the size of the area to correct.

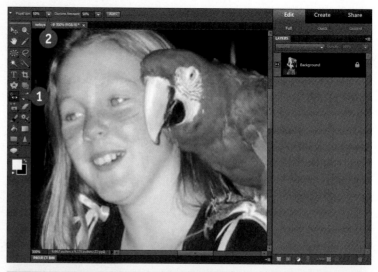

3 Click the and then drag the slider ( ) to the darkness setting you want.

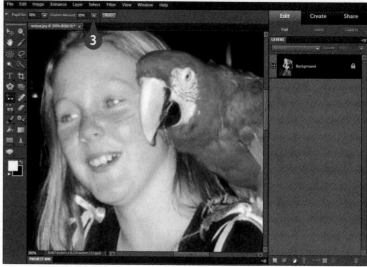

④ Click the eye you want to fix.

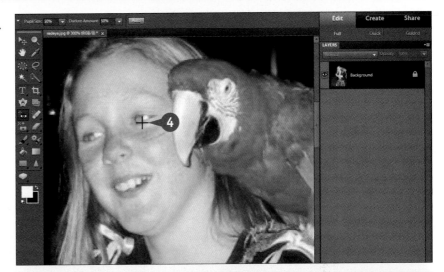

⑤ Release the mouse button.

● Photoshop Elements repairs the color.

If you need to change the settings, you can click **Undo** (⬛) to undo the color change.

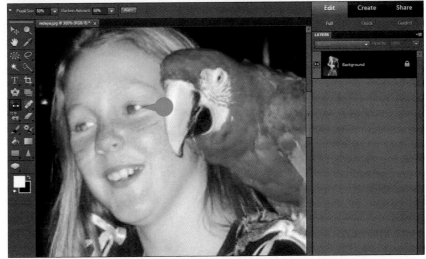

TIP

My pet photos have a yellow or green eye problem. How do I fix this?

① Click the **Burn** tool (⬛).

② Click the ⬛ to set your brush style and size options.

③ Click the **Range** ⬛ and select **Highlights** from the menu.

④ Click the eye you want to darken.

Photoshop Elements darkens the eye. You can click as many times as needed to get the desired color.

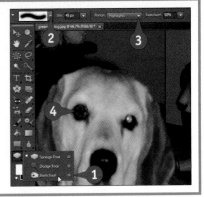

Retouch with the Clone Stamp Tool

You can clean up small flaws or erase elements in your image with the Clone Stamp tool. The tool copies information from one area of an image to another. For example, you can use the Clone Stamp tool to remove unwanted blemishes of all kinds by cloning an area near the flaw and then stamping over the flaw.

You can adjust the opacity of the tool to copy information partially to the new location. Lowering the opacity and then copying from multiple areas in an image can sometimes be the best way to cleanly erase an unwanted object.

Retouch with the Clone Stamp Tool

① In the Editor, click the **Clone Stamp** tool (⬛).

Note: For more on opening the Editor, see Chapter 1.

② Click the ▼ to choose a brush size and type, or set an exact brush size.

You can change the brush size while using the tool by pressing ⬚ and ⬚.

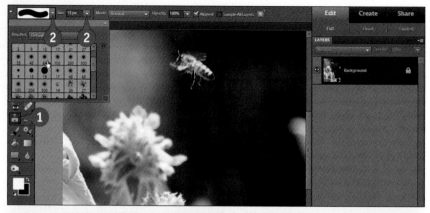

③ Click the ▼ to choose an opacity, which determines whether the tool covers an area completely or partially.

You can also type a value for the opacity.

④ Press and hold **Alt** and then click the area of the image from which you want to copy.

In this example, the Clone Stamp is used to remove a bee near a flower.

5 Click and drag the area of the photo that you want to correct.

Photoshop Elements copies the cloned area to where you click and drag.

6 Continue clicking new areas to clone and dragging over the area as many times as needed to achieve the desired effect.

Note: Short strokes can often produce better results than long strokes since they help avoid cloning from unintended areas.

You can click **Undo** (🔙) to undo the tool's effects.

TIPS

How can I make the Clone Stamp's effects look seamless?

To erase elements from your image with the Clone Stamp without leaving a trace, try the following:

• Clone between areas of similar color and texture.

• To apply the stamp more subtly, lower its opacity.

• Use a soft-edged brush shape.

What can I do with the Pattern Stamp?

You can use the Pattern Stamp, which shares space in the Toolbox with the Clone Stamp, to paint repeating patterns on your images. To find the Pattern Stamp tool, right-click the **Clone Stamp** tool (🔲) and then click **Pattern Stamp** (🔲) from the menu that appears. You can select a pattern, brush style, and brush size and then stamp the pattern on your photo.

Remove a Spot

You can use the Spot Healing Brush to quickly repair flaws or remove small objects in a photo. The tool works well on small spots or blemishes on both solid and textured backgrounds. You can adjust the brush size so that it covers the feature you want to remove.

The tool's Proximity Match setting analyzes pixels surrounding the selected area and replaces the area with a patch of similar pixels. The Create Texture setting replaces the area with a blend of surrounding pixels. The Content-Aware setting, which is often the most useful, is similar to Proximity Match but can also recognize patterns within the surrounding pixels and keep them intact.

Remove a Spot

1 In the Editor, click the **Spot Healing Brush** tool ( ).

Note: For more on opening the Editor, see Chapter 1.

2 Click the to choose a brush size and type that will cover the spot.

● You can also set an exact brush size here.

3 Click the type of healing effect you want to apply (● changes to ○).

④ Click the spot you want to correct.

You may have to click and drag across the spot to get the desired effect.

Photoshop Elements replaces the selected area with pixels similar to those nearby.

● You can click **Undo** (icon) to undo the change.

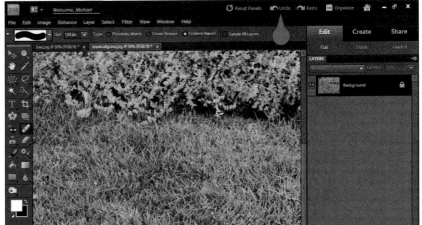

TIP

How do I correct larger areas of a photo?
Using the Healing Brush tool, follow these steps:

① Right-click the **Spot Healing Brush** tool (icon).

② Click the **Healing Brush** tool (icon).

③ Adjust the tool's settings.

④ Press and hold Alt and then click the area you want to clone.

⑤ Click and drag over the problem area to blend the cloned pixels into the new area.

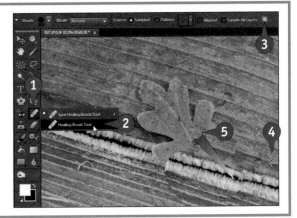

Sharpen an Image

You can use the Adjust Sharpness dialog box to sharpen an image suffering from focus problems. The tool enables you to control the amount of sharpening you apply.

To apply sharpening to just part of your image, for example to the main feature of your image, you can first select that part with a selection tool. To use the selection tools, see Chapter 6. Photoshop Elements also lets you to perform the opposite of sharpening by applying a blur filter. The blur filter is covered in Chapter 13.

Sharpen an Image

① In the Editor, select the layer to which you want to apply the enhancement.

Note: For more on opening the Editor, see Chapter 1. For more on layers, see Chapter 8.

In this example, the image has a single Background layer.

② Click **Enhance**.

③ Click **Adjust Sharpness**.

The Adjust Sharpness dialog box opens.

● A preview area displays the filter's effect.

● You can click the **Preview** check box to preview the effect in the main window (■ changes to ☑).

④ Click minus or plus (■ or ■) to zoom out or in. It is best to preview a sharpened image at 100% magnification.

⑤ Click and drag the sliders (●) to control the amount of sharpening you apply to the image.

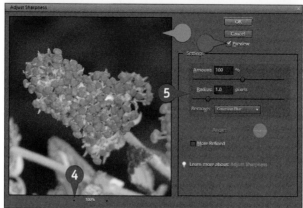

● Amount controls the overall amount of sharpening.

● Radius controls controls how far from any edges of high contrast sharpening is applied. A higher radius setting applies sharpening farther from edges in you image.

You can type values for the amount and radius settings.

● You can click the ▼ to remove a specific type of blur in the image. The default is Gaussian Blur, which applies sharpening across the image. Lens Blur concentrates the sharpening on details while Motion Blur removes blur caused by camera or subject motion.

6 Click **OK**.

Photoshop Elements applies the enhancement.

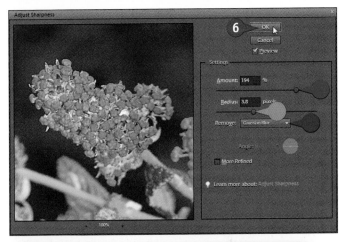

When should I apply sharpening?
Sharpening an image after you resize it can be a good idea because changing an image's size, especially enlarging, can add blurring. Adjusting sharpness can also help clarify scanned images. Although the tool cannot perform a miracle and make an unfocused image completely clear, it can sharpen slightly blurred images or blurring caused by applying other filters. It is best to apply sharpening as a final step.

What does the Auto Sharpen button in the Quick Fix window do?
The Auto button on the Sharpen panel sharpens an image by a preset amount. If you use the Quick Fix window to retouch a photo, you can easily apply the Auto Sharpen command. However, you can fine-tune the sharpening effects to your liking when using the Adjust Sharpness dialog box.

Extract an Object from a Background

You can extract an object in your photo from its background by using the Magic Extractor tool. You define the object and background by brushing lines of color over them, and then Photoshop Elements deletes the background automatically. When you perform the extraction, the area around your selected object is removed and replaced with transparent pixels.

Using the Magic Extractor can be quicker than selecting the object with one of the Lasso tools, inverting the selection, and then deleting the background. For more on the Lasso tools, see Chapter 6.

Extract an Object from a Background

1 In the Editor, click **Image**.

Note: For more on opening the Editor, see Chapter 1.

2 Click **Magic Extractor**.

You can also press Alt + Shift + Ctrl + V.

The Magic Extractor dialog box opens.

3 Click the **Foreground Brush** tool (⊿).

4 Click the ▶ to specify your brush size.

5 Click and drag to apply brushstrokes to the object you want to keep.

The more of the object you cover, the greater the chance of a successful extraction.

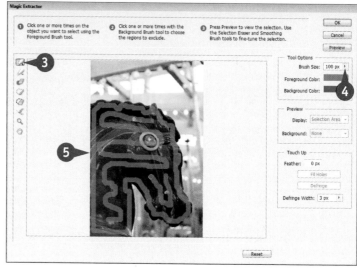

6 Click the **Background Brush** tool (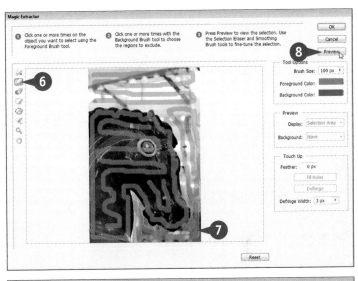).

7 Click and drag to apply brush lines on the background you want to remove.

8 Click **Preview**.

Photoshop Elements extracts the object from the background and displays a preview.

● To remove your your work and repeat the process, click **Reset**.

9 Click **OK** to complete the extraction and return to your image.

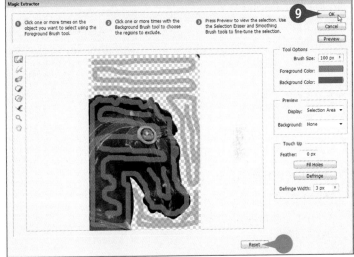

TIP

TIP

How can I clean up the edges of an object after extraction?

1 Use the Magic Extractor tools and commands to preview your extraction.

2 Use the **Zoom** (🔍) and **Hand** (🖐) tools to view the edges of the object.

3 Click the **Remove from Selection** (🖌) tool.

4 Click and drag to clean up the edges of the object.

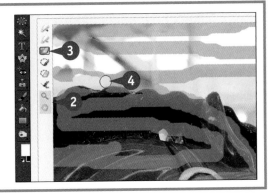

Merge Group Shots

You can take several photos of groups of people and then merge them so the good parts of the different versions are combined into a single optimized photo. This can help when some people have their eyes closed or are not smiling in photos.

The Group Shot tool works best when the different photos have similar backgrounds. This allows Photoshop Elements to align the different photos and place the different parts in the correct places.

To merge content between the photos, you paint over the good areas of the source photo to add those areas to another photo.

Merge Group Shots

1 In the Editor, open multiple versions of the same group photo.

Note: For more on opening the Editor, see Chapter 1.

2 Ctrl +click to select the photos in the Project Bin.

3 Click **Guided**.

● Make sure the Photomerge panel is open. You can click the ▶ to open it (▶ changes to ▼).

4 Click **Group Shot**.

Photoshop Elements opens the photos in the Photomerge Group Shot tool.

5 In the Project Bin, click and drag the photo that you want to fix to the Final window.

6 Click to select the source photo you want to copy from.

● The photo to select from appears in the Source window.

7 Click the **Pencil** tool (✐).

8 Click and drag to apply brushstrokes in the Source window to define the area you want replaced in the Final window.

● Photoshop Elements takes the defined area and merges it into the similar area in the Final window.

You can click **Undo** (↩) to undo the change.

9 Repeat Step **8** to replace different areas of the final photo.

You can select other photos in the Project Bin to replace more areas.

10 Click **Done** to exit the Photomerge Group Shot tool.

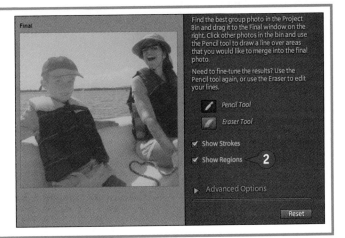

TIP

How can I view the areas that Photoshop Elements replaces in the Photomerge Group Shot window?

1 Complete Steps **1** to **8** in this section.

2 Click the **Show Regions** check box (■ changes to ✓).

Photoshop Elements places tinting in the Final window to show which areas were merged from which photos.

Combine Faces

The Faces tool enables you to put the eyes, nose, or mouth from one face onto another face. After you align the faces by using this tool, you can select the different features and then Photoshop Elements combines the faces automatically.

The tool works best when the faces you are combining are oriented in a similar fashion, for example both level and looking straight ahead. If faces are not oriented similarly, the tool distorts the faces slightly so that they are in better alignment and so that features can be matched correctly.

Combine Faces

1 In the Editor, open two or more face photos.

Note: For more on opening the Editor, see Chapter 1.

2 Ctrl +click to select the photos in the Project Bin.

3 Click **Guided**.

● Make sure the Photomerge panel is open. You can click the ▶ to open it (▼ changes to ▲).

4 Click **Faces**.

Photoshop Elements opens the photos in the Photomerge Faces tool.

5 Click and drag the photo you want to copy to into the Final window.

6 Click to select the photo you want to select from.

● The photo to select from appears in the Source window.

7 Click the **Alignment** tool (⊕).

Numbered crosses appear on the Source photo.

8 Click and drag the crosses to features on the face from where you want to copy.

9 Position the cursor over the Final window.

Numbered crosses appear on the Final photo.

10 Place the crosses on the same facial features as in Step 8.

11 Click **Align Photos**.

Photoshop Elements aligns the faces in the photos.

12 Click the **Pencil** tool (✐).

13 Click and drag the Source face to define a feature.

● Photoshop Elements places the feature on the Final face.

14 Repeat Steps 8 to 11 to add more features.

15 Click **Done** to exit the Photomerge Faces tool.

TIPS

How can I edit the facial features that Photoshop Elements merges in the Faces tool?

The Faces tool places the merged facial features in a separate layer above the original face. You can edit the added features by editing that layer in the Full Edit interface. For example, you can use the Eraser tool to remove extra skin around the eyes or mouth. To access the Full Edit interface, click **Full**.

How can I remove extraneous people or objects from a large scene?

If you have several versions of a scene shot from the same angle, you can use the Scene Cleaner tool to remove the people or objects from the scene. The tool enables you to select empty areas from one version of the scene and place them over the people or objects you want to remove in the other version of the scene. To access the Scene Cleaner, click **Scene Cleaner** in the Photomerge section of Guided Edit.

Recompose a Photo

You can recompose a photo to change its size while keeping important objects within it intact. Recomposition is an alternative to cropping for when you want to reduce an image's size without trimming or deleting certain subject matter. For more on using the Crop tool, see Chapter 5.

Before you apply the Recomposition tool, you designate areas of your photo that you want kept unchanged by painting over them. You also paint over areas that you would prefer be eliminated. Photoshop Elements can then intelligently rearrange the correct areas of the photo as you resize.

Recompose a Photo

① In the Editor, right-click the **Crop** tool (▣).

Note: For more on opening the Editor, see Chapter 1.

The Recompose tool shares space with the Crop tool in the Toolbox.

② Click the **Recompose** tool (▣).

If a dialog box opens with tips about using the tool, click **OK**.

③ Click **Mark for Protection** (▣).

④ Click the ▾ to specify a brush size.

⑤ Click and drag over the objects you want to keep unchanged.

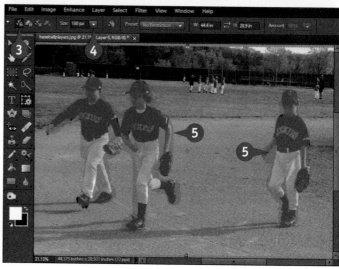

6 Click **Mark for Removal** (■).

7 Click the ▾ to specify a brush size.

8 Click and drag over the areas that can be deleted.

9 Click and drag the corner handles to recompose the image.

Photoshop Elements rearranges content in the image, keeping the protected objects intact.

10 Click ✔ or press Enter to commit the changes.

● You can fix misaligned edges in the recomposed image using the Spot Healing Brush tool or Healing Brush tool.

TIP

How do I edit my selections when using the Recompose tool?

1 With the Recompose tool selected, click **Erase Highlights Marked for Protection** (■).

2 Click and drag to erase protected coloring.

3 Click **Erase Highlights Marked for Removal** (■).

4 Click and drag to erase coloring marking deletable areas.

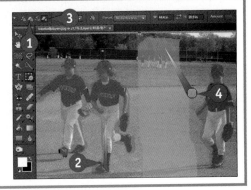

Fix Keystone Distortion

You can use the camera distortion tools in Photoshop Elements to fix keystone effects. This can occur when taking pictures with the camera tilted horizontally or vertically, which can cause rectangular objects — such as tall buildings — to appear trapezoidal.

The Correct Camera Distortion dialog box enables you to stretch and squeeze your image in various ways to eliminate distortion and straighten large objects. It also includes a vignette adjustment that removes shadowing around the edges of an image. Vignetting can be caused by camera or lens limitations.

Fix Keystone Distortion

① In the Editor, open a photo that has keystone distortion.

Note: For more on opening the Editor, see Chapter 1.

② Click **Guided**.

③ Click **Fix Keystone Distortion**.

The Fix Keystone Distortion panel opens.

④ Click the 🔽 to scroll to the bottom of the panel.

⑤ Click **Correct Camera Distortion**.

● You can click the 🔽 to view Before and After versions of the image.

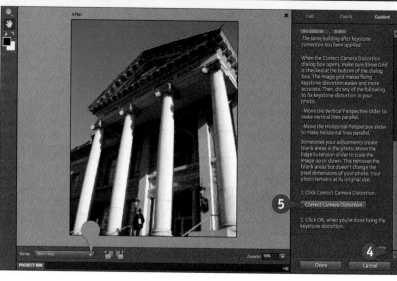

The Correct Camera Distortion window opens.

6 Click and drag the sliders ( ) to correct the horizontal and vertical perspectives.

7 Click and drag the to correct distortion that fisheye lenses can cause.

● You can click and drag the to scale the photo.

You can also type values for the horizontal and vertical perspectives, the distortion, and the scale.

8 Click **OK**.

Photoshop Elements corrects the photo.

9 Click **Done** to exit the tool.

● You can click **Reset** to undo the correction.

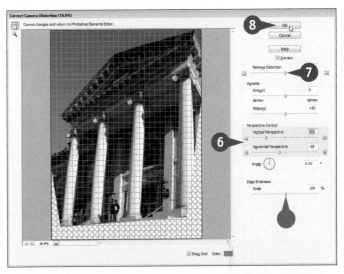

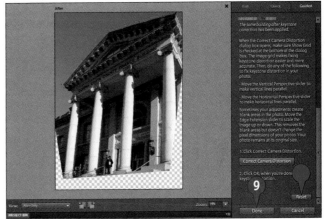

TIP

How can I use the Perspective command to correct buildings with keystone distortion?

1 Click **Image**.

2 Click **Transform**.

3 Click **Perspective**.

Handles appear on the edges and corners of the image.

4 Drag the top corner handles outward to fix the distortion.

5 Click or press **Enter** to commit the changes.

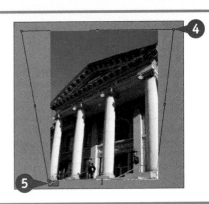

CHAPTER 10

Improving Lighting and Exposure

Does your photo suffer from shadows that are too dark or highlights that are too light? Or perhaps you have an old photo in which the entire image is faded? You can correct overall tone, contrast, exposure, and lighting problems by using features in Photoshop Elements. You can also make isolated changes to the lighting of objects in your photo with the Dodge and Burn tools.

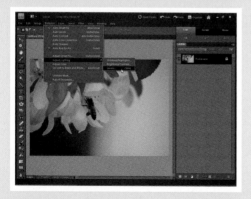
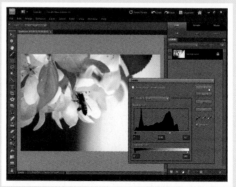

Enhance Lighting with Guided Edit

You can fix simple lighting problems in your images by using the step-by-step instructions and adjustments in the Guided Edit interface in Photoshop Elements. This feature enables you to compare before-and-after versions of an image as you change the lighting.

The Lighten or Darken Guided Edit uses the same editing settings found in the dialog box for the Shadows and Highlights command. For more about this command, see "Adjust Shadows and Highlights."

In addition to lightening or darkening a photo in Guided Edit, you can access adjustments that enable you to correct color, merge content from multiple photos into a single image, and more. For more about color correction, see Chapter 11. For more about merging content, see Chapter 9.

Enhance Lighting with Guided Edit

1 In the Editor, click **Edit**.

2 Click **Guided**.

Note: For more on opening the Editor, see Chapter 1.

The Guided Edit view opens.

● Make sure the Lighting and Exposure list is open. You can click the ▼ to open it (▶ changes to ▼).

3 Click **Lighten or Darken**.

● You can click **Auto** to have Photoshop Elements automatically adjust the lighting in your image by using its built-in optimization routines.

4 Click the ▮ and then click a **Before & After** setting to open Before and After views of the image.

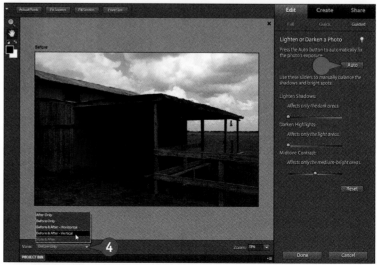

5 Click and drag the slider (⬛) to lighten shadows in the image.

6 Click and drag the slider (⬛) to darken highlights in the image.

7 Click and drag the slider (⬛) to increase or decrease the contrast in the image.

8 Click **Done**.

Photoshop Elements enhances the lighting in the image.

In this example, shadows in the barn and the highlighting in the sky are decrease to bring out details.

● You can click **Full** to switch to the Full Edit interface.

TIP

How do I automatically adjust lighting and color in one step?

1 Click **Enhance**.

2 Click **Adjust Smart Fix**.

The Adjust Smart Fix dialog box opens.

3 Click and drag the slider (⬛) to control the strength of the adjustment.

4 Click **OK**.

Photoshop Elements applies the adjustment.

Adjust Levels

You can use the Levels dialog box to fine-tune shadows, highlights, and midtones in your image. Input sliders enable you to manipulate the tonal qualities of an image, and the output sliders let you adjust contrast.

The Levels dialog displays a *histogram*, which is a graph that shows the distribution of lighter and darker colors in the image. The amount of darker colors is represented on the left and the amount of lighter colors on the right. Adjusting the Levels settings changes how the colors are distributed. You can adjust levels in just a part of your image by making a selection or selecting a layer before executing the command. For more on making selections, see Chapter 6. For more on working with layers, see Chapter 8.

Adjust Levels

1 In the Editor, click **Enhance**.

Note: For more on opening the Editor, see Chapter 1.

2 Click **Adjust Lighting**.

3 Click **Levels**.

Alternatively, you can press Ctrl+L.

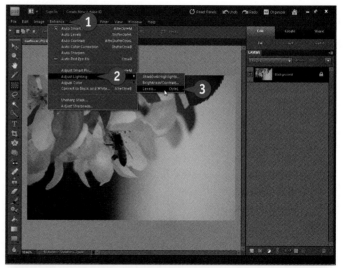

The Levels dialog box opens.

4 Make sure to click the **Preview** check box (■ changes to ☑).

The Preview option enables you to see your adjustments as you make them.

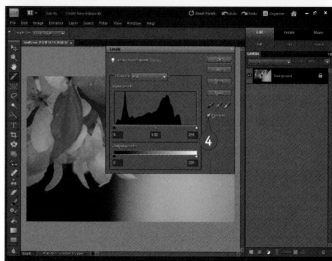

⑤ Click and drag the slider (■) to darken shadows and increase contrast.

⑥ Click and drag the slider (■) to adjust the midtones of the image.

⑦ Click and drag the slider (□) to lighten the bright areas of the image and increase contrast.

You can also type values to control the contrast and midtones.

● Photoshop Elements displays a preview of the adjustments in the workspace.

⑧ Click and drag the slider (■) to the right to lighten the image.

⑨ Click and drag the slider (□) to the left to darken the image.

⑩ Click **OK**.

Photoshop Elements applies the adjustments.

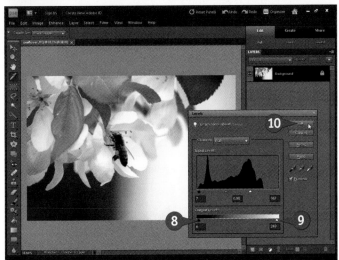

TIPS

How do I adjust the brightness levels of an image automatically?
Click **Enhance** and then **Auto Levels**. Photoshop Elements sets the lightest pixels to white and the darkest pixels to black and then redistributes the intermediate values proportionally throughout the rest of the image. You can use the Auto Levels command to make immediate corrections to shadows, midtones, and highlights.

Can I tell Photoshop Elements what pixels to use as the darkest, midtone, and brightest levels in my image?
Yes. The Levels dialog box includes three Eyedropper tools, one each for the darkest (📷), midtone (📷), and lightest tones (📷). You can click the Eyedropper tool for the tone you want to set and then click the appropriate pixel(s) in your image.

Adjust Shadows and Highlights

You can use the Shadows and Highlights feature to make quick adjustments to the dark and light areas of your image. The feature is less complicated than the Levels tool but also less flexible. The tool can be useful for fixing photos with poor exposure. The Lighten Shadows setting enables you to improve underexposed and overly dark photos, whereas Darken Highlights can help correct overexposed photos that are too light. Making subtle adjustments with the tool can also improve photos by bringing out details in the darker and lighter areas.

You can adjust shadows and highlights in just a part of your image by making a selection or selecting a layer before executing the command. For more on making selections, see Chapter 6. For more on working with layers, see Chapter 8.

Adjust Shadows and Highlights

1 In the Editor, click **Enhance**.

Note: For more on opening the Editor, see Chapter 1.

2 Click **Adjust Lighting**.

3 Click **Shadows/Highlights**.

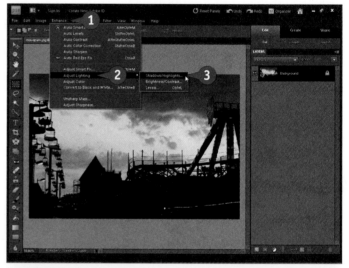

The Shadows/Highlights dialog box opens.

4 Make sure to click the **Preview** check box (■ changes to ✓).

The Preview option enables you to view your adjustments as you make them.

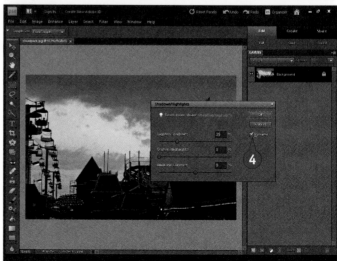

5 Click and drag the slider ( ) to lighten shadows in the image.

6 Click and drag the slider ( ) to darken highlights in the image.

7 Click and drag the slider ( ) to adjust midtone contrast in the image.

You can also type values for the shadows, highlights, and contrast.

8 Click **OK**.

Photoshop Elements applies the adjustments.

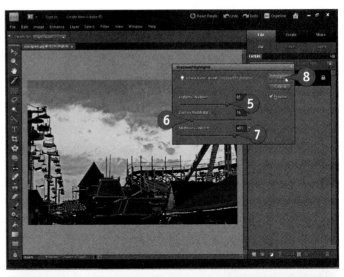

How do I cancel my adjustments without exiting the Shadows/Highlights dialog box?

If you press and hold Alt, Cancel changes to Reset. Click **Reset** to return the settings to their default values.

When I open the Shadows/Highlights dialog box, Photoshop Elements immediately adjusts my image. What is happening?

The Shadows/Highlights filter is set to automatically lighten shadows in your image by 25%. When you open the dialog box, you see this applied. You can reduce the effect by dragging the **Lighten Shadows** slider ( ) to the left.

Change Brightness and Contrast

You can use the Brightness/Contrast dialog box to adjust the brightness and contrast levels in a photo or a selected portion of a photo. *Brightness* refers to the intensity of the lighter pixels in an image, and *contrast* refers to the relative difference between dark and light areas in an image.

The Brightness/Contrast tool is easiest way to make simple adjustments to the lightness in your image in Photoshop Elements. To make more complex adjustments to the tonal qualities in an image, use the Levels dialog box. See the section "Adjust Levels" for more information.

Change Brightness and Contrast

1 In the Editor, click **Enhance**.

Note: For more on opening the Editor, see Chapter 1.

2 Click **Adjust Lighting**.

3 Click **Brightness/Contrast**.

The Brightness/Contrast dialog box opens.

If you want to restrict changes to a selection or layer, select the layer or make the selection before executing the command.

● The Preview check box is selected by default.

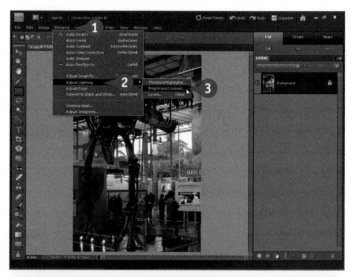

4 Click and drag the **Brightness** slider (■) to adjust brightness.

Drag the slider to the right to lighten the image.

Drag the slider to the left to darken the image.

● You can also type a number from 1 to 150 to lighten the image or from -1 to -150 to darken the image.

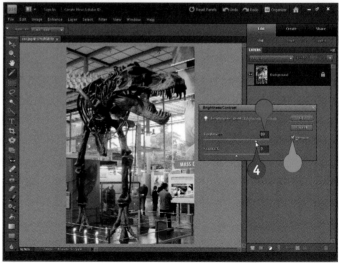

5 Click and drag the **Contrast** slider (■) to adjust contrast.

Drag the slider to the right to increase contrast.

Drag the slider to the left to decrease contrast.

● You can also type a number from 1 to 100 to increase contrast or from -1 to -50 to decrease contrast.

6 Click **OK**.

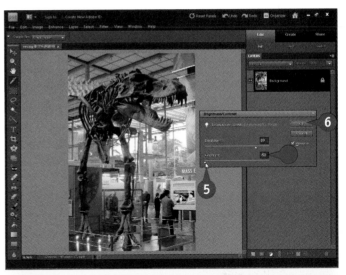

Photoshop Elements applies the adjustments to the image, selection, or layer.

TIPS

How can I automatically adjust the contrast of an image?
You can click **Enhance** and then **Auto Contrast**. Photoshop Elements automatically converts light and dark pixels for you. The Auto Contrast feature converts the very lightest pixels in the image to white and the very darkest pixels to black. Unlike with the Brightness/Contrast dialog box, you cannot fine-tune the contrast settings with Auto Contrast.

Does Photoshop Elements offer a tool for evaluating tones in an image?
Yes. You can use the Histogram panel to evaluate tonal qualities in your images. Click **Window** and then **Histogram** to open the panel. The Histogram is a graphical representation of the light and dark pixels in an image plotted by intensity. The density of each color intensity is plotted, with the darker pixels plotted on the left and the lighter pixels plotted on the right.

Lighten Areas with the Dodge Tool

You can use the Dodge tool to quickly brighten a specific area of an image. *Dodge* is a photographic term that describes the diffusing of light when printing a film negative. For example, you can selectively lighten a dark area of an image by brushing over the area with the Dodge tool.

You can limit the pixels affected by the Dodge tool by specifying what tones to correct — midtones, shadows, or highlights. You can also specify the strength of the lightening effect by selecting an exposure setting.

Making a selection prior to applying the Dodge tool can be useful so that lighting adjustments are made only to intended areas. For more about making selections, see Chapter 6.

Lighten Areas with the Dodge Tool

① In the Editor, right-click the **Sponge** tool (▣).

Note: For more on opening the Editor, see Chapter 1.

The Dodge tool shares space with the Sponge and Burn tools in the Toolbox.

② Click the **Dodge** tool (▪). You can also press the Ⓞ shortcut key.

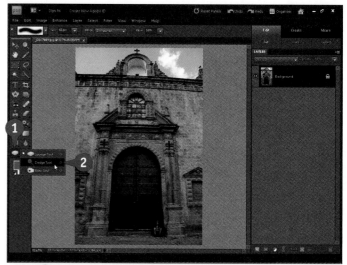

③ Click the down arrow (▼) and choose the brush you want to use.

● You can click the ▼ and select an exact brush size here.

You can change the brush size while using the tool by pressing [and].

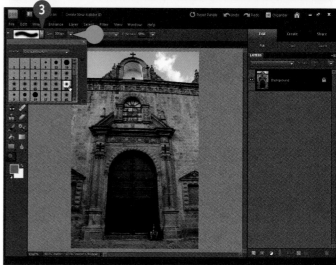

- You can click the ▼ and choose the range of tones you want to affect.

- You can click the ▼ and choose the tool's exposure, or strength.

4 Click and drag the mouse pointer (○) over the area you want to lighten.

- Photoshop Elements lightens the area.

  If you continue to click or click and drag over an area, the area is lightened more with each application of the tool.

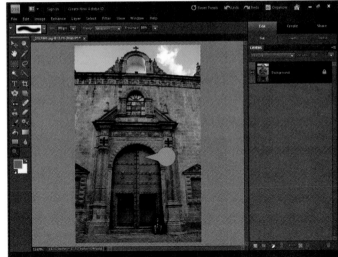

TIPS

Is there a way to gradually brighten an area?
If you set the Exposure level to a low value, you can drag repeatedly over the area you want to correct to gradually brighten the area, or you can click multiple times to gradually brighten just the area under the cursor.

How can I add extra highlights to the lighter area of an object?
You can apply the Dodge tool with the Range set to Highlights to brighten the lighter areas of an object in your image. Likewise, you can use the Burn tool (▣) with the Range set to Shadows to add shadows to the shaded side of an object. For more on the Burn tool, see the section "Darken Areas with the Burn Tool."

Darken Areas with the Burn Tool

You can use the Burn tool to darken a specific area of an image. *Burn* is a photographic term that describes the focusing of light when printing a film negative. For example, you can selectively darken a bright area of an image by brushing over the area with the Burn tool.

You can limit the pixels affected by the Burn tool by specifying what tones to correct — midtones, shadows, or highlights. You can also specify the strength of the darkening effect by selecting an exposure setting.

Making a selection prior to applying the Burn tool can be useful so that lighting adjustments are made only to intended areas. For more about making selections, see Chapter 6.

Darken Areas with the Burn Tool

1 In the Editor, right-click the **Sponge** tool ( ).

Note: For more on opening the Editor, see Chapter 1.

The Burn tool shares space with the Sponge and Dodge tools in the Toolbox.

2 Click the **Burn** tool ( ).

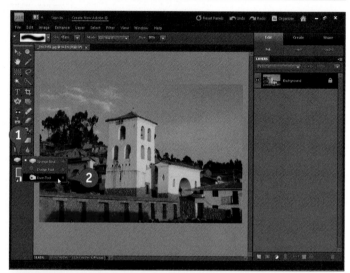

3 Click the ▼ to choose the brush you want to use.

● You can also select the range of colors you want to affect and the tool's exposure, or strength.

4 Click and drag the mouse pointer (○) over the area you want to darken.

Photoshop Elements darkens the area.

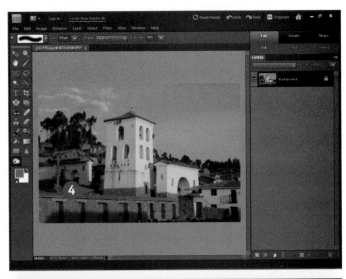

● If you continue to click or click and drag over an area, the area is darkened more with each application of the tool.

In this example, shadows are added to buildings on the left.

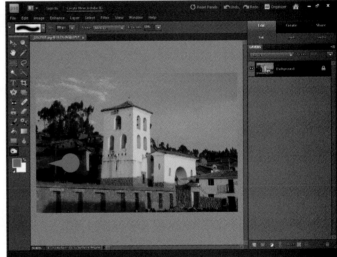

TIP

How do I invert the bright and dark colors in an image?

1 Click **Filter**.

2 Click **Adjustments**.

3 Click **Invert**.

You can also press Ctrl+I to apply the Invert command.

Photoshop Elements inverts the image. For more on filters in Photoshop Elements, see Chapter 13.

Add a Spotlight

You can use the Lighting Effects filter in Photoshop Elements to create the illusion of spotlights and directional lights in an image. Photoshop Elements offers 17 light styles that can help add ambiance to your images. After you assign a light style, you can control the direction of the light source and the focus of the beam.

You can select different real-world lights from the Light Types menu to achieve different effects. Omni lights shine directly over an object. Spotlights create an elliptical beam of light. Directional lights shine light from one angle.

Add a Spotlight

1 In the Editor, select the layer to which you want to apply the filter.

Note: For more on opening the Editor, see Chapter 1. For more on layers, see Chapter 8.

2 Click **Filter**.

3 Click **Render**.

4 Click **Lighting Effects**.

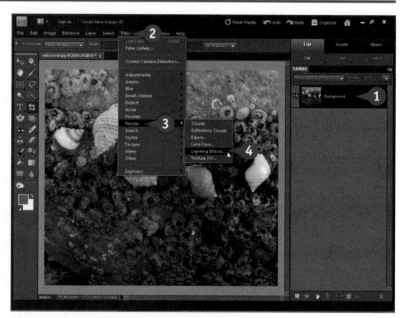

The Lighting Effects dialog box opens.

● Photoshop Elements displays a small preview of the effect.

5 Click the ▾ and choose a lighting style.

Note: Some light styles use multiple lights; you must position each light in the set and adjust the settings individually.

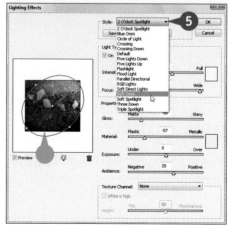

● Optionally, you can click the ▾ and choose a light type.

6 Adjust the position and shape of the lighting by clicking and dragging the handles in the preview window.

● You can click and drag the center point to change where the light is focused.

7 Click and drag the **Intensity** slider (◙) to control the light intensity.

You can also type a value for the intensity.

8 Click **OK**.

Photoshop Elements applies the filter.

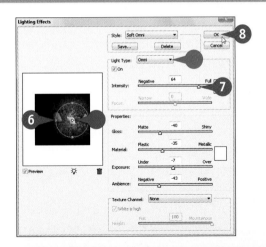

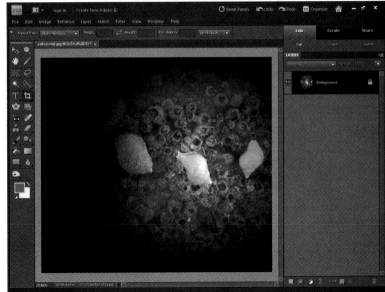

TIP

How can I add a lens flare to an image?
Lens flare occurs when light entering the lens at an extreme angle reflects off the multiple elements of the lens. To add a lens flare, follow these steps:

1 Click **Filter**, click **Render**, and then click **Lens Flare**.

2 In the Lens Flare dialog box, click and drag the slider (◙) to control the brightness.

3 Drag the mouse pointer (+) to position the lens flare in your image.

4 Click **OK**.

Photoshop Elements adds the lens flare effect.

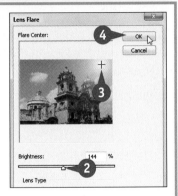

209

Fix Exposure

You can use the Photomerge Exposure tool to combine photos of the same scene taken with different exposure settings. Photoshop Elements intelligently merges the photos to create an image that has optimal lighting throughout.

Photoshop Elements analyzes the lighting in the photos and combines them to produce a single optimized image. The Photomerge Exposure tool also enables you to manually choose areas with good lighting and contrast from one photo and then copy them to another photo where they are poorly lit. Some digital cameras have a feature known as *exposure bracketing* that automatically takes several photos of a scene, with each photo having a slightly different exposure setting. It is best if you take the photos using a tripod and without zooming between shots, to keep the photos perfectly aligned.

Fix Exposure

1 In the Editor, click **Edit**.

2 Click **Guided**.

Note: For details about opening the Editor, see Chapter 1.

The Guided Edit view opens.

3 Ctrl +click to select the photos in the Project Bin.

4 Click **Exposure**.

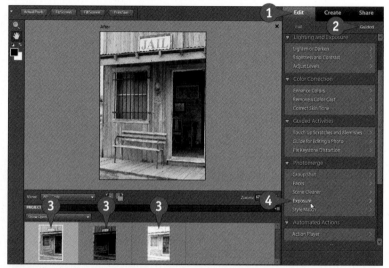

The Photomerge Exposure panel opens and automatically combines the photos to blend their exposures.

5 Click and drag the slider (▣) to adjust the details in the lighter areas of the composite.

6 Click and drag the slider (▣) to adjust the details in the darker areas of the composite.

7 Click and drag the slider (▣) to adjust the overall color intensity.

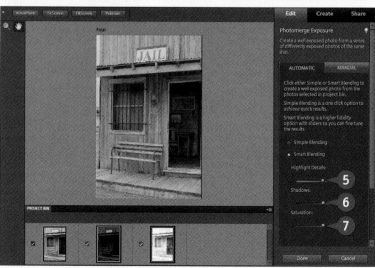

● Photoshop Elements applies the adjustments.

● You can click here to remove a photo from the composite.

8 Click **Done** to save the changes and return to the Guided Edit view.

● The merged image appears in the Project Bin.

● You can click **Full** to switch to the Full Edit interface.

TIP

How can I manually combine the elements in my photos?

1 Click **Manual**.

2 Click and drag a photo to the Background window.

3 Click to select a photo with objects to combine with the background. This photo appears in the Foreground window.

4 Click the **Selection** tool ( ).

5 Click and drag over an object to select it.

● Photoshop Elements merges the selected object with the background photo.

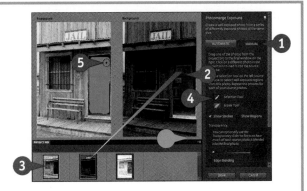

Using the Blur and Sharpen Tools

You can sharpen or blur specific areas of your image with the Blur and Sharpen tools. This enables you to emphasize or de-emphasize objects in a photo. You can use the Blur tool to make tiny specks and other small flaws less noticeable in your photos. You can use the Sharpen tool to increase the contrast of edges. However, excessive sharpening can produce noise that can be especially apparent in areas of light, solid colors.

You can blur or sharpen the entire image by using one of the Blur or Sharpen filters located in the Photoshop Elements Filter menu. See Chapter 13 for more. Making a selection prior to applying the Blur or Sharpen tools can be useful so that adjustments are only made to intended areas. For more about making selections, see Chapter 6.

Using the Blur and Sharpen Tools

Using the Blur Tool

1 In the Editor, click the **Blur** tool (⬛).

Note: For more on opening the Editor, see Chapter 1.

The Blur tool shares space in the Toolbox with the Sharpen and Smudge tools.

2 Click the ▾ and choose the brush you want to use.

● To change the strength of the tool, type a value from 1% to 100%.

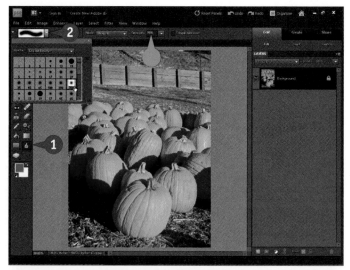

3 Click and drag the mouse pointer (○) to blur an area of the image.

Photoshop Elements blurs the area.

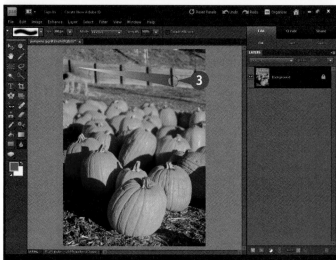

Using the Sharpen Tool

1 Right-click the **Blur** tool (🔵).

2 Click the **Sharpen** tool (🔺).

The Sharpen tool shares space in the Toolbox with the Blur and Smudge tools.

3 Click the ▼ and choose the brush you want to use.

● To change the strength of the tool, type a value from 1% to 100%.

4 Click and drag the mouse pointer (○) to sharpen an area of the image.

Photoshop Elements sharpens the area.

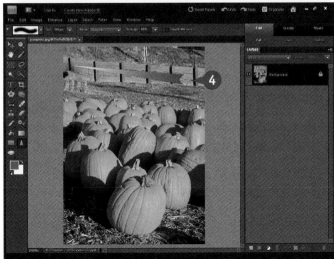

What is the Smudge tool?

The Smudge tool (👆) is another tool you can use to create interesting blur effects in your photos. It simulates dragging a finger through wet paint, shifting and smearing colors in your image. The Smudge tool shares space in the Toolbox with the Blur and Sharpen tools.

Is there a filter I can use to sharpen or blur an entire image?

Yes. Photoshop Elements includes a sharpening feature called Unsharp Mask that you can use to sharpen the appearance of pixels in a photo. For more on sharpening an image, see Chapter 9. You can also select from several blurring filters, including Gaussian Blur, to make your image appear blurry. For more on blurring an image, see Chapter 13.

CHAPTER 11

Enhancing Colors

Do your photos suffer from faded colors or unattractive colorcasts? This chapter shows you how to use the tools in Photoshop Elements to correct color problems in your images by adding, removing, or shifting colors. You can also remove color completely to turn a color photo black and white or add color to parts of a black-and-white image to make it more interesting.

Enhance Colors with Guided Edit

You can enhance or shift the colors in your images by using the step-by-step instructions and adjustments in the Photoshop Elements Guided Edit interface. The interface enables you to compare before-and-after versions of an image as you adjust the colors. The explanations included in the interface can make it less intimidating than the tools found in the Full Edit interface.

Guided Edit color-correction tools also enable you to correct a colorcast, which can be caused by certain lighting conditions or by changes that occur as a photo ages. You can also adjust skin tones that have odd tints or appear washed out.

Enhance Colors with Guided Edit

1 In the Editor, click **Edit**.

2 Click the **Guided** tab.

Note: For more on opening the Editor, see Chapter 1.

The Guided Edit interface opens.

● Make sure the Color Correction list is open. You can click the ▶ to open it (▶ changes to ▼).

3 Click **Enhance Colors**.

● You can click **Auto** to have Photoshop Elements automatically balance the colors and contrast by using its built-in optimization routines. You can press Ctrl + Z to undo the effect.

4 Click the down arrow (▾) and click a **Before & After** setting to open Before and After views of the image.

5 Click and drag the **Hue** slider () to shift the colors in the image.

6 Click and drag the **Saturation** slider (□) to change the color intensity in the image.

7 Click and drag the **Lightness** slider (□) to change the lightness of the colors in the image.

8 Click **Done**.

Photoshop Elements adjusts the colors in the image.

● You can click **Full** to switch to the Full Edit interface.

TIP

How can I limit my color adjustments to one type of color in my image?

1 Click **Enhance**, click **Adjust Color**, and then click **Adjust Hue/Saturation**.

2 In the Hue/Saturation dialog box, click the ▣ and choose a color type.

3 Click and drag the sliders (□) to make adjustments.

4 Click **OK**.

Photoshop Elements adjusts the color.

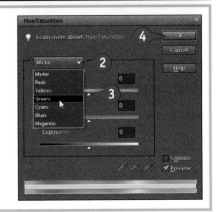

Adjust Skin Color

Y ou can improve skin colors that may appear tinted or washed out in your images. After you sample an area of skin with the eyedropper, Photoshop Elements adjusts the skin color to make it look more natural. Photoshop Elements also adjusts other colors in the image based on the sampled skin.

You can fine-tune the adjustment to increase or decrease the tan or blush in the skin tones as well as the overall temperature of the image. To adjust all the colors in your image, not just the skin tones, see the other sections in this chapter.

Adjust Skin Color

1 In the Editor, click **Enhance**.

Note: For more on opening the Editor, see Chapter 1.

2 Click **Adjust Color**.

3 Click **Adjust Color for Skin Tone**.

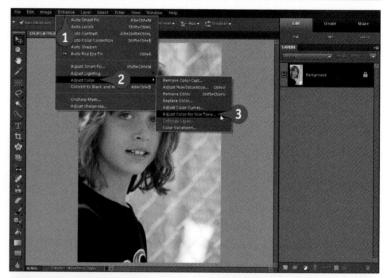

The Adjust Color for Skin Tone dialog box opens.

● The mouse pointer ( ) changes to an eyedropper ( ).

4 Click an area of skin in your image.

Photoshop Elements adjusts the skin tones and other colors in your image.

5 Click and drag the **Tan** slider (◉) to adjust the level of brown in the skin tones.

6 Click and drag the **Blush** slider (◉) to adjust the level of red in the skin tones.

7 Click and drag the **Temperature** slider (◉) to adjust the overall coloring of the skin tones.

8 Click **OK**.

Photoshop Elements makes adjustments to the skin in the image.

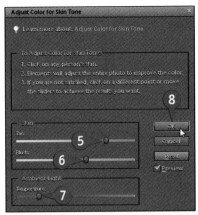

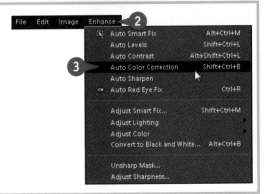

TIP

Can I have Photoshop Elements correct all the colors in my image automatically?

Yes. Follow these steps to apply the command.

1 Click the layer you want to adjust.

2 Click **Enhance**.

3 Click **Auto Color Correction**.

Photoshop Elements adjusts the image colors. You can press Ctrl + Z to undo the effect.

219

Adjust Color with the Sponge Tool

You can use the Sponge tool to make simple adjustments to the color saturation or color intensity of a specific area of an image. For example, you may want to make a person's clothing appear more colorful or tone down an element that is too colorful.

You apply the Sponge as you do the Brush tool, by clicking and dragging across a part of the image. You can adjust the size and softness of the brush to match the area you want to affect. You can click and drag multiple times to increase the effect of the tool.

Adjust Color with the Sponge Tool

Decrease Saturation

1 In the Editor, click the **Sponge** tool ( ).

Note: For more on opening the Editor, see Chapter 1.

The Sponge tool shares space with the Dodge and Burn tools in the Toolbox. You may need to right-click the Dodge or Burn tool and then select the Sponge tool from the menu.

2 Click the ▼ and select the brush style you want to use.

● To set a brush size, you can also click the ▼ and drag the slider ( ) that appears.

3 Click the ▼ and select **Desaturate**.

4 Click and drag the mouse pointer (○) to decrease the saturation of an area of the image.

In this example, a section of the part of a quilt is desaturated.

To confine the effect to a particular area, you can make a selection prior to applying the tool. See Chapter 6 for more on making selections.

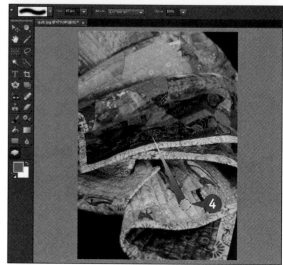

Increase Saturation

1 Perform Steps **1** and **2** on the previous page.

2 Click the ▪ and select **Saturate**.

3 Click and drag the mouse pointer (○) to increase the saturation of an area of the image.

In this example, the colors of part of a poncho are intensified.

To confine the effect to a particular area, you can make a selection prior to applying the tool. See Chapter 6 for more on making selections.

TIPS

What does the Flow setting do?
Clicking the **Flow** ▪ in the Options bar displays a Flow slider (▉) that you can use to control the intensity of the saturation. You can set the Flow anywhere from 1% to 100% to determine how quickly the sponge saturates or desaturates the pixels in your image. Start with the 50% Flow setting and then experiment with increasing or decreasing the percentage to get the amount of control you want.

How do I find the right brush style and size?
The Brushes panel displays a variety of brush styles with soft, hard, and shaped edges. To blend your sponging effect into the surrounding pixels, select a soft-edge brush style. To make your sponging effect appear more distinct, use a hard-edge brush style. Shaped edges can help you produce textured effects. Clicking the **Size** ▪ in the Options bar lets you modify the brush size. You can also press 〔 or 〕 while sponging to change your brush size.

Correct Color with Color Variations

You can use the Color Variations feature to quickly fix colorcasts and other color problems in a photo. Colorcasts result from unfavorable lighting conditions. For example, when you shoot a subject under fluorescent lights, your photograph may take on a greenish color. Age can also add casts to a photo.

If you make a selection before performing the Color Variations command, you affect only the selected pixels. Similarly, if you have a multilayered image, your adjustments affect only the selected layer. See Chapter 6 for more on making a selection, and see Chapter 8 for more on layers.

Correct Color with Color Variations

1 In the Editor, click **Enhance**.

Note: For more on opening the Editor, see Chapter 1.

2 Click **Adjust Color**.

3 Click **Color Variations**.

To apply color corrections to a particular layer, select the layer before opening the Color Variations dialog box.

Note: For more on layers, see Chapter 8.

The Color Variations dialog box opens.

4 Choose a tonal range to apply effects to the different tones of your image (● changes to ○).

● Alternatively, you can click the **Saturation** radio button (● changes to ○).

5 Click and drag the slider (⬛) left to make small adjustments or right to make large adjustments.

6 To add or subtract a color, click one of the thumbnails.

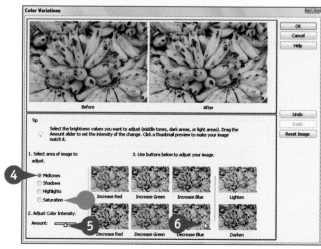

● The result of the adjustment appears in the After preview.

To increase the effect, click the thumbnail again.

● You can increase the brightness by clicking **Lighten**.

● You can decrease the brightness of the image by clicking **Darken**.

⑦ Continue adjusting other tonal ranges as needed.

⑧ Click **OK**.

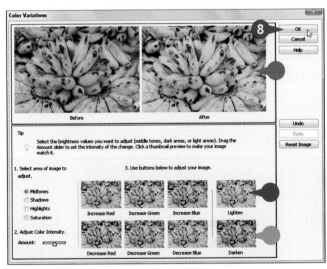

Photoshop Elements makes the color adjustments to the image.

In this example, the bananas in the photo have an intense, saturated color. The Color Variations dialog box enables you to decrease the intensity and give them a more natural yellow color.

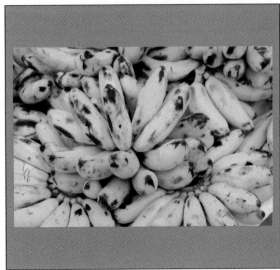

TIP

How can I undo color adjustments while using the Color Variations dialog box?
• If you have clicked a Decrease thumbnail image, you can click the corresponding **Increase** thumbnail image to undo the effect.
• If you have clicked an Increase thumbnail image, you can click the corresponding **Decrease** thumbnail image to undo the effect.
• Click **Undo** to cancel the last color adjustment.
• Click **Reset Image** to return the image to its original state — as it looked before you opened the dialog box.

Replace a Color

The Replace Color command enables you to change one or more colors in your image by using the Hue, Saturation, and Lightness controls. By shifting the controls, you can change the color of objects or backgrounds just slightly or to wildly different tints.

If you make a selection before executing the Replace Color command, only the selected pixels are affected. Similarly, if you have a multilayered image, your adjustments affect only the selected layer. See Chapter 6 for more on making a selection, and see Chapter 8 for more on layers. Another option for replacing colors is the Smart Brush. See Chapter 12 for details.

Replace a Color

1 In the Editor, click **Enhance**.

Note: For more on opening the Editor, see Chapter 1.

2 Click **Adjust Color**.

3 Click **Replace Color**.

To apply color corrections to a particular layer, select the layer before opening the Replace Color dialog box.

Note: See Chapter 8 to read more on layers.

The Replace Color dialog box opens. The mouse pointer ( ) changes to an eyedropper ( ).

4 Click in the image to select a color to replace.

● Photoshop Elements turns the selected color to white in the preview window.

5 Click and drag the **Fuzziness** slider ( ) to control how many pixels with similar colors are affected within the image or selection.

Dragging to the right selects more color and dragging to the left selects less color.

You can also type a value for the fuzziness.

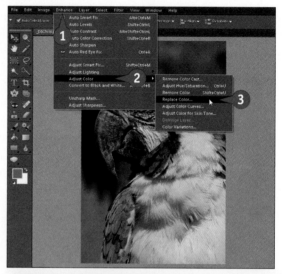

6 Click and drag the sliders (■) to change the colors inside the selected area.

You can also type values for the hue, saturation, and lightness.

Note: For more on these controls, see the section "Enhance Colors with Guided Edit."

7 Click **OK**.

Photoshop Elements replaces the selected color.

How can I replace more than one area of color?
You can press Shift and then click inside your image to add other colors to your selection. If you are viewing the Selection preview, the white area inside the preview box increases as you click. To deselect colors from your selection, press Alt and then click a color inside your image.

How can I replace a color using the painting tools?
You can click the **Paint Bucket** tool (🖌), select a foreground color, and then replace a color in your image with the selected color. You can retain details while applying the color by setting the mode to Color in the Options bar. For more on using the painting tools in Photoshop Elements, see Chapter 12.

Turn a Color Photo into Black and White

You can change a color photo into a black-and-white photo to create a dramatic effect or before publishing the photo in a noncolor newsletter or brochure. The conversion tool in Photoshop Elements enables you to adjust the contributions of the different colors to the effect and to control the lighting and contrast.

You may want to copy the color image file before making the change and saving so the full-color original file remains intact. See Chapters 2 and 17 to learn how to save files.

Turn a Color Photo into Black and White

1 In the Editor, click **Enhance**.

Note: For more on opening the Editor, see Chapter 1.

2 Click **Convert to Black and White**.

To confine the conversion to a particular area, you can make a selection prior to applying the command. See Chapter 6 for more on making selections.

The Convert to Black and White dialog box opens.

3 Click a style.

● Photoshop Elements displays a preview of the black-and-white version.

④ You can click and drag the sliders (■) to adjust the contributions of the original colors to the final black-and-white version.

⑤ You can also click this slider to increase or decrease the contrast.

⑥ Click **OK**.

Photoshop Elements converts the image to black and white.

Can I remove color from just one color channel?

Yes. Follow these steps.

① Click **Enhance**, click **Adjust Color**, and then click **Adjust Hue/ Saturation**.

② In the Hue/Saturation dialog box, click here and then choose a color channel.

③ Drag the **Saturation** slider (■) to the left.

You can also type a value for the saturation.

④ Click **OK** to desaturate the color channel.

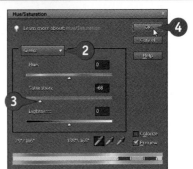

Add Color to a Black-and-White Photo

You can enhance a black-and-white photo by adding color with the painting tools in Photoshop Elements. For example, you can add color to a baby's cheeks or to articles of clothing. To add color, you must first make sure your image's mode is RGB Color. Setting the blending mode to Color for the layer you paint on enables you to add tints while keeping the details in the photo intact.

You can retain the original black-and-white version of your photo by making color changes on duplicate or adjustment layers. See Chapter 8 for more on layers.

Add Color to a Black-and-White Photo

1 In the Editor, click **Image**.

Note: For more on opening the Editor, see Chapter 1.

2 Click **Mode**.

3 Click **RGB Color**.

If your image has multiple layers, you may need to flatten the layers before proceeding. In the prompt box that opens, click **Flatten** to continue.

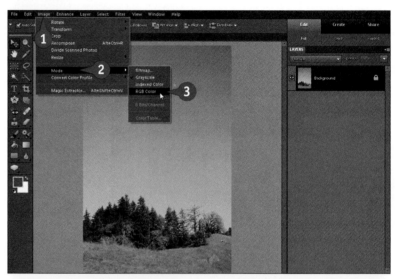

4 Duplicate the Background layer.

5 Click the **Brush** tool (![brush]).

6 Click the foreground color.

7 In the Color Picker dialog box, click a color range.

8 Click a color.

You can also type values for a color.

9 Click **OK**.

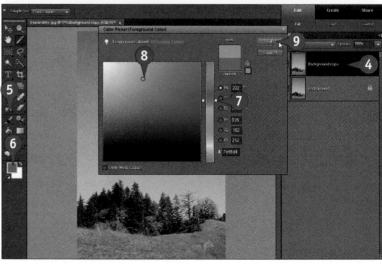

10 Click the ▾ to set the blending mode to Color. This enables you to retain the lighting details of the objects that you paint over.

To confine the effect to a particular area, you can make a selection prior to applying the tool. See Chapter 6 for more on making selections.

11 Click and drag to paint the color on the photo.

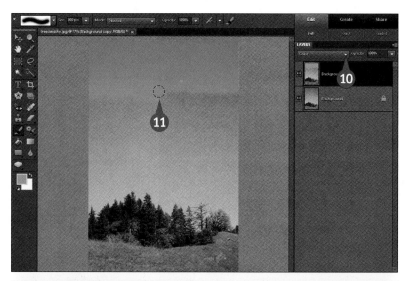

Photoshop Elements applies the color to the black-and-white image.

This example shows blue color added to a clear sky.

● You can click the visibility icon (👁) to hide the layer with the color and revert the image to black and white.

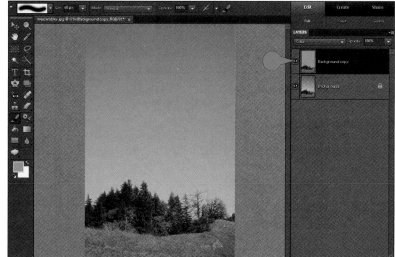

TIP

How do I tone down a layer color?
You can change the layer opacity in the Layers panel to make the color more transparent. Follow these steps.

1 Click the layer containing the color you want to edit.

2 Click the ▾ and then click and drag the slider (◼) that appears.

● Photoshop Elements automatically adjusts the color as you drag.

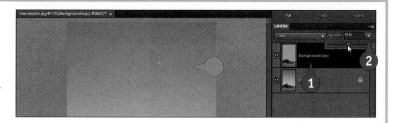

Adjust Color by Using Color Curves

You can manipulate the tones and contrast of your image with the Color Curves dialog box. In the dialog box, the colors in the image are represented by a sloping line graph. The top right part of the line represents the highlights, the middle part the midtones, and the bottom left part the shadows. You can adjust colors in your photo gradually by applying a sweeping curve or in dramatic ways with lots of sudden bends.

You can adjust curves in just a part of your image by making a selection or selecting a layer before executing the command. For more on making selections, see Chapter 6. For more on working with layers, see Chapter 8.

Adjust Color by Using Color Curves

1 In the Editor, click **Enhance**.

Note: For more on opening the Editor, see Chapter 1.

2 Click **Adjust Color**.

3 Click **Adjust Color Curves**.

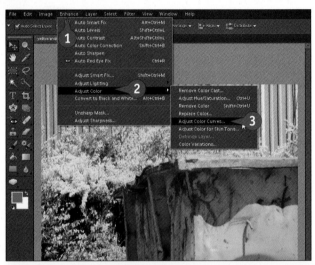

The Adjust Color Curves dialog box opens.

4 Click a style.

● Photoshop Elements displays a preview of the adjusted version.

● The curves graph changes depending on the style.

In this example, choosing the Increase Contrast style gives the graph a slight S shape.

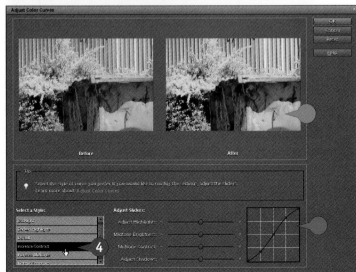

5 You can click and drag the sliders (◉) to make more adjustments to the tones and contrast in the image.

6 Click **OK**.

Photoshop Elements applies the adjustment to the image.

TIP

How can I give the colors in my image an out-of-this-world appearance?

You can choose the Solarize style in the Color Curves dialog box.

1 Follow Steps **1** to **3** in this section.

2 Click **Solarize** in the Select a Style menu.

3 Click **OK** to apply the effect.

See Chapter 13 for more on filters.

CHAPTER 12

Painting and Drawing on Photos

Want to add extra elements to your photos? Photoshop Elements offers a variety of tools you can use to paint and draw on your images as well as add shapes, colors, and gradients. Different brush shapes enable you to experiment with a variety of color textures. This chapter introduces you to some of those tools and their many uses.

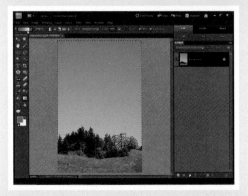
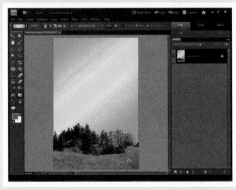

Set the Foreground and Background Colors

You can select colors to use with many of the painting and drawing tools in Photoshop Elements by setting the foreground and background colors. The Brush and Pencil tools apply the foreground color, and the Eraser tool applies the background color when used on the Background layer.

See the section "Add Color with the Brush Tool" for more on how to paint on a photo. See the section "Apply the Eraser" for more on using the Eraser.

Some filters in Photoshop Elements apply their effects to your image based on the current foreground and background colors. See Chapter 13 for more about filters.

Set the Foreground and Background Colors

Set the Foreground Color

① In the Editor, click the **Foreground Color** box (■).

Note: For more on opening the Editor, see Chapter 1.

The Color Picker dialog box opens.

② Click and drag the color slider (◀) to select a color range.

③ Click a color.

You can click outside the dialog box in the image window to select a color from your photo.

④ Click **OK**.

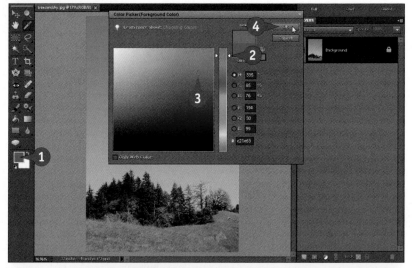

● The selected color appears in the Foreground Color box.

● Many tools including Text, Brush, and Shape tools use the current Foreground color when applied.

This example uses the Brush tool.

Note: For more on painting tools, see the section "Add Color with the Brush Tool."

Set the Background Color

1 Click the **Background Color** box (□).

The Color Picker dialog box opens.

2 Click and drag the color slider (◀) to select a color range.

3 Click a color.

You can click outside the dialog box in the image window to select a color from your photo.

You can also type values for a color.

4 Click **OK**.

● The selected color appears in the Background Color box.

● Tools such as the Eraser apply the background color to a photo.

The Eraser tool applies color only in the Background layer; in other layers, the eraser turns pixels transparent.

Note: See Chapter 8 for more on layers.

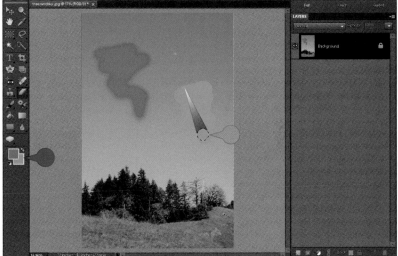

How do I reset the foreground and background colors?
Click the **Default** button (▣) to the lower left of the Foreground and Background icons or press D. Doing so resets the colors to black and white. You can also click the **Switch** icon (↰) or press X to swap the foreground and background colors.

Does Photoshop Elements offer a set of common colors?
Yes. You can select a color to paint or draw on your photo from the Color Swatches panel, which includes sets of commonly used colors. To view the panel, click **Window** and then **Color Swatches**. You can click the color you want to use, and the Foreground Color box in the Toolbox reflects your choice. To set the background color, you can Ctrl +click a color in the panel.

Add Color with the Brush Tool

You can use the Brush tool to add patches of solid color to your image. You can use the tool to cover unwanted elements or change the appearance of clothing or a backdrop. When applying the Brush tool, you can control the size of the brushstrokes by choosing a brush size. For realistic results, turn on the Airbrush feature to apply a softer line of color.

To limit where the brush applies color, create a selection before using the tool. For more, see Chapter 6. The Brush tool can also be used to edit a layer mask in your image. See Chapter 8 for more about layer masks.

Add Color with the Brush Tool

1 In the Editor, click the **Brush** tool (✏).

Note: For more on opening the Editor, see Chapter 1.

2 Click the **Foreground Color** box (■) to select a color with which to paint.

You can also press and hold **Alt** and then click inside your image to select a color.

3 Click **OK**.

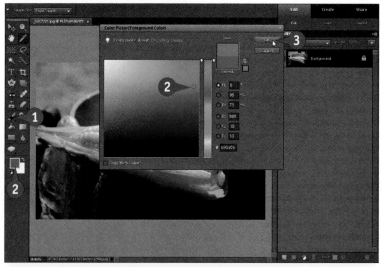

4 Click the ▼ and select a brush size and type.

● To set a brush size, you can also click here and adjust the slider that appears.

You can also type a brush size.

5 Press **Enter** to close the Brushes menu.

6 Click and drag the mouse pointer (◯) on the image.

Photoshop Elements applies color to the image.

7 Click here to reduce the opacity of the paint effect.

You can also type a value for the opacity.

8 Click and drag the mouse pointer (◯) on the image.

Photoshop Elements applies transparent color to the image.

To undo the most recent brushstroke, you can click **Edit** and then **Undo Brush Tool** or click the **Undo** button (⟲).

TIPS

How do I paint thin lines?

Use the Pencil tool (✎), which is similar to the Brush tool (🖌) except that it paints hard-edged lines. Like the Brush, the Pencil applies the foreground color. See the section "Draw a Line" for another way to draw lines.

What can I do with the Impressionist Brush tool?

The Impressionist Brush (🖌) creates artistic effects by blending existing colors in an image together. The Impressionist Brush does not add any foreground or background color to your image. You can select the tool from the menu that appears when you right-click on the Brush tool (🖌).

Change Brush Styles

You can select from a variety of predefined brush styles in Photoshop Elements to apply color to your image in different ways. Brush styles can have hard or soft edges. Brush styles with specialized tips can apply speckled patterns of color to your image. Photoshop Elements offers a variety of predefined brush sets that you can access in the Options bar.

You can also create a custom brush style by specifying spacing, fade, and other characteristics for your brush. This can be useful when you want to apply subtle or irregular patterns of colors.

Change Brush Styles

Select from a Predefined Set

1 In the Editor, click the **Brush** tool (![brush icon]).

Note: For more on opening the Editor, see Chapter 1.

2 Click the **Brush** ▪.

3 Click the ▼ and select a set of brushes.

The set appears in the Brushes menu.

4 Click a brush style to select it.

The mouse pointer changes to the new brush shape.

● You can click here to adjust the brush size, or you can type a brush size.

5 Click here to choose a color to apply with the brush. The actual color applied may vary depending on the brush type.

6 Click and drag the brush on the photo.

Photoshop Elements applies the brush to the area.

Customize a Brush

1 Click the **Show Options** button ().

2 Click and drag the slider (●) or type values to define the new brush attributes.

● You can limit the length of your brushstrokes with the Fade slider.

● You can randomize the painted color with the Hue Jitter slider.

● You can change the shape of the brush tip by clicking and dragging here.

3 Click and drag the brush on the photo.

Photoshop Elements applies the customized brush to the area.

Note: For more on applying the brush, see the section "Add Color with the Brush Tool."

TIP

How can I make a brush apply dots instead of a line?

1 Click the **Show Options** button (■) to open brush settings in the Options bar.

2 Click and drag the slider (●) to increase the Spacing value to greater than 100%.

● When you click and drag a brush shape, you get dots or patches instead of a contiguous line.

Add Color with the Paint Bucket Tool

The Paint Bucket tool enables you to fill areas in your image with solid color. You can use this technique to change the color of clothes, the sky, backgrounds, and more. By default, when you apply the Paint Bucket tool, it affects adjacent pixels in the image. You can set the Paint Bucket's tolerance value to determine the range of colors the paint bucket affects when you apply it. A low tolerance value affects a narrow range of colors, whereas a high tolerance value affects a wide range. You can also adjust the opacity of the tool to apply transparent color.

Add Color with the Paint Bucket Tool

Select the Paint Bucket Tool

1 In the Editor, click the **Paint Bucket** tool (🪣).

Note: For more on opening the Editor, see Chapter 1.

2 Click the **Foreground Color** box (⬛) to select a color for painting.

Note: For more, see the section "Set the Foreground and Background Colors."

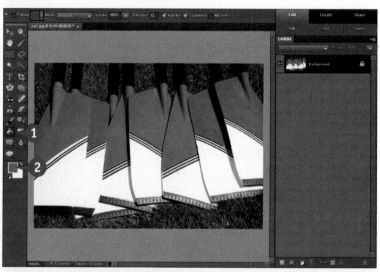

Set the Tolerance

3 Type a tolerance value from 0 to 255.

Tolerance is the amount by which neighboring pixels can differ from the selected pixel and still be affected.

To paint over a narrow range of colors, type a small value; to paint over a wide range of colors, type a large value.

4 Click inside the image.

Photoshop Elements fills an area of the image with the foreground color.

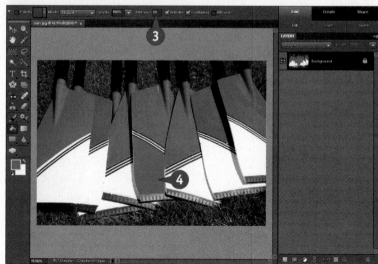

Set Image Opacity

5 To fill an area with semitransparent color, type a percentage value of less than 100% in the Opacity field.

6 Click inside the image.

Photoshop Elements fills an area with see-through paint.

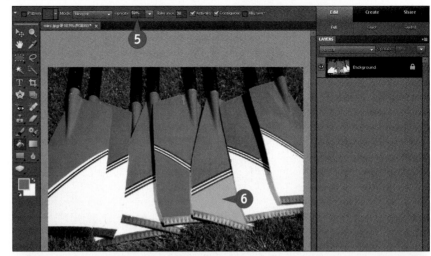

Fill Noncontiguous Areas

7 To fill noncontiguous but similar areas throughout the image, deselect the **Contiguous** check box (☑ changes to ■).

8 Click inside the image.

Photoshop Elements fills similar areas of the image, even if they are not contiguous with the clicked pixel.

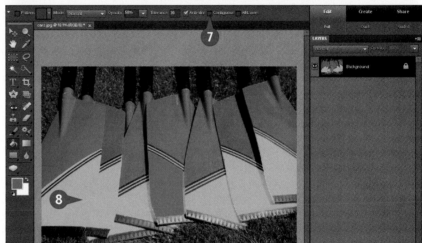

TIP

How can I reset a tool to the default settings?

1 Click the tool you want to select in the Toolbox.

2 Click the **Reset** ▾ on the far left side of the Options bar.

3 Click **Reset Tool** from the menu that appears.

For painting tools, this resets the opacity to 100%, the blending mode to Normal, and other attributes to their startup values.

● You can click **Reset All Tools** from the menu to reset all the Photoshop Elements tools to their default settings.

Using a Brush to Replace a Color

You can replace colors in your image with the current foreground color by using the Color Replacement tool. This gives you a free-form way of recoloring objects in your image while keeping the shading on the objects intact.

You can control the areas in your image that the tool affects by adjusting the Tolerance setting. A low tolerance value affects a narrow range of colors in the image, whereas a high tolerance value affects a wide range. You can also constrain how the tool is applied by selecting a brush size.

Using a Brush to Replace a Color

1 In the Editor, right-click the **Brush** tool (▨).

Note: For more on opening the Editor, see Chapter 1.

2 From the list that appears, click the **Color Replacement** tool (▨).

3 Click the **Foreground Color** box to select a color for painting.

4 Click the ▾ and select a brush size and type.

5 Type a tolerance from 1% to 100%.

The greater the tolerance, the greater the range of colors the tool replaces.

6 Click and drag in your image.

Photoshop Elements replaces the color.

7 Continue to click and drag in your image.

Photoshop Elements replaces more color.

TIP

How do I fill a selection with a color?

1 Make a selection with a selection tool.

2 Click **Edit**.

3 Click **Fill Selection**.

The Fill Layer dialog box opens.

4 Select the color you want to fill with and then set an opacity for the fill color.

5 Click **OK**.

● Photoshop Elements fills the selection.

Adjust Colors with the Smart Brush

You can simultaneously select objects in your photo and apply color adjustments to them with the Smart Brush tool. Different tool options enable you to increase, decrease, remove, or transform color in the objects. You can also darken areas of photos that are overexposed or brighten areas that have too much shadow.

The Smart Brush options in the Portrait category enable you to adjust facial colors to give photo subjects a tan, whiten teeth, or apply a lipstick tint to lips. Options in the Special Effects category apply striking, out-of-this world colors to objects.

Adjust Colors with the Smart Brush

Apply the Smart Brush Effect

1 In the Editor, click the **Smart Brush** tool (■).

Note: For more on opening the Editor, see Chapter 1.

● The Smart Paint menu opens.

2 Click the ▼ and select a category.

Photoshop Elements lists the painting effects in that category.

● A thumbnail image shows an example of each painting effect.

3 Click an effect.

4 Press Enter to close the Smart Paint menu.

5 Click the ▼ and select a brush style and size.

6 Click and drag over objects in your image to apply the tool.

Photoshop Elements selects the objects and applies the painting effect.

● You can make multiple selections with the tool.

● The effect is stored as a new adjustment layer.

● You can click **Inverse** to invert your selection and apply the effect to the other pixels in your image.

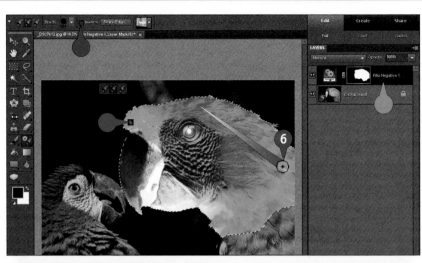

Undo the Smart Brush Effect

1 Click the Smart Brush adjustment layer to make sure the selection is active.

2 Click the **Subtract from Selection** option (■).

3 Click and drag over the selection.

Photoshop Elements deselects the area and reverts the Smart Brush effect.

TIP

How do I decrease the effect of the Smart Brush so that it is only partially applied?

1 In the Layers panel, click the adjustment layer the Smart Brush created.

2 Type a value less than 100% in the Opacity field.

● Photoshop Elements decreases the Smart Brush effect.

● You can click the visibility icon (◉) to turn off the adjustment layer and hide the effect.

Draw a Shape

You can create solid shapes in your image by using the many shape tools in Photoshop Elements. Shapes offer an easy way to add whimsical objects, labels, or buttons to an image.

When you add a shape to an image, Photoshop Elements places the shape on its own layer. This makes it easy to move and transform the shape later on. Because shape objects are vector graphics in Photoshop Elements, they can be resized without a loss in quality. For more on layers, see Chapter 8.

You can overlay text on a shape to create signs or labeled buttons. See Chapter 14 for more about adding text.

Draw a Shape

1 In the Editor, right-click the **Rectangle** tool (◼).

Note: For more on opening the Editor, see Chapter 1.

2 Click the **Custom Shape** tool (♥) in the menu that appears.

The Custom Shape tool shares space in the Toolbox with the other shape tools.

Note: See Chapter 1 for more on working with Toolbox tools.

3 Click here to open the Custom Shapes menu.

4 Click a shape.

5 Press Enter to close the menu.

● You can click ▶▶ to access hundreds of additional shapes in 24 categories.

6 Click the ▾ and select a color for your shape.

7 Press Enter to close the menu.

● You can click the **Style** ▾ to select a style, such as a 3-D style, for your shape.

8 Click and drag your mouse pointer (⊞) to draw the shape. You can adjust the ratio of the shape's height and width as you drag.

● Photoshop Elements places the shape on its own layer.

Note: For more on layers, see Chapter 8.

You can click and drag multiple times to create more than one shape.

TIP

How do I resize a shape after I draw it?

1 Click the shape's layer.

2 Click **Image**.

3 Click **Transform Shape**.

4 Click a transform command, or you can also press Ctrl + T.

You can then resize the shape just like you would a selection. See Chapter 7 for more on transformations.

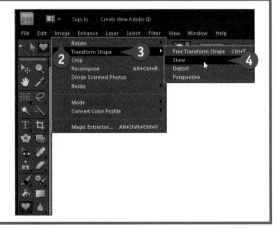

Draw a Line

You can use the Line tool in Photoshop Elements to draw straight lines in your image. You can customize the line with arrows, giving you an easy way to point out elements in your image.

When you add a line to an image with the Line tool, Photoshop Elements places the line in its own layer. This makes it easy to move and transform the line later on. Because line objects are vector graphics in Photoshop Elements, they can be resized and otherwise transformed without a loss in quality. For more on layers, see Chapter 8.

Draw a Line

1 In the Editor, right-click the **Rectangle** tool (■).

Note: For more on opening the Editor, see Chapter 1.

2 Click the **Line** tool (■).

The Line tool shares space in the Toolbox with the other shape tools.

3 Click here and then click **Start** or **End** to include arrowheads on your line (■ changes to ✔).

● You can also specify the shape of the arrowheads by typing values here.

4 Press Enter to close the menu.

5 Type a line weight.

6 Click the **Color** ▾ to choose a different line color.

● You can click the **Style** ▾ to set a style for your line. Styles such as 3-D and shadow are available.

7 Press `Enter` to close the menu.

8 Click and drag your mouse pointer (⊞) to draw the line.

● Photoshop Elements places the line on its own layer.

Note: For more on layers, see Chapter 8.

TIP

How can I add an outline along a selection in my image?

1 Click **Edit**.

2 Click **Stroke (Outline) Selection**.

3 In the Stroke dialog box, type a width for the line.

4 Click a location (● changes to ○).

5 Click **OK**.

● Photoshop Elements applies the stroke.

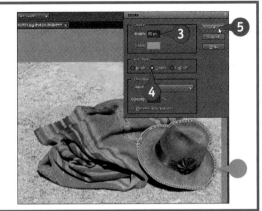

Apply the Eraser

You can use the Eraser tool to erase unwanted areas of your photo. When you apply the Eraser tool in the Background layer, the erased pixels are replaced with the current background color. When you erase in other layers, the Eraser tool turns the pixels transparent, revealing any underlying layers.

In the Options bar, you can control the size of the eraser and the softness of its edges. Using a soft-edged eraser can be useful for removing content around objects that have fuzzy edges, whereas a hard-edged eraser can be better for high-contrast objects. You can also change the opacity of the tool to only partially erase content in your image.

Apply the Eraser

Adjust the Eraser Settings

1 In the Editor, click the **Eraser** tool (▰).

Note: For more on opening the Editor, see Chapter 1.

2 Click the **Background Color** box (☐) to choose a color to appear in place of the erased pixels.

Note: For more, see the section "Set the Foreground and Background Colors."

3 Click the **Size** ▾ to choose an eraser size and type.

● You can also click here and adjust a slider to set an eraser size.

Erase the Background Layer

④ Click the Background layer.

⑤ Click and drag the mouse pointer (○) to erase.

Portions of the Background layer are erased and filled with the background color.

Erase a Normal Layer

⑥ Click a normal layer.

⑦ Click and drag the mouse pointer (○) to erase.

Portions of a layer are erased to reveal the underlying layer.

TIPS

What other eraser tools are available?

You can right-click the **Eraser** tool (⬛) to access other eraser types. You can use the Background Eraser tool (⬛) to sample a color in your image and erase only that color as you drag the tool over your image. The Magic Eraser tool (⬛) erases all the adjacent, similarly colored pixels when you click it.

Which eraser shape should I use?

In the Options bar, you can choose from three eraser shapes, or *modes*: Brush, Pencil, and Block. Brush mode, which is the default mode, enables you to apply the eraser to your image similar to the Brush tool. The Pencil mode acts like the Pencil tool while erasing, with the strokes having a harder edge. The Block mode turns the eraser mouse pointer into a hard-edged square shape for erasing.

Apply a Gradient

You can apply a *gradient*, which is a blend from one color to another, to give objects in your image a radiant or 3-D look. You can apply a gradient to a selected portion of an image or the entire image.

Setting the geometry of a gradient controls the direction of the color blend. A linear gradient changes as it moves across your image. A radial gradient changes color from a center point moving outward.

The Gradient Editor enables you to choose from predefined color combinations for your gradient, or choose your own custom colors. You can also edit the sharpness of the color transitions.

Apply a Gradient

① In the Editor, make a selection.

Note: For more on opening the Editor, see Chapter 1. See Chapter 6 for more on making selections.

If you do not make a selection, the gradient is applied to the entire image.

② Click the **Gradient** tool (■).

● A linear gradient (■) is the default. You can select different geometries in the Options bar.

③ Click the gradient swatch.

The Gradient Editor dialog box opens.

④ Click a preset gradient type from the top box.

● You can define a custom gradient by changing these settings.

⑤ Click **OK**.

6 Click and drag the mouse pointer (+) inside the selection.

This defines the direction and transition of the gradient.

Dragging a long line with the tool produces a gradual transition.

Dragging a short line with the tool produces an abrupt transition.

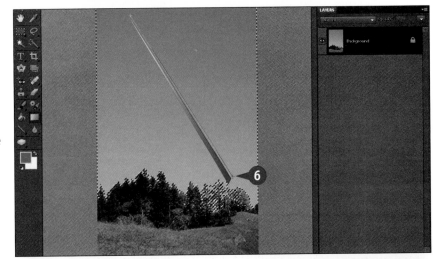

Photoshop Elements generates a gradient inside the selection.

TIP

How can I highlight an object in my image by using a gradient?

1 Place the object on its own layer.

2 Create a new layer below the object and then select the new layer.

3 Click the **Gradient** tool (■).

4 Click the **Radial Gradient** button (■).

5 Click and drag the mouse pointer (⊞) from the center of the object outward to create the gradient.

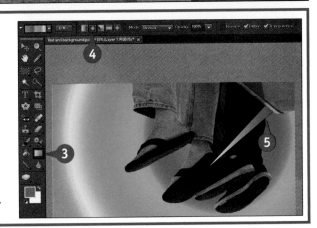

CHAPTER 13

Applying Filters

You can use the filters in Photoshop Elements to quickly and easily apply enhancements to your image, including artistic effects, texture effects, and distortions. Filters can help you correct defects in your images or enable you to turn a photograph into something resembling an impressionist painting. This chapter highlights a few of the more than 100 filters available in Photoshop Elements. For more on all the filters, see the help documentation.

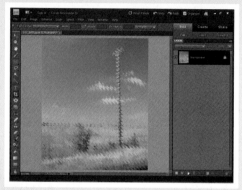

Blur an Image

You can use the Blur filters to apply a variety of blurring effects to your photos. For example, you can use the Gaussian Blur filter to obscure background objects while keeping foreground objects in focus.

To blur a background behind an object, select the object using a selection tool and then invert the selection. For more about making and inverting a selection, see Chapter 6. After inverting, you can apply the Blur filter.

Blurring a busy background makes an image look as if it has a short depth of field. A short depth of field keeps the foreground subject in focus while making the background out of focus.

Blur an Image

1. In the Editor, select the layer to which you want to apply the filter.

   In this example, the scenery around the flower has been selected.

2. Click **Filter**.

3. Click **Blur**.

4. Click **Gaussian Blur**.

   The Gaussian Blur dialog box opens, displaying a preview of the filter's effect.

5. Click the minus sign (🔍) or plus sign (🔍) to zoom out or in.

6. Click the **Preview** check box to preview the effect in the image window (■ changes to ✔).

7. Click and drag the **Radius** slider (🔘) to control the amount of blur added.

8. Click **OK**.

Photoshop Elements applies the filter.

Note: To apply the filter to just part of your image, select an element by using a selection tool. For more on selection tools, see Chapter 6.

TIP

How do I add directional blurring to an image?

1 Select the layer to blur.

2 Click **Filter**.

3 Click **Blur**.

4 Click **Motion Blur**.

The Motion Blur dialog box opens, displaying a preview of the filter's effect.

5 Click and drag the **Angle** dial to define the direction of the blur.

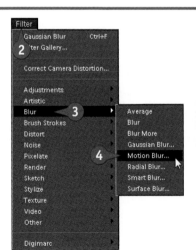

6 Click and drag the slider (■) to adjust the distance, which controls the amount of blur.

7 Click **OK** to apply the filter.

Distort an Image

You can use any of the Distort filters to stretch and squeeze your image, creating the appearance of waves, glass, swirls, and more. For example, the Twirl filter turns the image into a swirl of colors, and the Ripple filter adds wavelike effects. Settings in the filter dialog boxes enable you to increase or decrease the distortion. The Distort filters such as Glass and Ocean Ripple make your image appear as though viewed through a distorted, transparent surface, and the Shear filter lets you tilt your image at an angle.

To apply the filter to just part of your image, select that portion by using a selection tool. For more on selection tools, see Chapter 6.

Distort an Image

① In the Editor, select the layer to which you want to apply a filter.

② Click **Filter**.

③ Click **Distort**.

④ Click a filter.

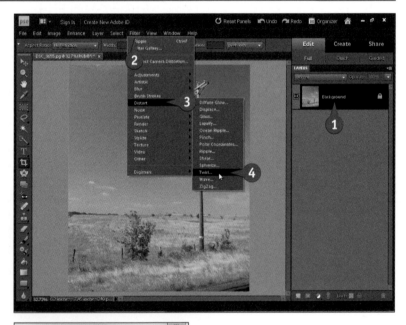

The filter's dialog box opens.

⑤ Make adjustments to the filter's settings to fine-tune the effect.

With some filters, you can preview the effect before applying it to the image.

⑥ Click **OK**.

Photoshop Elements applies the filter.

In this example, the Twirl distortion filter is applied.

In this example, the Ripple distortion filter is applied.

● You can also apply distortion effects with the new Reflection tool. To access it, click **Guided**. The tool is located under the Fun Edits heading.

TIPS

How many filters does Photoshop Elements offer?
Photoshop Elements has 106 filters grouped into 14 categories. You can experiment with each one to find out what effect it has on your image. You can also download additional filters from third-party companies. Some are of these filters are free, whereas others must be purchased.

Is there another way to distort a selection?
Yes. You can use the Distort command to reshape a selected element in your photo. After selecting the element, click **Image**, **Transform**, and then **Distort**. You can also press ctrl+ T . Photoshop Elements surrounds the selection with handles, which you can drag to distort the element. See Chapter 7 for more on distorting selections.

Turn an Image into a Painting

You can use many of the Artistic filters in Photoshop Elements to make your image look as if you created it with a paintbrush or other art media. The Watercolor filter, for example, applies a painted effect by converting similarly colored areas in your image to solid colors. The Palette Knife creates a similar but softer effect. The Colored Pencil filter applies a layer of crosshatched color to your image using the current background color.

To apply a filter to just part of your image, select that portion by using a selection tool. For more on selection tools, see Chapter 6.

Turn an Image into a Painting

1 In the Editor, select the layer to which you want to apply a filter.

In this example, the image has a single Background layer.

2 Click **Filter**.

3 Click **Artistic**.

4 Click a filter.

The Filter Gallery dialog box opens, displaying a preview of the filter's effect.

5 Adjust the filter's settings to fine-tune the effect.

● With some filters, you can preview the effect before applying it to the image. Click the minus sign (⊖) or the plus sign (⊕) to zoom out or in.

● You can select a different filter by clicking ▼ in the right pane.

6 Click **OK**.

Photoshop Elements applies the filter. In this example, the Dry Brush filter is applied.

TIP

How can I turn my image into a colorful Pop Art painting?

You can use the Pop Art tool in the Guided Edit panel to create a Warhol-like creation.

1. In the Editor, click **Guided**.

   The Guided Edit panel appears.

2. Under the Fun Edits heading, click **Pop Art**.

   The Create Pop Art steps appear.

3. Complete the sequence commands.

4. Click **Done**.

   Photoshop Elements turns the image into a Pop Art painting.

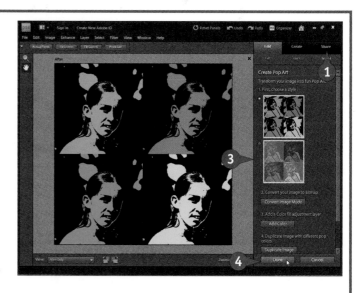

Turn an Image into a Sketch

The Sketch filters add outlining effects to your image. The Charcoal filter, for example, makes an image look as if you sketched it using charcoal on paper.

The Charcoal filter uses the foreground as the charcoal color and the background as the paper color. Changing these colors alters the filter's effect. For more on adjusting colors, see Chapter 11. Many other of the Sketch filters apply the foreground and background colors similarly.

To apply a filter to just part of your image, select that portion by using a selection tool. For more on selection tools, see Chapter 6.

Turn an Image into a Sketch

1. In the Editor, select the foreground and background colors that you want to apply with the sketch filter.
2. Select the layer to which you want to apply the filter.

Note: For more on layers, see Chapter 8.

In this example, the image has a single Background layer.

3. Click **Filter**.
4. Click **Sketch**.
5. Click **Charcoal**.

The Filter Gallery dialog box opens, displaying a preview of the filter's effect.

6. Click the minus sign (▣) or plus sign (▣) to zoom out or in.
7. Click and drag the sliders (▣) to control the filter's effect.
8. Click **OK**.

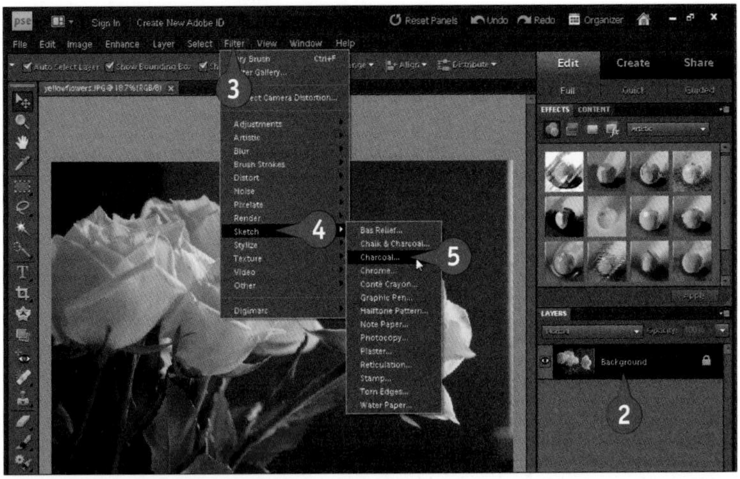

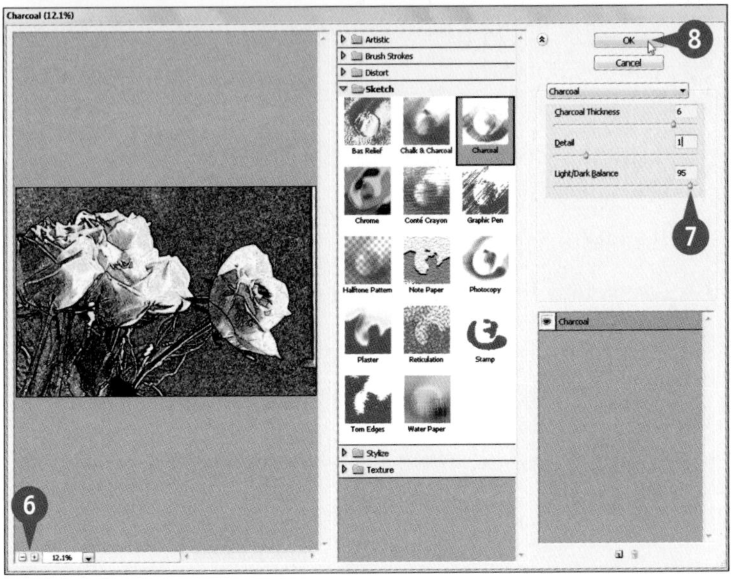

Photoshop Elements applies the filter.

In this example, the thickness of the charcoal strokes increases and the detail decreases.

TIP

What does the Photocopy filter do?

The Photocopy filter converts your image's shadows and midtones to the foreground color and converts highlights to the background color to make the image look like a photocopy.

1 Follow Steps **1** to **4** in this section, selecting **Photocopy** in Step **4**.

2 In the Filter Gallery dialog box, click and drag the sliders (⊟) to control the detail and darkness of the colors.

3 Click **OK**.

Photoshop Elements applies the filter.

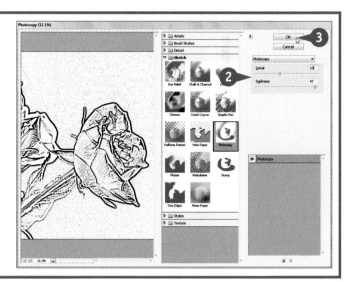

Add Noise to an Image

Filters in the Noise menu add graininess to or remove it from your image. You can add graininess with the Add Noise filter to reduce detail or add a static effect. You can adjust the amount of graininess added to control how much of your image continues to show through.

Other filters under the Noise menu remove extraneous elements from your image. For example, the Dust & Scratches filter applies blurring to get rid of dust and scratches. This can be helpful when retouching old scanned photos.

To apply the filter to just part of your image, select that portion by using a selection tool. For more on selection tools, see Chapter 6.

Add Noise to an Image

① In the Editor, select the layer to which you want to apply the filter.

   In this example, the Background layer is selected.

② Click **Filter**.

③ Click **Noise**.

④ Click **Add Noise**.

   The Add Noise dialog box opens, displaying a preview of the filter's effect.

⑤ Click the minus sign (□ or plus sign (□) to zoom out or in.

⑥ Click the **Preview** check box to preview the effect in the main window (■ changes to ☑).

7 Click and drag the **Amount** slider (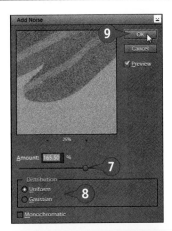) to change the noise, or type the amount of noise you want to apply to an image.

In this example, the Amount value is increased.

8 Click a Distribution radio button to select how you want the noise distributed (● changes to ○).

The Uniform option spreads the noise more evenly than Gaussian.

9 Click **OK**.

Photoshop Elements applies the filter.

TIPS

What does the Monochromatic setting in the Add Noise dialog box do?

If you click to select **Monochromatic** (■ changes to ☑), Photoshop Elements adds noise by lightening or darkening pixels in your image. Pixel hues stay the same. At high settings with the Monochromatic setting on, the filter produces a television-static effect.

Can you apply filters from the Photoshop Elements Effects panel?

Yes. If you open the Effects panel and click **Filters** (◙), you can access most of the filters also found under the Filter menu. You can choose different filter categories from the panel menu.

Pixelate an Image

The Pixelate filters divide areas of your image into solid-colored dots or shapes, generating an abstract effect. The Crystallize filter, one example of a Pixelate filter, re-creates your image by using colored polygons. You control the size of the polygons with a setting in the Pixelate dialog box.

You can apply the Pointillize filter to turn your image into a pointillist painting, with colors throughout the image turned into dots. The background color determines the color of the canvas on which the dots are placed. To apply a filter to just part of your image, select a portion by using a selection tool. For more on selection tools, see Chapter 6.

Pixelate an Image

1 In the Editor, select the layer to which you want to apply the filter.

In this example, the image has a single Background layer.

2 Click **Filter**.

3 Click **Pixelate**.

4 Click **Crystallize**.

The Crystallize dialog box opens, displaying a preview of the filter's effect.

5 Click the minus sign (⬛) or plus sign (⬛) to zoom out or in.

6 Click and drag the **Cell Size** slider (⬛) to adjust the size of the shapes.

The size can range from 3 to 300. In this example, the Cell Size has been increased.

7 Click **OK**.

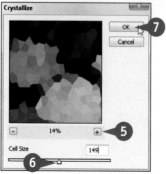

Photoshop Elements applies the filter.

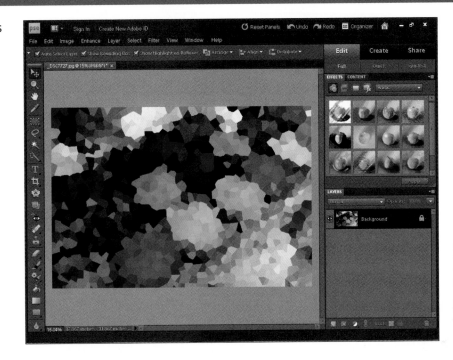

TIP

What does the Mosaic filter do?
The Mosaic filter converts your image to a set of solid-color squares.

① Click **Filter**.

② Click **Pixelate**.

③ Click **Mosaic**.

The Mosaic dialog box opens.

④ Click and drag the slider (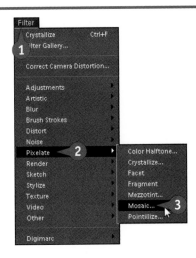) to specify the mosaic square size.

⑤ Click **OK** to apply the filter.

Note: By making a selection before applying, the Mosaic filter can be used to hide a face.

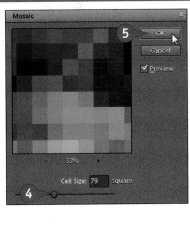

Emboss an Image

You can achieve the effect of a three-dimensional shape pressed into paper with the Emboss filter. You may find this filter useful for generating textured backgrounds. With settings for the filter, you can control the strength of the embossing by determining the height of the embossing and the types of edges it recognizes.

The Emboss filter is located under the Stylize submenu, which holds a grab bag of filters that can affect your image in a variety of different ways, some quite dramatically.

To apply the filter to just part of your image, select that portion by using a selection tool. For more on selection tools, see Chapter 6.

Emboss an Image

① In the Editor, select the layer to which you want to apply the filter.

In this example, the image has a single Background layer.

② Click **Filter**.

③ Click **Stylize**.

④ Click **Emboss**.

The Emboss dialog box displays a preview of the filter's effect.

⑤ Click the minus sign (⊟) or the plug sign (⊞) to zoom out or in.

⑥ Type an angle value to specify the direction of the shadow.

⑦ Click and drag the **Height** slider (■) to set the strength of the embossing, or type a number for the height.

⑧ Click and drag the **Amount** slider (■) to set the number of edges the filter affects.

⑨ Click **OK**.

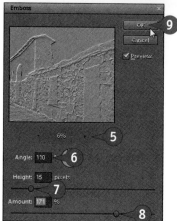

Photoshop Elements applies the filter.

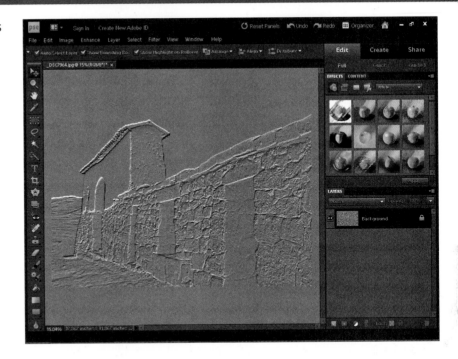

TIP

Do I have another way to create an embossed effect in an image?

Yes. You can use the Bas Relief filter to get a similar effect.

① Follow Steps **1** to **4** in this section, clicking **Sketch** in Step **3** and **Bas Relief** in Step **4**.

② In the Filter Gallery dialog box, click and drag the slider (🔲) to control the detail.

③ Click and drag the slider (🔲) to control the smoothness.

④ Click **OK**.

Photoshop Elements applies the filter.

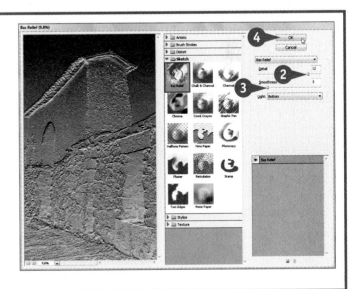

Apply Multiple Filters

You can apply more than one filter to an image by using the Filter Gallery interface. The interface enables you to preview a variety of filter effects and apply them in combination. For example, you can apply the Diffuse Glow filter to add bright lighting across an image or the Find Edges filter to apply contrast to edges of objects. You can experiment with the filter settings to get just the right look.

Many filters open the Filter Gallery interface when you apply them, including the Charcoal Sketch filter, which is covered earlier in this chapter.

Not all the effects listed under the Photoshop Elements Filter menu appear in the Filter Gallery. Ones not shown can be accessed in the Filter menu.

Apply Multiple Filters

① In the Editor, select the layer to which you want to apply the filters.

In this example, the image has a single Background layer.

Note: To apply the filters to just part of your image, make a selection with a selection tool. For more on selection tools, see Chapter 6.

② Click **Filter**.

③ Click **Filter Gallery**.

The Filter Gallery dialog box opens, with the most recently applied filter selected.

The left pane displays a preview of the filtered image.

④ Click an arrow to display filters from a category (▶ changes to ▼).

⑤ Click a thumbnail to apply a filter.

● The filter appears in the filter list.

6 Click the **New Effect Layer** button (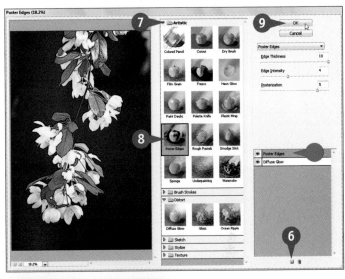).

● The new effect appears in the filter list.

You can click and drag effects in the list to change their order and change the look of your image.

Note: For more on rearranging layers, see Chapter 8.

7 Click a different triangle to display filters from another category (▶ changes to ▼).

8 Click a thumbnail to apply another filter.

You can repeat Steps **6** to **8** to apply additional filters.

9 Click **OK**.

Photoshop Elements applies the filters.

TIP

How can I apply filters to text?

1 Select a type layer.

2 Select a filter under the Filter menu.

A dialog box opens, asking if you want to simplify the type layer.

3 Click **OK**.

Photoshop Elements converts the type layer to a regular layer.

4 Apply the filter as you would to any other layer.

CHAPTER 14

Adding Text Elements

Do you want to add letters and words to your photos and illustrations? Photoshop Elements enables you to add text to your images and precisely control the appearance and layout of text. You can also stylize your text by using effects and other tools in Photoshop Elements.

Add Text

Adding text enables you to label elements in your image or use letters and words in artistic ways. You insert text in Photoshop Elements using the Type tool. The Toolbox contains horizontal and vertical versions of the tool.

Text that you add appears in its own layer. You can manipulate text layers in your image to move or stylize text. Text in Photoshop Elements is vector-based, so you can resize and transform it without a loss in quality.

Photoshop Elements comes with a number of expensive typefaces not typically preinstalled on computers.

Add Text

1 In the Editor, click the **Horizontal Type** tool (T).

Note: For more on opening the Editor, see Chapter 1.

2 Click in the image where you want the text to begin.

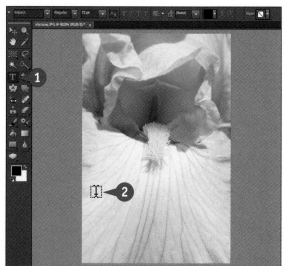

3 Select a font, style, and size for your text from these menus.

4 Click the **Color** down arrow (▪).

5 Click a color for your text.

When you position your mouse pointer (▸) over a color, it changes to an eyedropper (✐).

6 Type your text.

To create a line break, press Enter.

7 When you finish typing your text, click ✓ or press Enter on your keyboard's number pad.

● You can click ⊘ or press Esc to cancel.

● Photoshop Elements places the text in its own layer.

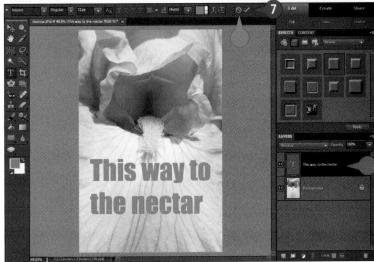

TIPS

How do I reposition my text?
You can move the layer that contains the text with the Move tool (⬙). Click the layer of text, click the **Move** tool, and then click and drag to reposition your text. For more on moving a layer, see Chapter 8.

How do I add vertical text to my image?
Right-click the **Horizontal Type** tool (⊤) and then click the **Vertical Type** tool (⊥) in the menu that appears. You can also click the Vertical Type tool in the Options bar. Your text appears with a vertical orientation, and lines are added from right to left.

You can change the orientation of existing text in your image by selecting a text layer and then clicking the **Change the Text Orientation** button (⊥). This converts horizontal text to vertical text and vice versa. Using vertical text can be useful when applying some Asian language characters.

Change the Formatting of Text

You can change the font, style, size, and other characteristics of your text. This can help emphasize or de-emphasize your text.

Photoshop Elements has access to all the fonts on your computer's operating system. A number of fonts are added when you installed Elements.

Available styles for text include italic, bold, and other options that can vary depending on the font being used. The default size measurement is the point, which is 1/72 of an inch. You can enter other units of measurement in the size field in the Options bar, such as "5 cm," and Photoshop Elements converts the value to points.

Change the Formatting of Text

1 In the Editor, click the **Horizontal Type** tool (▦).

Note: For more on opening the Editor, see Chapter 1.

2 Click the text layer that you want to edit.

Note: For more on how to open the Layers panel, see Chapter 1.

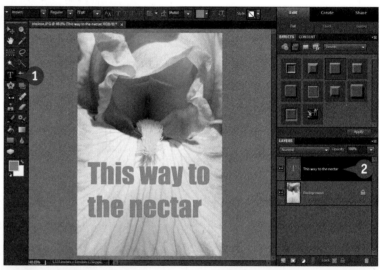

3 Click and drag to select some text from the selected layer.

● You can double-click the layer thumbnail to select all the text.

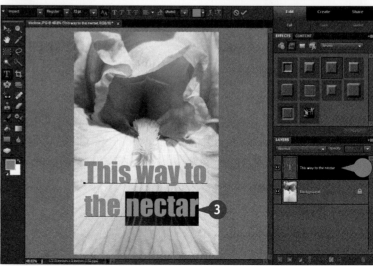

④ Click the ▼ and choose a font.

⑤ Click the ▼ and choose the text's style.

⑥ Click the ▼ and choose the text's size.

⑦ Click the **Anti-Aliased** button (▣) to control the text's anti-aliasing.

⑧ When you finish formatting your text, click ✔ or press [Enter] on your keyboard's number pad.

● You can click ⊘ or press [Esc] to cancel.

Photoshop Elements applies the formatting to your text.

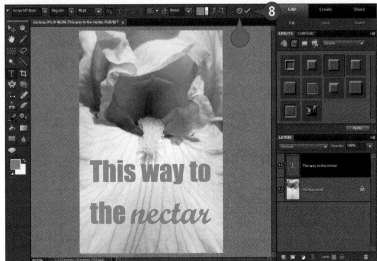

TIPS

What is anti-aliasing?
Anti-aliasing is the process of adding semitransparent pixels to curved edges in digital images to make the edges appear smoother. You can apply anti-aliasing to text to improve its appearance. Text that you do not anti-alias can sometimes look jagged. You can control the presence and style of your text's anti-aliasing with the Options bar. At very small text sizes, anti-aliasing can be counterproductive and cause blurring.

How do I change the alignment of my text?
When creating your text, click one of the three alignment buttons in the Photoshop Elements Options bar: Left Align Text (▤), Center Text (▤), or Right Align Text (▤). You may find these options useful when you create multiline passages of text.

Change the Color of Text

You can change the color of your text to make it blend or contrast with the rest of the image. You can change the color of all or just part of your text.

By default, Photoshop Elements colors your text the current foreground color. For more about setting the foreground color, see Chapter 12.

You can also change the color of your text by changing the opacity setting of a text layer. Lowering the opacity of a layer makes it more transparent, and therefore makes text in that layer lighter in color and see-through. For more about changing opacity of layers, see Chapter 8.

Change the Color of Text

1 In the Editor, click the **Horizontal Type** tool (T).

Note: For more on opening the Editor, see Chapter 1.

2 Click the text layer that you want to edit.

Note: For more on how to open the Layers panel, see Chapter 1.

3 Click and drag to highlight some text.

● You can double-click the layer thumbnail to highlight all the text.

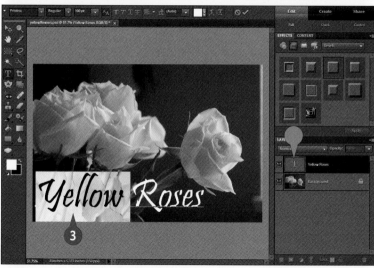

4 Click the ▾ and choose a color.

When you position your mouse pointer ( ) over a color, it changes to an eyedropper ( ).

● You can click **More Colors** to open the Color Picker for more color options.

● You can click here to open the Select Color dialog box.

5 Press **Enter** to close the color menu.

6 Click ✓ or press **Enter** again.

● You can click ⊘ or press **Esc** to cancel.

Photoshop Elements changes the text to the new color.

TIP

How do I change type color by using the Color Swatches panel?

1 Click **Window** and then **Color Swatches** to open the panel.

2 Click the text layer in the Layers panel.

3 Click and drag in the image window to highlight the text you want to recolor.

4 Click a color in the Color Swatches panel.

The text changes color.

Create Warped Text

You can easily bend and distort layers of text by using the Warped Text feature in Photoshop Elements. This can help you stylize your text to match the theme of your image. For example, text in a sky can be distorted to appear wind-blown.

Style options include Arc and Arch, which curves text in one direction across the image, and Flag and Wave, which curves the text back and forth across the image. Which direction the warping occurs depends on whether the warp is set to horizontal or vertical.

Create Warped Text

1 In the Editor, click the **Horizontal Type** tool ( ).

Note: For more on opening the Editor, see Chapter 1.

2 Click the text layer that you want to warp.

Note: For more on how to open the Layers panel, see Chapter 1.

3 Click the **Create Warped Text** button ( ).

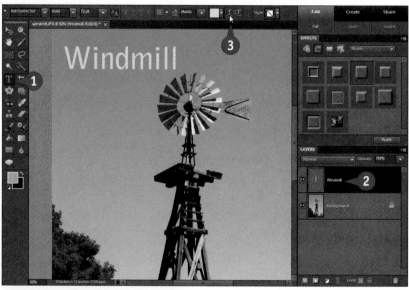

The Warp Text dialog box opens.

4 Click the **Style** and choose a warp style.

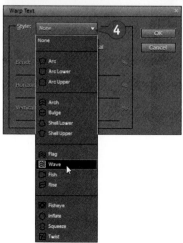

⑤ Click a radio button to select an orientation for the warp effect (● changes to ○).

⑥ Adjust the Bend and Distortion values by clicking and dragging the sliders (▣).

You can also type Bend and Distortion values. The Bend and Distortion values determine how Photoshop Elements applies the warp.

For all settings, a value of 0% means Photoshop Elements does not apply that aspect of a warp.

⑦ Click **OK**.

Photoshop Elements warps the text.

You can still edit the format, color, and other characteristics of the type when you apply a warp. See the other sections in this chapter for more.

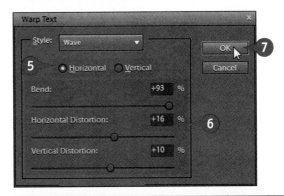

TIP

How do I unwarp text?

① Follow Steps **1** to **3** in this section.

② In the Warp Text dialog box, click the **Style** ▣ and choose **None**.

③ Click **OK**.

Your text unwarps.

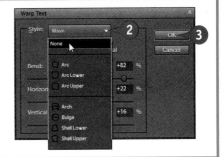

Create Beveled Text

You can give your text a raised look by adding a beveled effect. Photoshop Elements offers several beveled options in the Effects panel.

Beveling adds sloping and ridges to the edges of your text. You can edit the amount of beveling applied by double-clicking the effects icon for the beveled text layer and adjusting the controls in the Style Settings dialog box that appears. This enables you to make the beveled edges more pronounced or more subtle. For more on effects in Photoshop Elements, see Chapter 15.

Create Beveled Text

① In the Layers panel, click a text layer.

② In the Effects panel, click the **Layer Styles** button (▣).

Note: For more on how to open the Layers and Effects panels, see Chapter 1.

③ Click here and then choose **Bevels**.

Photoshop Elements displays the bevel effects.

④ Click a bevel effect.

⑤ Click **Apply**.

Photoshop Elements applies the beveling to the text.

● Photoshop Elements adds an icon (▨) to the layer to show that the layer includes an effect. You can double-click the icon to edit the effect.

Add a Shadow to Text

Y ou can cast a shadow behind your text to give the letters a 3-D look. Photoshop Elements offers several shadow options in the Effects panel.

A drop shadow effect adds soft-edged color beneath the text. By default the color is black, similar to a regular shadow. After adding a drop shadow effect, you can edit the shadow by double-clicking the effects icon for the text layer and adjusting the controls in the Style Settings dialog box that appears. This enables you to adjust the size of the shadow, how far it offsets beneath the text, its opacity, and even its color. For more on effects in Photoshop Elements, see Chapter 15.

Add a Shadow to Text

① In the Layers panel, click a text layer.

② In the Effects panel, click the **Layer Styles** button (▣).

Note: For more on how to open the Layers and Effects panels, see Chapter 1.

③ Click here to choose **Drop Shadows**.

Photoshop Elements displays the Drop Shadows effects.

④ Click a shadow effect.

⑤ Click **Apply**.

Photoshop Elements applies a shadow to the text.

● Photoshop Elements adds an icon (▣) to the layer to show that the layer includes an effect. You can double-click the icon to edit the effect.

CHAPTER 15

Applying Styles and Effects

You can apply special effects to your images by using the built-in styles and effects in Photoshop Elements. The effects enable you to add shadows, glows, and a 3-D appearance to your art. You can also add special effects to your layers with layer styles.

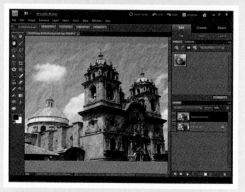

Frame a Photo with a Drop Shadow

You can apply a drop shadow to make your photo appear to float above the image canvas. You can also apply a drop shadow to just a layer. See the section "Add a Drop Shadow to a Layer" for more. When shadowing text, see Chapter 14. Photoshop Elements places dark, diffuse coloring beneath your image.

After you apply the drop shadow, you can edit its effects by opening the style settings in the Layers panel. You can control the transparency of the shadow, the distance the shadow appears from the image above it, and the color of the shadow.

Frame a Photo with a Drop Shadow

1 In the Editor, open the Effects panel.

Note: For more on opening the Editor or panels, see Chapter 1.

2 Click the **Photo Effects** button (■).

3 Click the down arrow (■).

4 Click **Frame**.

The Frame effects appear.

5 Double-click the **Drop Shadow Frame** effect.

● Photoshop Elements duplicates the selected layer, adds extra space around the photo, and applies the effect.

● Photoshop Elements applies the drop shadow over a canvas with the current background color, which is white in this example.

Note: For more on setting the background color, see Chapter 12.

TIP

How do I change the color of a drop shadow?

1 After applying the drop shadow style, double-click the **Style** icon (■) to open the Style Settings dialog box for the style.

2 Click the color box to open the Select Shadow Color dialog box to select a shadow color.

3 Click **OK**.

Photoshop Elements changes the shadow color.

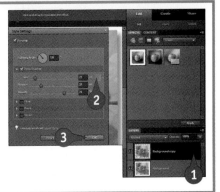

Add a Drop Shadow to a Layer

You can add a drop shadow to a layer to give objects in your photo a 3-D look. Style settings enable you to control the placement of the shadow. You can decrease the opacity to make the shadowing more subtle, increase the offset distance to make the photo appear farther off the canvas, or change the shadow color to something other than black.

Photoshop Elements offers a number of predefined drop-shadow styles in the Effects panel that apply shadowing with hard and soft edges and that are different distances from the layer.

Add a Drop Shadow to a Layer

① In the Editor, open the Layers panel.

Note: For more on opening the Editor, see Chapter 1.

② Open the Effects panel.

③ Click the **Layer Styles** button (⬛).

④ Click the layer to which you want to add a drop shadow.

⑤ Click the ▾.

⑥ Click **Drop Shadows**.

The Drop Shadow styles appear.

7 Click a drop shadow style.

8 Click **Apply**.

Photoshop Elements applies the drop shadow to the layer.

9 Double-click the **Style** icon (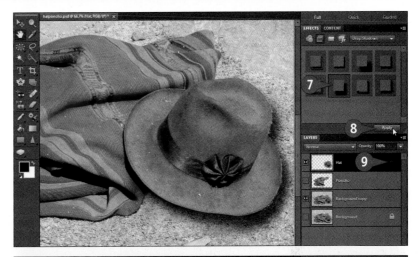) in the affected layer.

The Style Settings dialog box opens.

10 Click and drag the **Lighting Angle** dial to specify the direction of the shadowing.

11 Click and drag the **Distance** slider (■) to increase or decrease the distance of the shadow from your layer.

12 Click **OK**.

Photoshop Elements applies the style settings.

How can I add color shading to a layer by using layer styles?

1 Click a layer.

2 Open the Effects panel.

3 Click the **Layer Styles** button (■).

4 Click the ■ and then choose **Photographic Effects**.

5 Double-click an effect.

Photoshop Elements applies the shading.

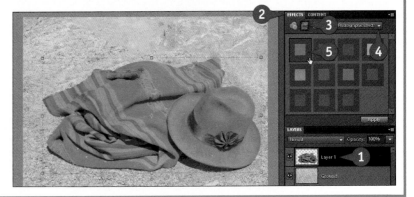

Create a Vintage Photo

You can apply an effect that removes color and adds a wrinkled texture to your photo, creating the look of an older snapshot. Photoshop Elements creates a duplicate layer before applying the effect, so you can easily compare before and after images and also blend the layers. You can select a blend mode to combine the vintage version with the original version for a more subtle appearance. For more about blending, see Chapter 8.

For a similar old-fashioned effect, you can select the Old Photo category in the Effects panel and then apply the Old Photo effect.

Create a Vintage Photo

1 In the Editor, open the Effects panel.

Note: For more on opening the Editor or panels, see Chapter 1.

2 Click the **Photo Effects** button (◼).

3 Click the ▾.

4 Click **Vintage Photo**.

An Old Paper effect appears.

⑤ Double-click the **Old Paper** effect.

● Photoshop Elements duplicates the selected layer and then applies the effect.

● You can reduce the opacity of the new layer to make the effect more subtle.

Note: See Chapter 8 for more on layer opacity.

TIP

How can I add the vintage effect to just part of a photo?

① Make a selection by using one of the selection tools.

② In the Effects panel, double-click the **Old Paper** effect.

Photoshop Elements applies the effect to the selected area.

Add a Fancy Background

You can add a fancy background to your image with one of several texture effects in Photoshop Elements. The backgrounds that Photoshop Elements provides include rainbow designs, molten textures, and a brick pattern. For a more subtle use of the effect, you can duplicate a layer, apply the background to the top copy, and then reduce the opacity of that layer. For more about duplicating layers and opacity, see Chapter 8.

You can scale the background effect applied to your image to make the pattern appear larger or smaller behind the rest of the image content. See the tip on the next page for details.

Add a Fancy Background

1 In the Editor, open the Layers panel.

2 Open the Effects panel.

Note: For more on opening the Editor or panels, see Chapter 1.

3 Click the **Layer Styles** button (▦).

4 Click the layer to which you want to add the fancy background. You must select something other than the default Background layer.

5 Click the ▼.

6 Click **Patterns**.

The Pattern styles appear.

7 Double-click a style.

If you selected the Background layer in Step **4**, a dialog box opens, asking if you want to make your background a normal layer.

8 Click **OK** and then click **OK** again in the dialog box that follows.

Photoshop Elements applies a pattern to the selected layer, creating a background behind the other layers.

TIPS

How can I reduce the strength of an effect that I just applied?

In cases where the effect is applied to a duplicate layer, you can reduce the opacity of the new layer to lessen the effect. Reducing the opacity to less than 100% allows the original content underneath to show through.

How can I change the size of a layer's background pattern?

To adjust the size of your pattern, click the pattern layer in the Layers panel. Then click **Layer**, click **Layer Style**, and then click **Scale Effects**. You can adjust the Scale setting in the Scale Layer Effects dialog box to resize the pattern. For example, you can increase the Scale setting to make the bricks in a brick pattern larger.

Add an Outline to a Layer

You can add a color outline to a layer in your image. You can make the objects in the layer stand out by adding an outline that contrasts with the background. You can also emphasize text with an outline color that contrasts with the color of the text.

After applying the effect, you can open the Style Settings dialog box to customize the color, size, and opacity of the outline. Another way to add fancy coloring to the outer edge of a layer is to apply an outer glow. See the section "Add an Outer Glow to a Layer" for details.

Add an Outline to a Layer

1 In the Editor, open the Layers panel.

2 Open the Effects panel.

Note: For more on opening the Editor or panels, see Chapter 1.

3 Click the layer to which you want to apply the outline.

In this example, a text layer is outlined.

Note: For more on using text, see Chapter 14.

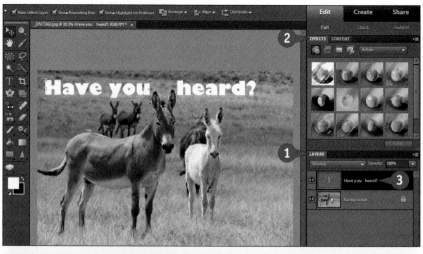

4 Click the **Layer Styles** button (🔲).

5 Click the ▼ and then choose **Strokes**.

The Stroke styles appear.

6 Double-click a stroke style.

Photoshop Elements applies the outline to the layer.

7 Double-click the **Style** icon () in the affected layer.

The Style Settings dialog box opens.

8 Click and drag the slider (⬤) to adjust the size of the outline, or type a size.

9 Click here to open the Select Stroke Color dialog box.

10 Click here to select a color, or type values to create a color.

11 Click **OK**.

12 Click **OK**.

Photoshop Elements applies the style settings.

How do I add a second effect, such as a beveling, to the layer that I have outlined?

1 Double-click the **Style** icon (⬛) for the layer to open the Style Settings dialog box.

2 Click the **Bevel** check box (⬛ changes to ✓).

3 Click and drag the slider (⬤) to adjust the size of the beveling.

4 Click **OK**.

Photoshop Elements applies beveling to the layer.

Add an Outer Glow to a Layer

The outer glow style adds fancy coloring to the outside edges of a layer's content, which can help highlight the layer. The effect can give an object in your image a ghostly or electric look and feel, depending on the color and size of the outer glow.

Photoshop Elements offers various outer glow styles to start with in the Effects panel. If you are not pleased with a style after applying it, you can open the Style Settings dialog for the style and adjust the color, size and opacity of the outer glow. To add a solid color to the edge of a layer, see the section "Add an Outline to a Layer."

Add an Outer Glow to a Layer

① In the Editor, open the Layers panel.

Note: For more on opening the Editor or panels, see Chapter 1.

② Open the Effects panel.

③ Click the layer to which you want to apply the outer glow.

④ Click the **Layer Styles** button (▣).

⑤ Click the ▾ and then choose **Outer Glows**.

Photoshop Elements displays the Outer Glow styles.

⑥ Double-click an outer glow style.

Photoshop Elements applies the outer glow to the layer.

⑦ Double-click the **Style** icon (■) in the affected layer.

The Style Settings dialog box opens.

⑧ Click and drag the slider (■) to increase or decrease the outer glow size.

You can also type a size.

⑨ Click **OK**.

Photoshop Elements applies the style settings.

TIP

Can I add an inner glow to layer objects?

Yes. An inner glow adds color to the inside edge of a layer object.

① Click a layer.

② Open the Effects panel.

③ Click the **Layer Styles** button (■).

④ Click the ■ and then choose **Inner Glows** from the menu.

⑤ Double-click an inner glow style.

Photoshop Elements applies the inner glow.

Add a Fancy Covering to a Layer

You can apply any of a variety of layer effects that can make a layer appear covered in colorful metal or glass. The glass effects are located in the Glass Buttons category in the Layer Styles. Photoshop Elements offers 14 different glass colors to choose from. A metal effect called Diamond Plate is located under the Complex category and gives your layer a look of textured chrome. You can find other metallic effects under the Patterns category.

In some cases, you can apply multiple effects to a layer simultaneously. For example, after adding a glass covering, you can further customize the layer with a drop shadow.

Add a Fancy Covering to a Layer

Cover with Glass

1 In the Editor, open the Layers panel.

2 Open the Effects panel.

Note: For more on opening the Editor and panels, see Chapter 1.

3 Click the layer that you want to cover.

4 Click the **Layer Styles** button (■).

5 Click the ■ and then select **Glass Buttons**.

Photoshop Elements displays a number of glass styles.

298

6 Double-click a style.

Photoshop Elements applies the style to the layer.

Cover with Metal

1 Click the layer that you want to cover.

2 Click the ▼ and then select **Complex**.

Photoshop Elements displays various styles.

3 Double-click the **Diamond Plate** style.

Photoshop Elements applies the style to the layer.

TIP

How do I remove a style from a layer?

1 Click a layer that has a style applied indicated by a Style icon (▨).

2 Click **Layer**.

3 Click **Layer Style**.

4 Click **Clear Layer Style**.

Photoshop Elements removes the style from the layer.

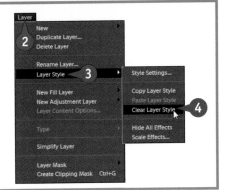

Add a Watermark

Photoshop Elements can automatically add watermarks to a collection of photos. Watermarks are semi-opaque words or designs overlaid on images to signify ownership and discourage illegal use. Before you can begin, you need to create a source folder and a destination folder for your images. To work with folders, see your operating system's documentation.

Photoshop Elements enables you to choose custom text — for example, your name or company name — to use as your watermark and also specify a font and color. You can decrease the opacity of the watermark text to let the image content below the text show through.

Add a Watermark

① Place the images to which you want to add watermarks into a source folder.

② Create an empty destination folder in which to save your watermarked files.

③ In the Photoshop Elements Editor, click **File**.

Note: For more on opening the Editor, see Chapter 1.

④ Click **Process Multiple Files**.

The Process Multiple Files dialog box opens.

⑤ Click **Browse** next to the Source box.

The Browse for Folder dialog box opens.

⑥ Click the source folder containing your images.

⑦ Click **OK**.

⑧ Click **Browse** next to the Destination box and then repeat Steps **5** to **7** for the destination folder.

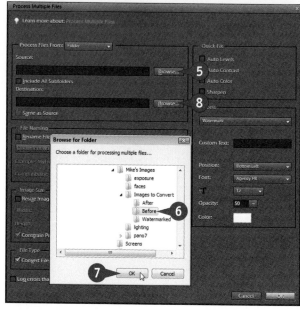

9 Click the ▼ and then choose **Watermark**.

10 Type your watermark text.

11 Select the position, font, and size for the text.

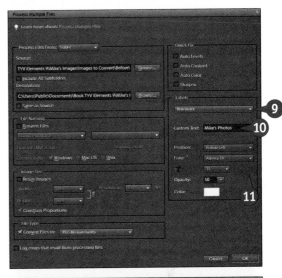

12 Click here and specify an opacity from 1 to 100. The lower the opacity, the more transparent the watermark will be.

You can also type an opacity value.

13 Click the color box and then choose a watermark color.

You may want to select a color that contrasts with the colors in your photo.

14 Click **OK**.

Photoshop Elements adds watermarks to the photos in the source folder and saves them in the destination folder.

TIPS

How can I automatically add captions to my photos?

In the Process Multiple Files dialog box, you can select **Caption** under the top menu in the Labels panel. With Caption chosen, Photoshop Elements applies text associated with the photo to the top of the photo. Similar to applying a watermark, you can specify the positioning, font, size, opacity, and color of the caption.

What kinds of captions can I add to my photos?

You can add the filename, date modified, and description as a caption. You can add this information by itself — for example, just the filename — or in combination by clicking one or more check boxes (■ changes to ☑).

Apply a Photomerge Style

Photoshop Elements can apply the color and tone styles from one image to another with the new Photomerge Style Match tool. The tool is useful if you like the ambience of the scene in one photo and want to duplicate the look and feel in a very different photo.

After you apply the style match, you can selectively remove it from areas of your image with the Style Eraser tool or add it back with the Style Painter tool. These tools enable you to apply the matched colors and tones to specific objects in your image.

Apply a Photomerge Style

1. Open the image to which you want to apply the style.

2. Click **File**.

3. Click **New**.

4. Click **Photomerge Style Match**.

Photoshop Elements displays a set of images in the Style Bin.

● You can click **Add Styles Images** (⊞) to add images to the Style Bin.

5. Click and drag a image to the Sample window.

● Photoshop Elements merges the color and tones from the sample image.

6 Click and drag the sliders () to adjust how the style is merged.

● You can click **Reset** to undo the merge and select a different sample image.

7 Click **Done**.

Photoshop Elements applies the final style settings to the image.

● The merged style is placed in its own layer. You can adjust the opacity of the layer to lessen the effect of the merge.

Note: See Chapter 8 for more about changing layer opacity.

TIP

How can I remove a merged style from parts of an image?
Follow these steps:

1 Complete Steps 1 to 5 to merge the styles.

2 Click the **Style Eraser** tool (▨).

3 Click and drag to remove the style.

● You can use the **Style Painter** tool (▨) to reapply erased styles.

CHAPTER 16

Presenting Photos Creatively

You can use photos that you have edited in Photoshop Elements in a variety of creative projects. You can showcase your favorite photos in a slide show, complete with professional looking transitions, captions, and music. With a photo book, you create a hard-copy keepsake that you can give as a gift to friends and family. A flipbook enables you to combine several images into a short movie, and the Photomerge Panorama feature stitches a sequence of photos into a single panoramic image.

Create a Slide Show

You can use the Organizer to combine images from your collection into a custom slide show that includes music, text, graphics, and even narration. The resulting slide show can be shared with friends and family online, as a DVD, or as an Adobe PDF document.

Once you choose the photos to create a slide show in the Organizer, you can select a default slide duration and transition to be applied to all the slides. You can rearrange the slide order by clicking and dragging thumbnails in the Slide Show Editor.

Create a Slide Show

1 In the Organizer, **Ctrl**+click the images you want to put in your slide show.

Note: For more on using the Organizer, see Chapter 3.

2 Click **Create**.

3 Click **Slide Show**.

Note: The slide show feature is not available in the Mac version of Photoshop Elements.

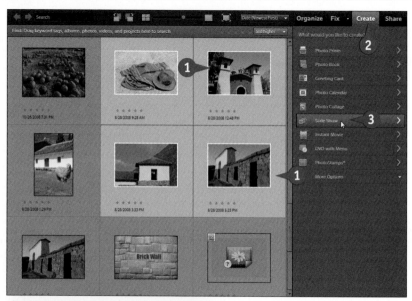

The Slide Show Preferences dialog box opens.

4 Choose a duration, a transition, and other options.

5 Specify the quality of the preview photos. Choosing a lower quality results in a shorter load time.

6 Click **OK**.

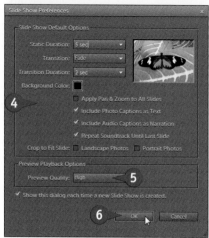

The Slide Show Editor dialog box opens.

● To add more photos to your slide show, you can click **Add Media**.

● Photoshop Elements displays thumbnails for the slides and icons for the transitions along the bottom of the Slide Show Editor.

7 Click a slide to which you want to add text.

8 Click **Add Text**.

The Edit Text dialog box opens.

9 Type your text.

10 Click **OK**.

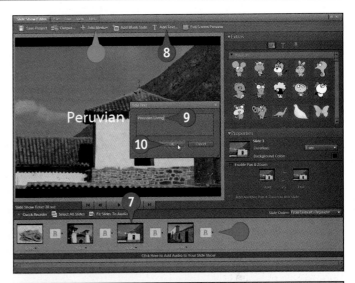

Photoshop Elements adds the text to the selected slide.

The text properties appear.

11 Click and drag inside the text to position it.

12 Choose formatting options for your text.

13 Repeat Steps **7** to **12** for the other slides in your slide show.

TIPS

How do I rearrange the photos in my slide show?

In the Slide Show Editor you can click and drag the photo thumbnails at the bottom to change their order in the slide show. To remove a slide entirely, right-click it and then choose **Delete Slide**. If you have a lot of slides, you can click **Quick Reorder** to view and rearrange them in a larger window.

How do I add music to my slide show?

To add music or narration to a slide show, click **Add Media** and then choose one of the audio options in the Slide Show Editor. You can add an audio file that plays in the background while the slide show runs. Organizer supports MP3, WAV, WMA, and AC3 audio file formats. You can click **Fit Slides To Audio** located below the Play button (▶) to sync your slide show with the audio.

continued ▶

Create a Slide Show (continued)

When creating a slide show, you can edit the transition effect and slide duration for each slide as well as set the show to loop continuously. Transition effects control how one slide flows to the next. You can also caption your slides with text or add clip art to give them extra decoration.

Organizer saves your slide show as either a WMV file or a PDF file. The WMV format can be viewed with Windows Media Player. You can view PDFs with a variety of applications, including the free Adobe Reader. Slide shows are easy to share with others by copying the finished file onto a disk or e-mailing it.

Create a Slide Show (continued)

⑭ If the Extras panel is closed, click **Extras** to open it.

⑮ Click a slide to which you want to add clip art.

⑯ Click and drag the clip art to the slide.

You can click and drag the clip art to reposition it.

● You can choose options here to resize or recolor the clip art.

⑰ Click a transition icon between the slides.

The transition properties appear.

⑱ Click the down arrow (▾) to choose a transition duration.

⑲ Click the ▾ to choose a transition style.

⑳ Click the **Play** button (▶) to preview your slide show.

Photoshop Elements cycles through the slides.

● You can click **Full Screen Preview** to preview the slide show at maximum size. To exist Full Screen Preview, you can press Esc.

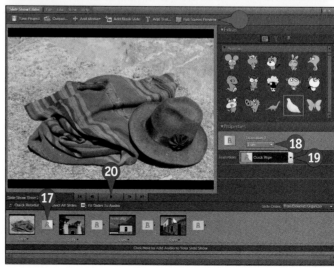

21 Click **Save Project**.

A dialog box opens, asking you to name your slide show.

22 Type a name.

23 Click **Save**.

24 Click here to close the Slide Show Editor and return to the Organizer. You can also press Ctrl+Q.

● You can click **Output** to save the slide show as a PDF file or movie or burn it to a CD or DVD.

● Photoshop Elements saves your slide show in the Organizer and labels it with a 🖫.

You can double-click the slide show to continue to edit it.

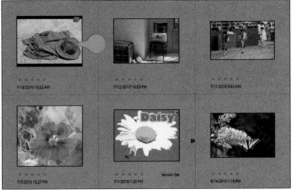

TIP

How do I add a title page to my slide show?

1 Click a slide thumbnail.

2 Click **Add Blank Slide**.

● Photoshop Elements adds a blank slide to your slide show.

3 Click **Add Text**.

4 In the dialog box that opens, type a title for your page.

5 Click **OK**.

You can click and drag the new title page to reposition it.

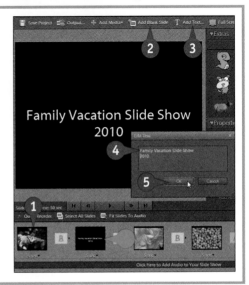

Create a Photo Book

Photoshop Elements lets you arrange the favorite photos from your collection into a professional-looking photo book. This enables you to have a hard copy of your photos that you can share with friends and family.

You can select from a variety of styles, colors, and layouts for your book pages. Photoshop Elements can automatically assemble photos selected in the Organizer into the pages of your book. You can then review the pages of the book and make custom changes to the positioning of the photos and add text to describe what is happening in each image.

Create a Photo Book

Set Up the Book

1. In the Organizer, Ctrl+click the images you want to include in your photo book.

Note: For more on using the Organizer, see Chapter 3.

2. Click **Create**.

3. Click **Photo Book**.

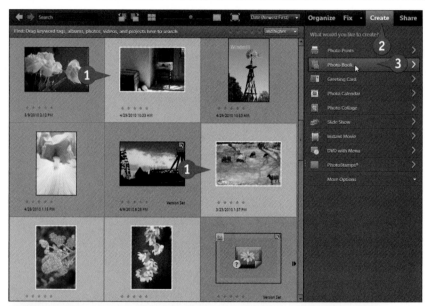

The Photo Book dialog box opens in the Editor.

4. Click a book size.

5. Click a book theme.

● By default, Photoshop Elements automatically fills the pages with your images.

6. Type the number of pages in your photo book. Page limits vary with the type of book.

7. Click **OK**.

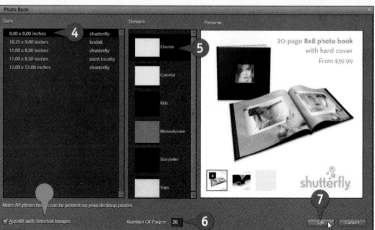

Photoshop Elements adds the photos to the book.

8 Click the ▾ to magnify the currently selected page.

9 Click the arrows to cycle through the pages sequentially.

10 Click a page to edit.

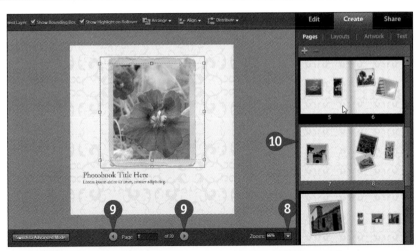

Edit a Photo

11 Click the ▾ and select **Show Files selected in Organizer**.

12 Click and drag a file to a photo on the page.

continued ▶**311**

TIP

How do I change the title page text?

1 Complete Steps **1** to **9** and click the first page in your book under the Pages tab to view it.

2 Click **Text**.

3 Double-click the title page text to select it.

4 Type to change the text.

5 Click ✓ to finish editing the title page text.

After you complete your photo book, you can save it as a project in Photoshop Elements. The photo book appears in the Organizer along with your images and other creations. To get an idea of what the final photo book will look like, or to create a do-it-yourself book, you can print the pages on your printer. To get a professionally printed version, you can order your book through one of the printing partners in the Photo Book interface.

Create a Photo Book (continued)

● Photoshop Elements replaces the photo.

⑬ Click the **Move** tool (▶).

⑭ Click and drag inside a photo.

● You can click a selection handle to resize the photo.

● You can click and drag the rotation handle to turn the photo.

Photoshop Elements moves the photo.

Add Text

⑮ Click **Text**.

⑯ Select the font, size, and other formatting.

⑰ Click where you want to add text on the page.

⑱ Type your text.

⑲ Click ✓ to finish adding the text.

Finish the Book

20 Click **Pages**.

21 Click to select other book pages.

22 Repeat Steps **12** to **19** to edit photos and add text.

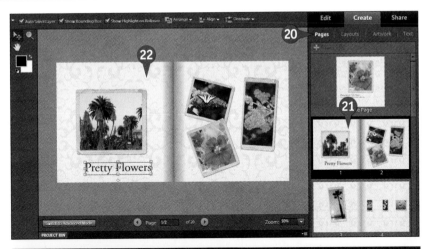

23 Click **File** and then **Save** to save your photo book.

24 Click **Done** to return to the Editor.

● You can click **Print** to print the photo book with your printer.

● You can click **Order** to have the book professionally printed and shipped to you.

How do I change the layout of a page?

1 Click **Pages** and click the page whose layout you want to change.

2 Click **Layouts**.

Photoshop Elements displays a list of layouts.

3 Double-click a layout.

● Photoshop Elements applies the layout to the page.

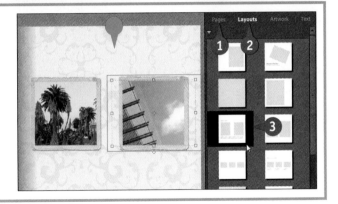

Create a Flipbook

You can take a sequence of action photos and turn it into a flipbook, which is a short movie. You can specify the frame rate of the movie as well as the dimensions.

To create the animated frames for a flipbook, you can duplicate objects in your image and place them into separate layers. You can move or scale the different layers to create a set of time-lapse images. In the following example, a sheep layer was duplicated and scaled. Then different versions of the layered image were saved to create four frames.

Another way to combine images into a movie is to create a slide show. See "Create a Slide Show" for details.

Create a Flipbook

1 In the Organizer, **Ctrl**+click to select the photos you want to include in your flipbook.

Note: For more on using the Organizer, see Chapter 3.

2 Click **Create**.

3 Click **More Options**.

4 Click **Flipbook**.

Note: The flipbook feature is not available in the Mac version of Photoshop Elements.

The Flipbook dialog box opens.

5 Type a playback speed between 1 and 30. *Fps* stands for frames per second.

● You can also click and drag the slider (■) to set a playback speed.

● Your photos are ordered as they were in the Organizer. You can click the **Reverse Order** check box (■ changes to ✓) to reverse the order.

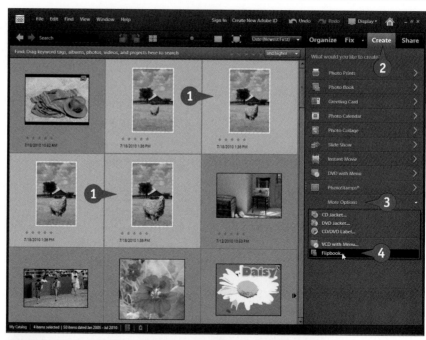

6 Choose an output setting based on how the flipbook will be viewed. The setting determines the dimensions of the movie.

● You can click **Details** for an explanation of the current setting.

7 Click the **Play** button (▶) to preview your flipbook.

8 Click **Output**.

The Save dialog box opens.

9 Type a filename for your flipbook.

● Flipbooks can only be saved in the Windows Media View (WMV) format.

10 Click the ▾ and choose where to save the flipbook.

11 Click **Save**.

Photoshop Elements saves the flipbook.

TIP

What are my options for previewing a flipbook?

● You can click and drag the slider (◉) to cycle back and forth through the flipbook photos.

● You can click the **Previous** button (◀) to go to the previous photo.

● You can click the **Next** button (▶▶) to go to the next photo.

● You can click to deselect the **Loop Preview** check box (☑ changes to ■) to stop the preview from looping.

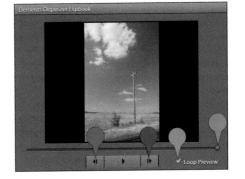

Create PhotoStamps

You can turn an image into U.S. Postal Service-approved stamps by using the PhotoStamps feature. After you upload the photo you want displayed on the stamp to the service, you can customize the stamp and then purchase a set.

Customization options enable you to zoom in on an image detail, rotate your image, adjust the border and coloring of the stamp, and choose the postage amount. After you design the stamp, you can order sheets of it through the Adobe Photoshop Services Web site.

Create PhotoStamps

1 From the Organizer, click the photo you want to use on your stamps.

Note: For more on using the Organizer, see Chapter 3.

You can **Ctrl**+click to select multiple photos.

2 Click **Photo Stamps**.

3 In the PhotoStamps dialog box that opens, click **Upload My Photos**.

Photoshop Elements uploads the photo(s) to the PhotoStamps Web site.

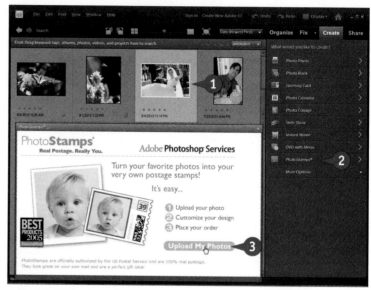

4 In the confirmation dialog box that opens, click **Continue**.

The Adobe Photoshop Services page opens in a browser window.

5 Click the **Create Product** link beneath your photo.

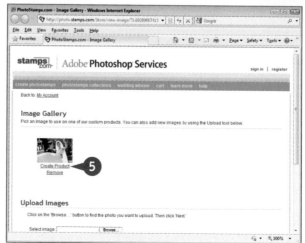

⑥ On the Image Details page that appears, click the **PhotoStamps** link.

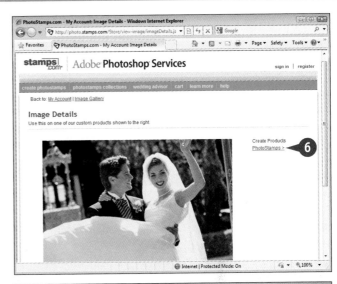

The Customize Your PhotoStamps page appears.

⑦ Click options to customize your stamps.

You can zoom into or out of your photo, rotate it, add a border, or change the color of the postage amount.

⑧ Click **Continue**.

Your stamps are added to your shopping cart.

On the pages that follow, you can enter payment and shipping information to purchase the stamps.

TIPS

How can I order prints of my Photoshop Elements photos?

You can obtain prints of your photos by clicking the **Create** tab and then **Photo Prints**. A panel appears that enables you to order prints through Shutterfly or Kodak Gallery. You need an Internet connection to use these services. The panel also lets you print your photos on a local printer or create a picture package that arranges multiple photos on a single page.

How can I create a calendar featuring my images?

You can create a calendar by clicking the **Create** tab and then **Photo Calendar**. A panel appears that enables you to design and order calendars through Shutterfly or Kodak Gallery. With both services, you use tools on external Web sites to build the calendar pages. You need an Internet connection to do this.

Create a Photo Panorama

You can use the Photomerge feature in Photoshop Elements to stitch several sequential images together into a single panoramic image. This enables you to capture more scenery than is usually possible in a regular photograph.

Photoshop Elements automatically merges the edges of your images together by taking into account the type of lens used and the geometry of the scenery. You can specify a merging technique or have the program choose it automatically with the Auto setting. New to this version of Photoshop Elements is a feature that fills in any extra space on the sides of the resulting panoramic image.

Create a Photo Panorama

1 In the Editor, click **File**.

Note: For more on opening the Editor, see Chapter 1.

2 Click **New**.

3 Click **Photomerge Panorama**.

The Photomerge dialog box opens.

4 Click **Auto** (● changes to ○).

With the Auto setting, Photoshop Elements evaluates the images and attempts to choose the best method for stitching your photos together.

5 Click **Browse**.

The Open dialog box opens.

6 Click the ▾ to choose the folder that contains the images you want to merge.

7 Ctrl +click the images you want to merge into a panoramic image.

8 Click **OK**.

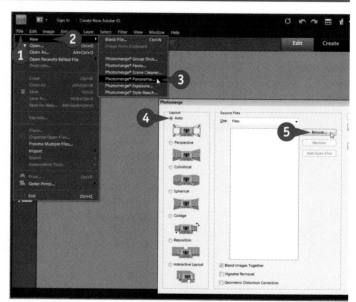

● The filenames of the images appear in the Source Files list.

9 Click **OK** to build the panoramic image.

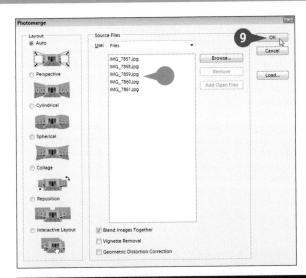

Photoshop Elements merges the images into a single panoramic image.

● Parts of each original image appear in separate layers in the Layers panel.

Note: For more on layers, see Chapter 8.

● The stitching process can leave empty areas along the edges of the panorama.

10 In the Clean Edges dialog box that appears, click **Yes** to automatically fill in the edges.

How can I create photos that merge successfully?

To merge photos successfully, you need to align and overlap the photos as you shoot them. Here are a few hints. For more tips, see the Photoshop Elements help documentation.

- Use a tripod to keep your photos level with one another.
- Experiment with the different layout modes in the Photomerge dialog box.
- Refrain from using lenses that distort your photos, such as fisheye lenses, and do not change zoom settings between frames.
- Shoot your photos so they overlap 15-30%.

CHAPTER 17

Saving and Sharing Your Work

Photoshop Elements enables you to save your images in different file formats for use on the Web and in other applications. You can also share your photos by e-mailing them, putting them in an online gallery, or printing them. For safekeeping, you can export your photos to a separate folder on your computer, back them up to a CD or DVD, or back them up online. Saving a second copy of your photo collection is a good idea in case your computer malfunctions.

Save a JPEG for the Web

You can save an image in the JPEG — Joint Photographic Experts Group — format and then publish it on the Web. JPEG is the preferred Web format for saving photographic images. Many digital cameras also use it for saving their photos.

Photoshop Elements saves JPEG images at 72 dpi. When saving, you can adjust a JPEG quality setting to determine the file size of the resulting image. If you are saving a non-photographic image, such as a line drawing or illustration with lots of solid color, consider saving your image in the GIF or PNG format. See the other sections in this chapter for more information.

Save a JPEG for the Web

1 In the Editor, click **File**.

Note: For more on opening the Editor, see Chapter 1.

2 Click **Save for Web**.

The Save For Web dialog box opens.

Your original image appears on the left and a preview of the JPEG version is on the right.

3 Click the ⊡ to choose **JPEG**.

4 Click the ⊡ to choose a quality setting.

● Alternatively, you can select a numeric quality setting from 0 (low quality) to 100 (high quality).

The higher the quality, the larger the resulting file size.

⑤ Check that the file quality and size are acceptable in the preview area.

● You can resize the resulting image by typing dimensions or a percentage and then clicking **Apply**.

⑥ Click **OK**.

The Save Optimized As dialog box opens.

⑦ Click the ▾ to choose a folder in which to save the file.

⑧ Type a filename. Photoshop Elements automatically assigns a .jpg extension if you do not specify an extension.

⑨ Click **Save**.

Photoshop Elements saves the JPEG file, and the original image file remains open.

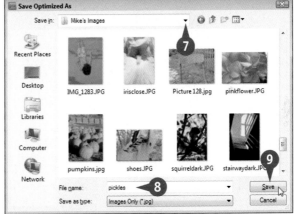

What is image compression?

Image compression involves using mathematical techniques to reduce the amount of information required to describe an image. This results in smaller file sizes, which is important when transmitting information on the Web. Some compression schemes, such as JPEG, reduce image quality somewhat, but the loss is usually negligible compared to the savings in file size. You can avoid unnecessary loss in quality by saving a image in the PSD or TIFF format as you work and saving to JPEG when you are ready to publish on the Web.

How can I adjust the view of my image in the Save For Web dialog box?

You can use the Hand tool (✋) in the upper left corner to shift the position of your image in the Save For Web dialog box, or use the Zoom tool (🔍) to zoom in or out.

Save a GIF for the Web

You can save an image as a GIF — Graphics Interchange Format — file and then publish it on the Web. The GIF format is good for saving illustrations that have a lot of solid color. The format supports a maximum of 256 colors.

Photoshop Elements saves GIF images at 72 dpi. Unlike JPEG images, GIF images can include transparency. Transparency can allow images to appear as interesting shapes when on a Web page. If you are saving a photographic image with lots of continuous colors, consider saving your image in the JPEG format. See "Save a JPEG for the Web" for more information.

Save a GIF for the Web

1 In the Editor, click **File**.

Note: For more on opening the Editor, see Chapter 1.

2 Click **Save for Web**.

The Save For Web dialog box opens.

3 Click the 🔽 to choose **GIF**.

4 Click the 🔽 to choose the number of colors to include in the image.

GIF allows a maximum of 256 colors.

● You can click here to choose the method Photoshop Elements uses to select the GIF colors.

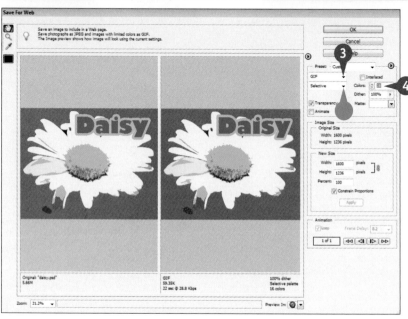

5 Check that the file quality and size are acceptable in the preview area.

● You can resize the resulting image by typing dimensions or a percentage and then clicking **Apply**.

● Click the **Transparency** check box (☐ changes to ☑) to ensure that any transparent areas of your image remain that way in your final GIF image.

6 Click **OK**.

The Save Optimized As dialog box opens.

7 Click here to choose a folder in which to save the file.

8 Type a filename. Photoshop Elements automatically assigns a .gif extension if you do not specify an extension.

9 Click **Save**.

Photoshop Elements saves the GIF file, and the original image file remains open.

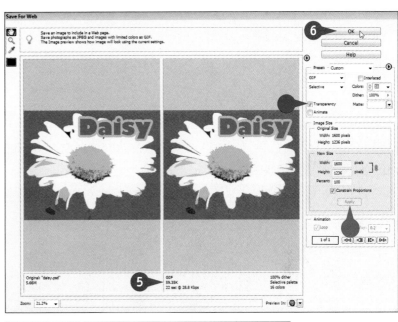

TIPS

How do I minimize the file sizes of my GIF images?

The most important factor in creating small GIFs is limiting the number of colors in the final image. GIF files are limited to 256 colors or fewer. In images that have just a few solid colors, you can often reduce the total number of colors to 16 or even 8 without any noticeable reduction in quality. See Step **4** in this section to set the number of colors in your GIF images.

How can I use GIF transparency in my Web images?

GIF images that include transparency allow the background of a Web page to show through. Transparent GIFs enable you to add nonrectangular elements to your Web projects. Because Background layers cannot contain transparent pixels, you need to work with layers other than the Background layer to create transparent GIFs. See Chapter 8 for more on layers.

You can save an image as a PNG — Portable Network Graphics — file and then publish it on the Web. PNG was devised as a high-quality alternative to GIF and JPEG.

Unlike GIF, PNG can support more than 256 colors. However, PNG is not as universally supported as GIF and JPEG are in Web browsers. If you want to minimize the file size of a photograph, consider saving it as a JPEG instead because the JPEG format offers better compression, which results in smaller file sizes. See "Save a JPEG for the Web" for details.

Save a PNG for the Web

1 In the Editor, click **File**.

Note: For more on opening the Editor, see Chapter 1.

2 Click **Save for Web**.

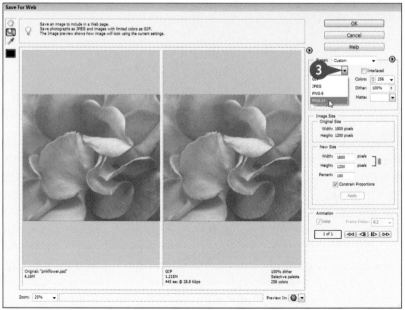

The Save For Web dialog box opens.

3 Click the ☑ to choose **PNG-8** or **PNG-24**.

Note: See the tip in this section for more on the different PNG settings.

④ Check that the file quality and size are acceptable in the preview.

● You can resize the resulting image by typing dimensions or a percentage and then clicking **Apply**.

● Click the **Transparency** check box (☐ changes to ☑) to ensure that any transparent areas of your image remain that way in your final PNG image.

⑤ Click **OK**.

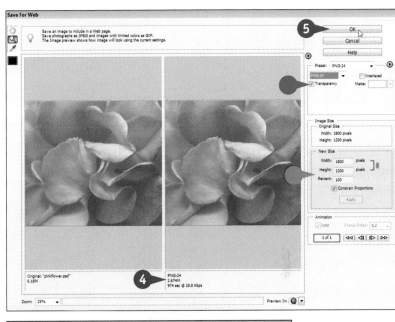

⑥ Click the ▾ to choose a folder in which to save the file.

⑦ Type a filename. Photoshop Elements automatically assigns a .png extension if you do not specify an extension.

⑧ Click **Save**.

Photoshop Elements saves the PNG file, and the original image file remains open.

TIPS

What is the difference between the PNG-8 and PNG-24 settings?
PNG-8 stands for PNG 8-bit. With it, you can limit the number of colors in the final PNG image and thereby decrease the resulting file size. Similar to GIF, PNG-8 can include a maximum of 256 colors. PNG-24 stands for PNG 24-bit. This format includes a wider range of colors than 8-bit and leads to better image quality, but it generally results in much larger file sizes.

How does the PNG format support transparency?
Like GIF files, PNG files can include transparency. But unlike GIFs, the PNG format supports a more advanced feature called alpha-channel transparency, which allows a background behind an image to show through partially. You can add partial transparency to your image by decreasing the opacity of a layer. For more on layers and opacity, see Chapter 8.

Convert File Types

You can quickly and easily convert images from one file type to another in Photoshop Elements by using the Process Multiple Files feature. This makes it easy to convert a collection of PSD files to the JPEG format for sending by e-mail or posting on the Web.

You can specify that the images are resized as they are processed. This enables you to shrink the file size of the resulting images. You can also rename the converted files using a serial number, the current date, and other options. During the process, Photoshop Elements opens each image, makes the necessary conversions, and then saves the updated image to a file location of your choosing.

Convert File Types

1 Place the images that you want to convert in a folder.

Note: To work with folders, see your operating system's documentation.

2 In the Editor, click **File**.

Note: For more on opening the Editor, see Chapter 1.

3 Click **Process Multiple Files**.

If a dialog box appears warning about Multi Page Documents and Project Files, click **OK**.

The Process Multiple Files dialog box opens.

4 Click **Browse**.

The Browse for Folder dialog box opens.

5 Click here to open folders on your computer (⊳ changes to ◢).

6 Click the folder containing your images.

7 Click **OK**.

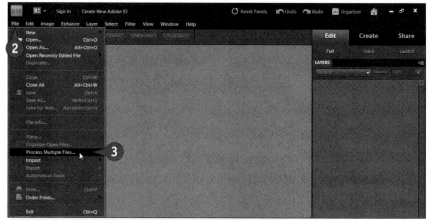

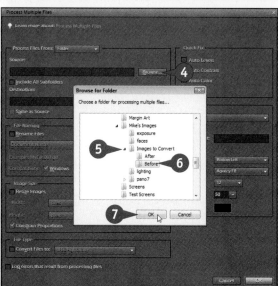

8 Click **Browse** and then repeat Steps **6** to **8** to specify a destination folder where you want your processed images to be saved.

● You can optionally click the **Resize Images** check box (■ changes to ☑), type a new width and height, and then Photoshop Elements resizes the images before saving.

● You can also click the **Rename Files** check box (■ changes to ☑) and choose a naming scheme for the converted images.

Note: For more on resizing images, see Chapter 5.

9 Click the **Convert Files to** check box (■ changes to ☑).

10 Click the ▼ to choose a file format to convert to.

11 Click **OK**.

● Photoshop Elements processes the images.

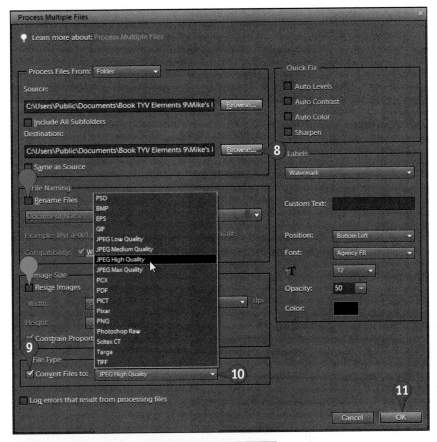

How can I automatically fix color and lighting problems in my converted photos?

There are automatic optimization settings under the Quick Fix heading in the Process Multiple Files dialog box. You can select them to have Photoshop Elements improve the color, contrast, and sharpness of your photos before they are converted. For more on these settings, see Chapter 9.

How can I quickly add labels to my converted photos?

Under the Labels heading in the Process Multiple Files dialog box are tools for adding captions and watermarks to your converted photos. You can automatically add filename, description, and date information as captions as well as specify the size and style of the caption font. For more on adding watermarks, see Chapter 15.

E-Mail Images with Photo Mail

You can embed your images in an e-mail message and then send them to others by using the Photo Mail feature in Photoshop Elements. With Photo Mail, you can select custom stationery that inserts colors, graphics, and captions next to your images. Photoshop Elements enables you to store recipient information in a contact book so you do not have to enter the same e-mail information every time you send an image.

This feature requires that you already have an e-mail program, such as Microsoft Outlook, set up on your computer. Photoshop Elements does not come with e-mail capability.

E-Mail Images with Photo Mail

1 In the Organizer, click **Share**.

Note: For more on using the Organizer, see Chapter 3.

2 Click **Photo Mail**.

Note: Photoshop Elements may display a dialog box asking you to choose your e-mail client. If so, choose the software with which you prefer to send e-mail and then click **Continue**.

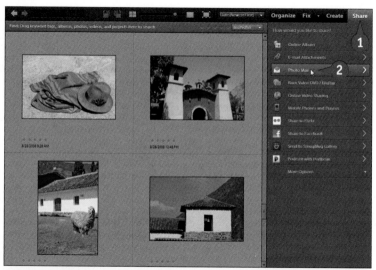

The Photo Mail pane opens.

3 Click and drag images you want to mail from the main Organizer window into the Photo Mail pane.

● Photoshop Elements totals the file sizes and estimates how long they will take to send.

4 Click **Next**.

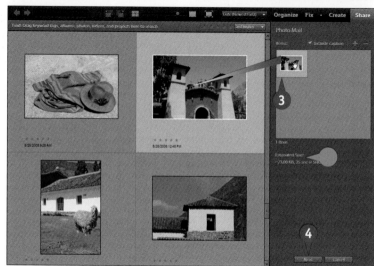

5 Type a message to accompany your images.

6 Click the **Contact Book** button (▨) to define your recipient.

The Contact Book dialog box opens.

7 Click **New Contact**.

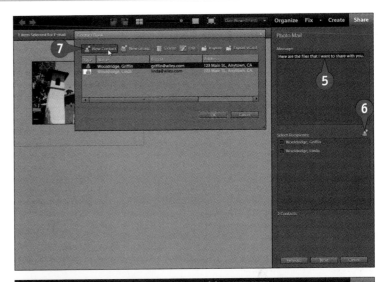

The New Contact dialog box opens.

8 Type the contact details for your recipient.

9 Type an e-mail address for your recipient.

10 Click **OK**.

● The recipient appears in the Contact Book.

11 Click **OK** in the Contact Book dialog box.

TIPS

Can I send my images as e-mail attachments?

If you want to send your photos as plain e-mail attachments rather than as embedded items in an e-mail message, click the **E-mail Attachments** option in the Organizer's Share pane. Sending attachments is similar to sending Photo Mail but without the steps where you select stationery and a layout.

How can I keep the file sizes of my images small when e-mailing them?

If you are worried about the file sizes of your images when e-mailing, choose the **E-mail Attachments** option rather than the Photo Mail option in the Organizer's Share pane. In the E-mail Attachments option, you can adjust both the dimensions of your photos and the JPEG compression applied prior to sending.

continued ▶

Photo Mail includes more than 50 stationery designs that you can apply to the photos that you e-mail. You can select stationery with animal, seasonal, or party themes. Photoshop Elements embeds your images and the stationery into the e-mail message by using HTML, which is the language used to create Web pages.

A few older e-mail programs do not display HTML that is embedded in e-mail. Recipients using such e-mail programs will not be able see the styles and graphics offered in the Photo Mail feature.

E-Mail Images with Photo Mail (continued)

The new contact appears in the Select Recipients list.

12 Click the check box for each intended recipient (■ changes to ☑).

13 Click **Next**.

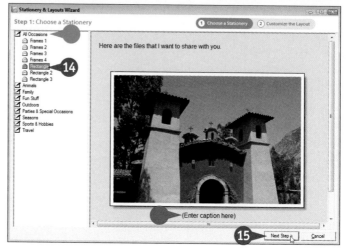

The Stationery & Layouts Wizard opens with the Choose a Stationery options.

● You can click a category to open stationery options.

14 Click a stationery with which to style your e-mail.

● You can click text inside the stationery design to caption your images.

15 Click **Next Step**.

The Customize the Layout options appear.

⑯ Click the layout options to organize and size your images.

● You can optionally customize your text.

● You can click here to set other options. The available options vary depending on the stationery selected in Step 14.

⑰ Click **Next**.

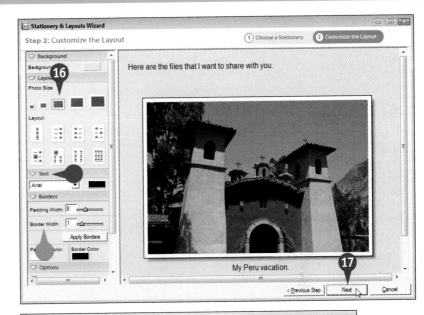

Photoshop Elements opens a new message in your e-mail client software.

● The recipient is added to the To field.

● Your message text, layout design, and images are included in the body of the message.

Note: For more on sending your message, see the documentation for your e-mail application.

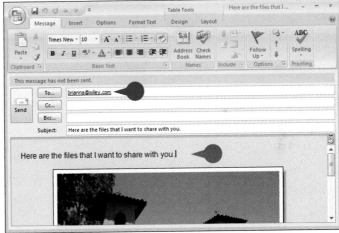

TIP

How can I view a history of what I have e-mailed?

① Click **Find**.

② Click **By History**.

③ Click **E-mailed to**.

● A dialog box opens, showing a history of e-mail messages sent through Photoshop Elements. You can double-click an entry to view the photos that were sent.

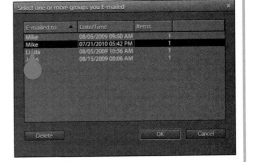

Print Photos

You can print your Photoshop Elements images to create hard copies of your work. You can then add your photos to a physical photo album or frame them.

After you select your photos to print, you can choose the paper size and the printed size for your photos on the page. Photoshop Elements automatically arranges the images on the page for printing. You can zoom and pan your photos within the print dimensions to focus on just the content you want printed. Additional printing options enable you to include a filename, caption, or date with the photo.

Print Photos

1. In the Organizer, **Ctrl**+click to select the photos you want to print.

Note: For more on using the Organizer, see Chapter 3.

2. Click **File**.

3. Click **Print**.

   You can also print by pressing **Ctrl**+**P**.

   This example shows printing from the Organizer. You can also open an image and follow steps from **2** forward to print from the Editor.

Note: See Chapter 1 for more on the Editor and Organizer.

   The Prints dialog box opens.

4. Select your printer and paper settings. These vary depending on the make and model of your printer.

5. Click the ▼ and select a print type.

   In the print type menu, you can select Contact Sheet to arrange your photos in rows and columns. You can select Picture Package to access more photo layouts.

6. Click the ▼ and select a print size.

7 Click a photo to adjust.

8 Click and drag the slider () to zoom the photo.

● You can click here to rotate the photo.

You can click and drag to pan your photo within the print size boundary.

9 Type the number of copies to print.

10 Click **Print**.

Photoshop Elements prints the photos.

TIP

How can I add captions and other text to my printed photo?

1 In the Print dialog box, click **More Options**.

2 Click **Printing Choices**.

3 Click here to print a caption if your photo has one (■ changes to ☑).

● You can click here to print the date the photo was taken or the filename.

● You can use these settings to print a solid border around the photo.

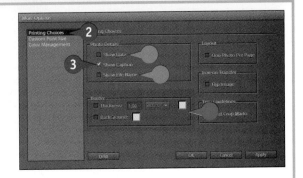

Export Photos

You can export the photos in the Organizer to a folder. This is helpful if you want to move the photos to another computer or give them to another person. Photoshop Elements enables you to export your photos in a variety of file formats. You can export JPEG or PNG versions for sharing electronically. TIFF or PSD versions are best for saving high-quality originals. A size menu lets you export to a variety of common image dimensions. When exporting JPEG photos, you can control the quality of the exported files.

Export Photos

1 **Ctrl**+click to select the photos you want to export in the Organizer.

Note: For more on using the Organizer, see Chapter 3.

If you do not select any photos, Photoshop Elements exports all the photos currently displayed.

2 Click **File**.

3 Click **Export As New File(s)**.

The Export New Files dialog box opens, showing the selected photos listed.

4 Click a file type option (● changes to ○).

● Some file types allow you to specify a size or quality.

5 Click **Browse** to choose a destination folder for the images.

6 To select more images to export, click **Add**.

The Add Media dialog box opens.

7 Click the check box next to the photos you want to add (■ changes to ☑).

● You can use the Add Media From settings to limit the displayed photos.

8 Click **Done**.

Photoshop Elements adds the photos.

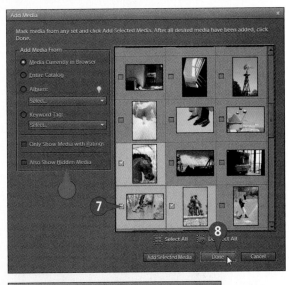

● To remove a photo from the export list, click the photo and then click **Remove**.

9 Click **Export**.

Photoshop Elements exports your images.

TIP

How do I customize the names of my exported images?

1 In the Export New Files dialog box, click the **Common Base Name** check box (● changes to ○).

2 Specify a base name for your photo filenames.

3 Click **Export**.

Photoshop Elements exports your images and appends a hyphen and number to your base name to create each filename.

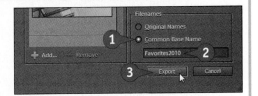

Back Up Photos

You can back up your collection of digital photos by using the Organizer's backup tool. This feature walks you through the steps for backing up your photo files to a CD, DVD, or external hard drive. Regularly backing up your work to external media is a good idea in case the hard drive or other main storage on your computer fails.

A standard CD can hold up to 650MB of data. A standard DVD can hold up to 4.7GB of data, or about seven times more than a CD. Photoshop Elements can also burn to the new Blue-ray disc format, which can hold up to 50GB. How many of your images a disc will hold depends on the size of the images and the format at which they are saved.

Back Up Photos

① In the Organizer, open the catalog you want to back up.

Note: For more on catalogs, see Chapter 3.

② Click **File**.

③ Click **Backup Catalog to CD, DVD or Hard Drive**.

Photoshop Elements may display a warning about missing files. If this happens, click **Reconnect** to perform a check. See the tip for more details.

The Backup Catalog to CD, DVD, or Hard Drive dialog box opens.

④ Click the **Full Backup** radio button (● changes to ○).

● For subsequent backups, you can select the **Incremental Backup** option. Incremental Backup backs up files that have changed or been added since the last backup and is faster than a full backup when you have saved a catalog previously.

⑤ Click **Next**.

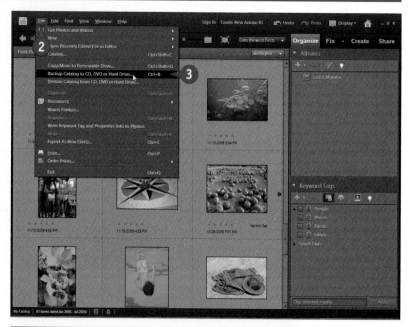

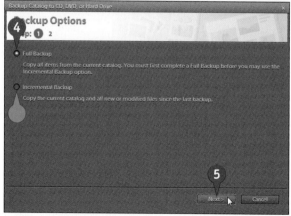

6 Click the drive to which you want to copy the backup files.

● You can type a name for the backup in this text box.

● Depending on your backup drive selection, the wizard displays an estimated file size and creation time.

7 Click **Save Backup**.

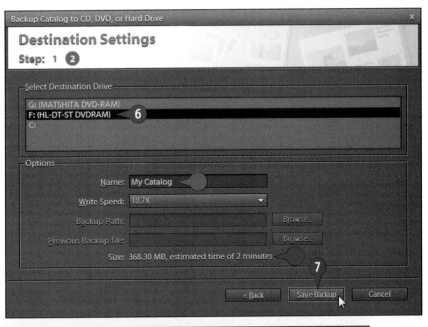

Photoshop Elements backs up your photos.

A prompt box alerts you when the procedure is complete.

Depending on the media you used, you may have the option of verifying your backup when the backup is finished.

The Organizer prompts me to find missing files before backing up my photos. What do I do?
If any of the catalog photos no longer contain valid links to original files, the backup tool displays a prompt box, asking you to reconnect any missing files. A file can appear to be missing if you move it after adding the photo to the Organizer or if you rename the file outside the Organizer. You can click **Reconnect** to allow Photoshop Elements to look for the missing links and then continue with the backup.

How do I restore my backed-up files?
You can click **File** and then **Restore Catalog from CD, DVD or Hard Drive** to restore backups of your photos to your computer. The Restore dialog box offers options for restoring backed-up photos and catalogs to their original location or to a new location of your choosing.

Sign Up for Online Services

Photoshop Elements enables you to sign up for an online account at Photoshop.com. With the service, you can create online galleries of your photos to share with friends and back up your photos online for safekeeping. At Photoshop.com, you can also access tutorials and view examples of interesting imaging projects from other Photoshop Elements users.

Once you sign up for a Photoshop.com account, you can sign into the account through the Photoshop Elements interface. After you are signed in, you can create your online galleries or back up your photos without leaving the Photoshop Elements application. A Photoshop.com account also gives you a unique Web address where others can view the photos that you post online.

Sign Up for Online Services

1 In the Organizer, click **Create New Adobe ID**.

Note: For more on using the Organizer, see Chapter 3.

> You can also click **Create New Adobe ID** on the Welcome screen or in the Editor to sign up.

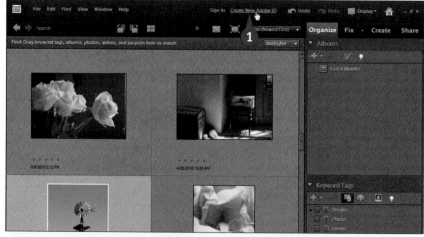

> A Create Your Adobe ID dialog box opens.

2 Type your signup information.

3 Create a personalized Web address, or URL, for accessing your account.

> You can use letters, numbers, and underscores to create your Web address but no other special characters.

4 Click **Create Account**.

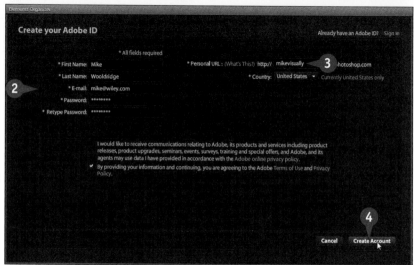

An Account Benefits dialog box opens.

● You can click **Plus** to sign up for a premium account, which offers more storage space and other premium features.

⑤ To continue with a free account, click **Free**.

An Account Verification dialog box opens.

Adobe sends a verification message to your e-mail address.

⑥ To complete the signup, you must access the Web address contained in the verification e-mail.

● After you verify the e-mail address, you can sign in here.

⑦ Click **Done** to close the dialog box.

To sign in to your account from Photoshop Elements, see the tip below.

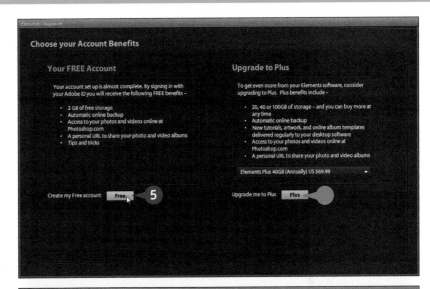

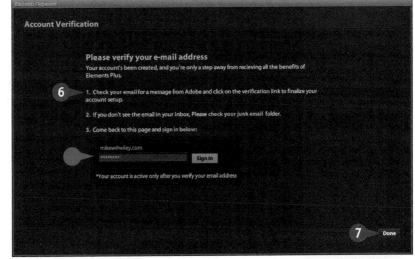

TIP

How do I sign in to my Photoshop.com account from Photoshop Elements?

① In the Organizer or Editor, click **Sign In**.

② In the dialog box, type the e-mail address associated with your account.

③ Type your password.

④ Click **Sign In**.

A confirmation dialog box opens, and welcome text appears in the menu bar.

Share a Photo Album Online

You can share an album that you created in the Photoshop Elements Organizer on Photoshop.com. Photoshop Elements uploads the album photos to your Photoshop.com account and then displays them in a custom template. You can announce the album via e-mail to your contacts. For more about creating albums in the Organizer, see Chapter 3.

Contacts can view your online photo albums at the personalized Web address for your account. See the section "Sign Up for Online Services" for more. Because sharing albums involves uploading photos, the feature works best with a fast Internet connection.

Share a Photo Album Online

1 Sign in to your Photoshop.com account in Photoshop Elements.

Note: See the section "Sign Up for Online Services" for more.

2 In the Organizer, click **Organize**.

3 Click the ▼ to open the Albums panel.

4 Click an album to share.

5 Click **Share** (◼).

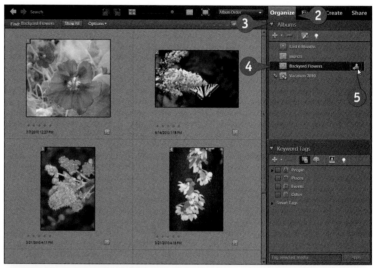

The Album Details panel appears, showing a preview of the album.

6 Type a name for the online album. Photoshop Elements uses the current name as the default.

● You can click here to choose a different template for your gallery.

7 Click here to share your album to Photoshop.com (◼ changes to ✓).

● In the Slideshow Settings dialog box, you can edit the title and subtitle, and turn on or off captions.

8 Type a message to send to your contacts.

9 Click here to select the contacts (■ changes to ☑).

Note: See the section "E-mail Images with Photo Mail" for more on adding contacts.

● You can optionally allow viewers to download photos or order prints from within the gallery.

10 Click **Done**.

● Photoshop Elements uploads the album photos to your gallery at Photoshop.com for sharing. This may take a few minutes or more, depending on the size of your album and your upload speed.

An e-mail is sent to each contact, inviting the recipient to view the gallery.

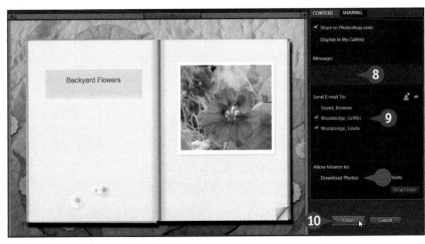

TIP

How do I stop an album from being shared?

1 In the Organizer's Albums pane, click **Stop Sharing** (▣).

A Stop Sharing icon appears next to each shared album.

Photoshop Elements displays a confirmation dialog box.

2 Click **OK**.

Photoshop Elements changes the status of the photos so that they are no longer accessible online.

You can automatically back up albums that you create in the Organizer at your Photoshop.com account. This safeguards your photos in case you lose them on your local computer. Backed-up albums are also synchronized, which means any changes you make to the albums in Photoshop Elements are also made to the backed-up copies.

Because backing up and synchronizing albums involves uploading photos to Photoshop.com, the features work best with a fast Internet connection. Another way to safeguard your photos is to back them up to external media such as a CD or DVD. See "Back Up Photos" for details.

Back Up and Synchronize Photos Online

1 Sign in to your Photoshop. com account in Photoshop Elements.

2 In the Organizer, click **Edit**.

3 Click **Preferences**.

4 Click **Backup/Synchronization.**

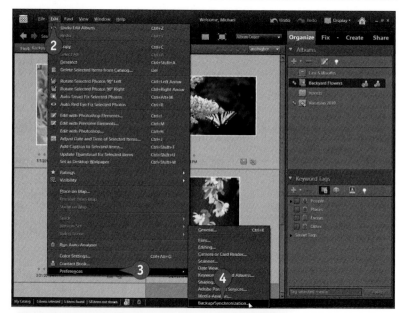

The Backup/Synchronization Preferences dialog box opens.

● You can click here to turn on Backup/Synchronization (■ changes to ☑).

● Albums shared on Photoshop. com are automatically backed up and synchronized.

5 Click here to back up and synchronize an album (■ changes to ☑).

6 Click here to view advanced options.

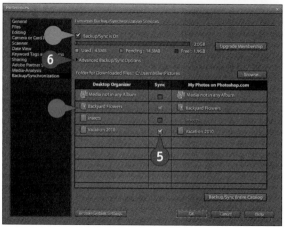

● You can click here to
automatically back up and
synchronize new albums
(■ changes to ☑).

● You can click here to limit
the types of files that are
backed up and synchronized.

7 Click **OK**.

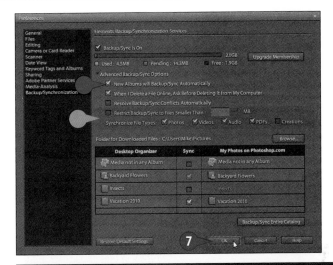

Photoshop Elements backs
up and synchronizes the
selected albums at
Photoshop.com. It may take
some time for the files to
transfer from your computer
to Photoshop.com.

● Photoshop Elements marks
the selected albums with a
Backup/Synchronize icon (■).

How do I check my Photoshop.com account details from within Photoshop Elements?

1 Sign in to your Photoshop.com account in Photoshop Elements. See the section "Sign Up for Online
Services" for more.

2 Click **Welcome** on the menu
bar.

3 Type your password in the
dialog box that opens.

4 Click **My Account**.

Your account details appear.

● A graph shows you how much
storage space you are using.

Index

A

Account Benefits dialog box, 341
Account Verification dialog box, 341
Add Caption dialog box, 58
Add Noise filter, 264
Add to Quick Selection button, Quick Selection tool, 131
Adjust Date and Time option, contextual menu, 57
Adjust Sharpness dialog box, 182
Adjust Smart Fix dialog box, 197
adjustment layer, 145, 160–161, 163
Advanced Photo Downloader dialog box, 27
After Only view, Quick Fix pane, 172
Airbrush feature, 236
Album Details panel, Organizer, 60–61
albums
    adding photos to in Full Screen mode, 83
    create new, 60–61
    creating category of, 71
    removing photos from, 61
    saving open photos as, 39
    sharing online, 342–343
    stopping from sharing, 343
    viewing, 61
Albums panel, Organizer, 70
alignment, text, 277
Amount slider, Emboss dialog box, 268
anchor points, 116
anti-aliasing, 277
Arrange commands, layers, 153
art, 24
Auto Color Correction command, 219
Auto Contrast feature, 203
Auto Hide button, 52
Auto setting, Photomerge dialog box, 318
Auto Sharpen button, Quick Fix window, 183
Auto-Analyzer feature, Organizer, 33

B

Background layer, 132, 138, 147, 251
backing up photos, 338–339, 344–345
Backup Catalog to CD, DVD, or Hard Drive dialog box, 338

Backup/Sync check box, Album Details panel, 60
Bas Relief filter, 269
Before & After setting, Guided Edit interface, 216
Before Only view, Quick Fix pane, 172
beveled text, 282
Bin Actions button, Project Bin, 39
Bitmap (BMP) format, 35
bitmap images, 7
Black and White – High Contrast tool, 174
black-and-white photo, 226–229
Blank File option, File menu, 36
blank image, 25, 36–37
blending layers, 162–163
Block mode, eraser, 251
Blur filters, 256–257
Blur tool, 13, 212–213
Blush slider, Adjust Color for Skin Tone dialog box, 219
BMP (Bitmap) format, 35
brightness, 199, 202
Browse For Folder dialog box, 32
Brush menu, Quick Selection Tool, 120
Brush mode, eraser, 251
brush styles, 238–239
Brush tool, 13, 236–237, 242–243
Brushes panel, 221
Burn tool, 205–207
By Caption or Note option, Find menu, 65
By Filename option, Find menu, 65
By History option, Find menu, 65
By Media Type option, Find menu, 65

C

calendar, photo, 317
camera, digital, 24, 26–27
canvas size, image, 102–103
captions, 59, 301, 335
card reader, 24, 26–27
Catalog Manager dialog box, 48–49
Catalog option, File menu, 48
catalogs, 44, 48–49
Clone Stamp tool, 13, 178–179
collage, 5